INTO THE FIRESTORM

OSPREY
PUBLISHING

INTO THE FIRESTORM

THE ALLIED HEROES WHO FLEW
WORLD WAR II'S MOST DARING MISSIONS

SCOTT McGAUGH

OSPREY PUBLISHING
Bloomsbury Publishing Plc
Kemp House, Chawley Park, Cumnor Hill, Oxford OX2 9PH, UK
Bloomsbury Publishing Ireland Limited,
29 Earlsfort Terrace, Dublin 2, D02 AY28, Ireland
Bloomsbury Publishing Inc.
1359 Broadway, 5th Floor, New York, NY 10018, USA
E-mail: info@ospreypublishing.com
www.ospreypublishing.com

OSPREY is a trademark of Osprey Publishing Ltd

First published in Great Britain in 2026
First published in the United States in 2026

For legal purposes the Acknowledgments on p. 255–258 constitute an extension of this copyright page.

Library of Congress Cataloging-in-Publication Data is available.

ISBN: HB 9781472872456; eBook 9781472872449; ePDF 9781472872432;
XML 9781472872418; Audio 9781472872425

26 27 28 29 30   10 9 8 7 6 5 4 3 2 1

Index by Alan Rutter

Typeset by Lumina Datamatics Ltd
Printed and bound in Great Britain by Clays Ltd, Elcograf S.p.A.

Osprey Publishing supports the Woodland Trust, the UK's leading woodland conservation charity.

To find out more about our authors and books visit www.ospreypublishing.com.
Here you will find extracts, author interviews, details of forthcoming events and the
option to sign up for our newsletter.

For product safety related questions contact productsafety@bloomsbury.com

To Marjorie,
my life's mission

Contents

Foreword

General Mike Minihan, USAF (Ret.)
Commander, Air Mobility Command

During my 34 years of service in the United States Air Force, I had the honor of leading the world's largest flying operation, enabled by more than 1,000 aircraft and more than 107,000 Total Force Airmen. Like the heroes in *Into the Firestorm*, we were proud to carry out strategic mobility operations for this great nation.

I'm a proud Airlifter. "Tactical Airlifter" to be exact. A title I earned the hard way, through decades of blood, sweat, and tears in the cockpit of the C-130 Hercules. In the beginning, I cut my teeth "low and slow" while being pulled by propellers in the same squadrons, the legacy of which is uncovered in this book.

America's Air Force and Army still honor the deeds of our Airman and Soldier forefathers from World War II. Drop zones near Pope Army Airfield, North Carolina, are named Sicily, Normandy, Nijmegen, Luzon, Salerno, Ste-Mere-Eglise, and Holland (the Netherlands). The landing zone near Fort Polk, Louisiana, is named Geronimo. An Air Force cargo loader is named The Tunner, after General William Tunner (whom readers will meet on missions over the Himalayas). Our uniforms are occasionally adorned with heritage patches bearing original World War II Troop Carrier Squadron insignia.

We often mock the airborne vulnerability we share with every generation of airlifters who have flown before us. "If you ain't got bullets, you gotta have guts" was a popular, unauthorized flight suit patch. Another depicted the famous Air Force Weapons School patch with a C-130 – flying airlift, cargo, and medevac missions – in a fighter's crosshairs proudly exclaiming "Target."

With that vulnerability comes freedom. Freedom to unconditionally commit yourself to mission and crew. Freedom to celebrate and appreciate the contributions of the entire USAF "Fly, Fix, Support Team." Empowering others to tap their courage to "aim the pointy end at the scary place," and simply accomplish the tasked mission.

American Airlifters today are strengthened by the fearlessness, tenacity, and bravery they have inherited from the Allied troop carrier aircrews of World War II. They bear the battle scars of Afghanistan and Iraq and the "air bridge" miracles of Bosnia, Kosovo, Ukraine, and Israel. Not unlike the terror and triumph of World War II's heroes you will meet in *Into the Firestorm*.

Like no other, this book reveals and lays bare the extraordinary sacrifices, valor, and audacity of the first and greatest generation of tactical airlifters. The fearlessness of those who flew the "Hump" and the mettle of those who executed Operations *Overlord*, *Market Garden*, and *Varsity*. A lineage today's USAF Airlifters strive to meet and honor every single day.

So strap in. *Into the Firestorm* is "IP inbound at the 1-minute advisory," "on centerline," and "on airspeed." Doors are open. Jumpers are standing, hooked up, and in the door. In the pages ahead, the navigator will yell "Green Light!" as *New York Times* bestselling author Scott McGaugh buckles us into the co-pilot's seat to fly into the flak-filled skies of World War II, alongside America's and Britain's bravest "sitting ducks."

Preface

As a boy, they were strangers.

I only knew them as Mr Bateman, Mr Rhinehart, and Mr Lively when they and their wives visited to play bridge with my parents, or when the men went fishing with my father. A business owner, architect, general contractor, and a children's dentist. Yet only seven years before my birth, all four had served along with twenty-two million US and United Kingdom volunteers and draftees in World War II.

Perhaps they had been among those who had flown at the edge of manhood, writing letters home at every opportunity. Some to their wives, perhaps pregnant with their first child. A few to their unborn sons or daughters. Sometimes to their parents, struggling to express their gratitude for a boyhood filled with love and infused with responsibility. Others to buddies in case they died thousands of miles from home.

Will you see that whoever packs my clothes puts them all in … You can have my radio until I return if you want it. Also see that my German pistol is packed. I would appreciate it also if you would mail my Teddy Bear and perfume to my wife. Also, destroy that Exeter [England] address under the glass on my desk. Well kid, that's all I can think of except you get my fountain pen out of my desk drawer.[1]

Others wrote while lying in a hospital bed encased in a full body cast or wrapped in burn bandages after they had crashed and somehow had survived the fireball. Perhaps to return to the battlefield or fight another war, the victory of which would be marked by walking up to their front door back home months later.

Perhaps they had met other young men who had volunteered long before Americans tasted war. Men like David Lord who had already flown Royal Air Force missions in India, North Africa, and Burma before he returned to Britain to train for Normandy missions. Or Gordon Thring, a farmer's son who had been a school teacher before enlisting in the Royal Canadian Air Force.

All that changed when I joined other community leaders in 1996 to bring the decommissioned USS *Midway* aircraft carrier to my hometown of San Diego to become a museum.[2] I unexpectedly stepped into the universe of men and women who quietly and anonymously serve and sacrifice for our country. Serve and sacrifice for me and my family.

The next thirty years have become a personal mission to preserve the legacy of these heroes. To unveil their stories on a far more personal, intimate level than most history books.

Years ago, a retired two-star US Navy admiral and I were chatting one day. His last assignment before retirement had been commanding the US Navy Reserves worldwide, including hundreds of hotshot aviators who mainlined speed, thought they always could outrun weather, and whose nametag should have read "Invincible."

"Do you know what the two most dangerous words are in the English language?" he asked. I had no idea. "Watch this."

In researching *Into the Firestorm* and my previous book (*Brotherhood of the Flying Coffin*), it became quite clear that the DNA of these US and British pilots must have been infused with a heavy dose of "watch this." The confidence and bravery that empowered them to fly into enemy territory, defenseless, only a few hundred feet above the battlefield, and through enemy fire. Over and over again.

While on my book's research trek, I wondered what my father as well as Messrs Bateman, Rhinehart, and Lively had experienced. Fortunately, others late in life lifted the curtain.

"I have memory slippage," conceded World War II C-47 pilot Del Tiedeman a few years ago. "But with the war, very little has slipped."

In a newspaper interview, he remembered watching his good friend and former co-pilot, 1st Lieutenant John Crosetti, struggling to keep control of his aircraft so his pathfinder paratroopers could jump over Holland in Operation *Market Garden*. Both engines were spewing smoke from direct hits by the enemy and fire had reached the fuselage.

Finally, he ordered his aircrew to bail out, just before his plane nosed into a deep dive. "There was no way you can crawl out of an airplane in a dive," Tiedeman reflected seventy-five years later.

That memory haunted the retired construction executive for more than seven decades. Like another memory when he witnessed German artillery fire tear the wing off a combat glider, sending it cockpit first into the ground. Its epitaph became the tormented screams of pain from a surviving crewman who had lost both his legs.

Del Tiedeman died in 2021 at the age of 100.

Into the Firestorm honors his legacy and all the US and British aircrews who anonymously flew together over World War II's front lines.

Author's Notes

Capturing the legacy of those in battle becomes a mosaic of triumph and tragedy as intricate and interconnected as a cathedral's stained glass.

As complex and interlaced as the missions and fates of intrepid American and British men like Lawrence McMahon (KIA, Tunisia), David Lord (posthumous Victoria Cross and Distinguished Flying Cross), Howard Beaver (four Bronze Stars), John Gilliard (KIA, Distinguished Flying Cross), George Merz (crashed at sea), Geoffrey Buckland (300 missions over the Burmese jungle).

Into the Firestorm is their story. It is not a chronicle of Allied troop carrier commands and their air wings, troop carrier groups and squadrons, or British airborne squadrons and groups. Others have ably compiled the "unit histories" that are part of this book's foundation.

As such, I've referred to specific unit assignments only when they establish context or provided clarity for the reader. In a similar vein, I have intentionally skirted the use of military acronyms, abbreviations, and combat lingo to keep the story focused on these remarkable heroes.

Similarly, an airman's rank is a moving target as many received promotions during their active-duty service. Further, accounts did not always cite the individual's rank at a particular time. Their bravery and actions supplanted the need for 1st or 2nd Lieutenant and (RAF) Flight Lieutenant or Flying Officer at every turn. Out of respect, of course, I generally include rank whenever possible on the first reference, but generally refer to role (pilot, navigator, wireless operator, crew chief, even "kicker outers," etc.) upon subsequent references. In a similar vein, British and American ranks and ratings vary quite a bit, so I have kept those references as concise as possible for clarity's sake.

Winston Churchill once observed that "history is written by the victors." Yet written accounts, composed in a mission's aftermath or summarized and analyzed years later, rarely are consistent. Typos, omissions, and a faded typewriter ribbon can become enemies of a single pilot's after-mission account. A report taken by an intelligence officer, transcribed by a clerk, and forwarded for review and perhaps editing for the permanent record can be difficult to decipher and evaluate decades later. Names can become mangled, statistics transposed, and carbon copies can fade beyond legibility. The author has made every attempt to be selective and vigilant for corroborating confirmation.

War statistics, in particular, are moving targets. Numbers of aircraft, personnel, tonnage, and even the time of day often vary from one "official" account to the next. I've made every attempt to determine the most widely accepted statistics to make a particular point.

Today, far too few World War II veterans walk among us. Inevitably, this book is largely based on their accounts in their post-mission letters, after-action reports, journals, sometimes a memoir. Oftentimes buttressed by an oral history recording or a local newspaper feature, often when they are confronting their mortality late in life.

Narrative in italics signifies the "inner dialogue" or thoughts by a pilot or member of the crew. They are not fictionalized but drawn from their accounts when describing personal considerations, priorities, goals, and other thoughts in the moment. "Documentary support," historian and two-time Pulitzer recipient Barbara Tuchman called it.

Bias can appear in official documents that often gloss over issues, challenge, and failures. Opinions also can seep into official recordkeeping. A post-mission troop carrier group report on supply missions in Bastogne praised "close cooperation," "an excellent job of close [fighter] cover," and "readily available intelligence information." Yet the commanding officer of that group considered the report a "whitewash," and robustly criticized senior officers regarding cooperation, fighter cover, and intel reports. Considered judgment and inevitable selection from multiple sources by authors sometimes are more frequent than readers realize.

Similarly, the British and American military documents differ in style, detail, use of names, initials, and similar details. Again, I've kept references and citations as straightforward as possible.

Further, *Into the Firestorm* is not an attempt to include every Allied mission in every World War II region around the world. This book straps the reader into enough cockpits to understand and appreciate the nature of what these men faced – from Europe to the Himalayas to the Sahara Desert – and how each contributed to the Allied victory.

For the sake of clarity and to keep the story moving, in instances of redundant sources I sometimes employed a "John Hoye personal account" citation with general information on the source or multiple sources of his personal story.

Nearly all World War II photographs are in the public domain and many are widely available. Where appropriate, single sources such as the Silent Wings Museum are noted.

Finally, I have made every attempt to be as accurate as possible in honor of these heroes. Any misfires are mine and I welcome suggested corrections.

List of Illustrations

5 British and American C-47 aircrews faced danger from the
   moment they were airborne. Here, an RAF C-47 Dakota
   crashed shortly after takeoff in England where two crewmen
   were killed and two miraculously survived. (Photo by
   WATFORD/Mirrorpix/Mirrorpix via Getty Images)

6 A C-47's cockpit offered cramped quarters for the pilot
   and co-pilot. They were practically trapped from the time
   they buckled in on combat missions. A small escape hatch
   in the cockpit offered scant hope if a crash was imminent,
   especially when fire in cabin prevented them from
   parachuting out the rear cargo door. (Silent Wings Museum)

7 Aircrews and paratroopers often reported to their aircraft
   several hours before sunrise. A paratrooper could weigh 260
   pounds, including the equipment and supplies he carried.
   Paratroopers sat on two facing bench seats shoulder to
   shoulder, sometimes for hours before jumping into battle.
   (Library of Congress)

8 C-47 and Dakota aircrews' first objective was to fly in a
   tight formation, typically 200 feet back and 200 feet to the
   right or left of each other, often before sunrise. A wingspan
   of ninety-five feet left little margin of error in bad weather,
   severe turbulence, enemy fire, or when towing gliders to
   battle. (Silent Wings Museum)

9 Aircrews' cargo reflected the nature of the battle the troops
   were fighting on the ground. In Burmese jungle warfare, a
   single piece of artillery required seven mules, delivered by
   aircrews in flying stables. Army artillery pack units could
   unload and assemble a small howitzer "from mule to firing
   position" in five minutes. (National Archives)

10 Highly choreographed US and British aircrew migrations
   from as many as 24 airfields from England and France
   delivered 1,600 plane loads of troops and gliders in one hour
   in Operation *Market Garden* and two entire divisions in only
   four hours in Operation *Varsity*. (National Archives)

11 Mission orders prohibited evasive action by aircrews when
   delivering paratroopers and gliders past the front line. Flying

holding two benches. Enemy small arms fire and shrapnel
frequently pierced the plane's thin ribbed skin (less than one-
quarter inch thick between ribs). The planes' control surfaces
were fabric covered. (US Army Signal Corps)

17   RAF and American aircrews considered the Dakota/C-47
a remarkably sturdy aircraft. On several occasions, pilots
returned from missions on one engine or successfully crash
landed their crippled aircraft. (Silent Wings Museum)

18   For many British and American C-47 aircrews in World
War II, flying former prisoners of war to England or France
became their final mission. Here, their passengers are greeted
by volunteers from the Women's Auxiliary Air Force at
an RAF airfield in England. (Photo by Haywood Magee/
Picture Post/Hulton Archive/Getty Images)

Introduction

They were the faceless warriors of World War II.

Anonymous American and British aircrews in defenseless aircraft who flew combat missions over the Himalayas into China, to the edge of the Sahara Desert, into Burmese jungles, and in the middle of three wars fought in the European Theater of Operations.

There, ground troops waded ashore, battled from one tree to the next, and hunkered down in foxholes as enemy fire split the air and shrapnel screamed. They inspired Pulitzer Award-winning books and blockbuster movies. Likewise, the harrowing dedication of bomber crews and fighter pilots at 20,000 feet has been well documented in print and by Hollywood.

In between, a largely unknown war raged, often less than 1,000 feet off the ground. Not much higher than the Seattle Space Needle, Eiffel Tower, and little more than twice the height of London's Big Ben. An airborne war fought in a bedlam of exploding flak, cloud banks, enemy fighters, and often within range of German machine gunners. Sometimes close and slow enough to see the enemy's faces aiming rifles skyward.

Fought by the American and British aircrews who delivered tens of thousands of Allied paratroopers and thousands of combat gliders through wicked enemy crossfire to their designated drop and landing zones *behind the front lines*. Often without fighter support and saddled in aircraft that lacked guns, armor, protected fuel tanks, and maneuverability. Yet willing to fly into the firestorms of World War II, no matter the cost.

Flown by impossibly young pilots, some only a few years out of high school. First or 2nd lieutenants and flying officers gripping the yoke of stripped-down commercial airliners flying long-range combat missions, often through the night. Far into enemy territory carrying paratroopers poised to jump or step down into a modified bomber's "jump hole," or towing 3.5-ton combat gliders at the end of a one-inch nylon rope. On missions predicted to suffer up to seventy percent casualty rates.

They were microcosms of the Allies' Greatest Generation. The 10,000 mostly American and British aircrews that included young Americans like Brownie Bolton, Mayo Wood, and Albyn Plutt who volunteered from towns, villages, and crossroads – Bayard, Bradford, Sugar Cove, and Poplar Bluff – known only to their residents. And Royal Air Force heroes – Maurice McHugh, George Cairns, and Reginald Lawn – from St Kilda, Ontario, and Liverpool equally dedicated to service to their country in the name of freedom.

Unlike the fighter and bomber pilots who could "fight back," these aircrews were ordered to fly straight, low, take no evasive action, and arrive "on time and on target." For too many, they were one-way missions. For some, missions ended in prisoner-of-war camps. Others simply disappeared in a fireball.

They flew a commercial airliner modified to become a C-47 "Skytrain" in the US and called a "Dakota" in the UK, commonly referred to as a "Biscuit Bomber," "Gooney Bird," and even "Flying Boxcar," according to one commanding officer's report. In aircraft with which many established a lifelong bond: "Bar Fly," "Kwicherbichen," "Honeybun III," "Mild & Bitter," "Night Fright," "The Captain & The Kids," "Pegasus," "Nookie Wagon," "Squirrelie," and "Buck O Bolts," to name a few. Others flew modified British bombers in combined airborne and attack missions.

In Asia, they flew over the "Roof of the World," crossing the Himalayas from India into China, fighting Arctic-worthy blizzards, air so thin that brain damage became an enemy, and hurricane-force turbulence. Often at night with no escorts. On missions over Burma that risked vanishing in the enemy's jungle. And to the edge of the Sahara's blinding dust storms that tempted fate and tested devotion to duty.

All powered by courage in a modified commercial airliner across a network spanning 180,000 square miles. These pilots, co-pilots, navigators, wireless operators, crew chiefs, and despatchers forged a remarkable legacy in less than three years. They flew through World War II and into the dawn of the Cold War, yet have remained unsung heroes. Long overdue for recognition as perhaps the most anonymous cadre of the Allies' Greatest Generation.

We were only 500 feet above the [Normandy] beach coming in ... "Green Light!" and in that very instant I could hear bullets hitting [our C-47], a rather dry sound like peas being dropped into a pot. Our plane lurched forward on being released from the glider, and we banked sharply down and to the right, under the arcs of tracers.

With the realization that we were still flying, I began to get really scared. Now that we had a chance for life I was afraid we wouldn't make it. But after that few minutes in the thick of battle all we had facing us was an uneventful, practically routine flight [back to England]. No yelling, no rejoicing this time when we touched down at Membury. Just a quiet, heavy sensation. 'Well, that's two out of the way.' We went outside with flashlights to check on holes in our planes ... one mean-looking hole [was] in the fairing about ten inches from our right gas tank ... 31 of the 50 planes had been shot up, some badly ...

I was forced to turn back in a C-47 on account of heavy ice and violent updrafts associated with turbulence ... Ice was encountered at 16,000 feet ... A free air temperature of plus 2 degrees Centigrade ... [After changing course to a lower altitude] updrafts struck the airplane ... very clear ice formed, blacking out all radio reception and covering the side windows of the windshield so that the wings were no longer discernable. I judged this ice came from freezing rain ...

Into the Firestorm is the first book to reveal their story. It is based on their after-action reports, rarely seen military archives, journals, oral histories, photos, and letters home. The personal stories of young men like the former store clerk holding his aircraft steady through a curtain of enemy fire. Or a pilot towing a combat glider whose pilot had been the best man at his wedding. Another pilot climbing to give his aircrew the opportunity to bail out, then dying in his plane's subsequent meteoric crash, never meeting his infant son.

Readers become co-pilots alongside young men once dazzled by the prospect of becoming a fighter or bomber pilot, but who ultimately flew what had been passenger planes or not-yet-invented gliders into battle. Grocery clerks, accountants, farmhands, and college students trusted a general who had been the second choice of his father and of West Point when he had wanted to make the military his career.

Subsequent chapters reveal how aircrews became test pilots over Sicily; fought fog banks and the Germans over Normandy and southern France; and flew into hell over Holland. Then leading the invasion into the Fatherland and only weeks later evacuating starving refugees and liberated prisoners from German stalags. And on daring missions over southeast Asia jungles, the Balkans, and North Africa.

For some, battle scars lingered far beyond the end of World War II.

When he returned home, one pilot slept with a forearm across his throat after sleeping in the Middle East and Africa amid rumors that the enemy slit the throats of sleeping troops. Every noise in the middle of the night required identification before sleep would return. He bypassed restaurants with long lines and abhorred Spam and orange marmalade. He inspected the silverware before ordering at a restaurant and hated hot weather, mosquitos, and anything sticky.

Yet he also served in the Korean War and Vietnam. He retired from the military in 1969 as a lieutenant colonel with two Silver Stars and two Purple Hearts, among other awards.

Into the Firestorm chronicles the largely unknown legacy of these men, nearly all of whom now have made their "final flight." This is their story, in their voices. The stories of wartime heroes we all should have invited over to dinner.

Chronology

Sept 1, 1939	Germany invades Poland
Sept 3, 1939	Britain declares war on Germany
July 10, 1940	Battle of Britain begins
Nov 13, 1940	British Halifax bomber joins the RAF, some modified to tow gliders
Feb 10, 1941	British Short Stirling bomber joins the RAF, some modified to tow gliders
Feb 25, 1941	General Hap Arnold authorizes the US glider program
Mar 11, 1941	US Lend-Lease Act authorized, 2,000 C-47s will be sent to Britain
May 31, 1941	Britain authorizes two paratrooper brigades and glider force
June 20, 1941	General Arnold becomes Chief of the US Army Air Forces
Sept 12, 1941	British Horsa glider maiden flight
Dec 7, 1941	Japan attacks Pearl Harbor
Dec 8, 1941	US declares war on Japan
Dec 11, 1941	US declares war on Germany
Dec 23, 1941	US C-47 maiden flight, 10,174 built in World War II
Apr 1942	Supply flights over Himalayas begin in the China-Burma-India (CBI) Theater

May 1, 1942	US CG-4A glider first flight, 13,900 built in World War II
Nov 8, 1942	Operation *Torch*, C-47 airborne paratroopers fly from England to North Africa to support Allied ground war
Jan, 1943	British Albemarle joins the RAF, designed to tow gliders
Feb, 1943	British C-47 Dakotas begin arriving from US
Apr, 1943	C-46 begins flying the Himalayas route in the CBI Theater
July 9, 1943	Operation *Husky*, the invasion of Sicily
Jan 4, 1944	Operation *Carpetbagger* begins, clandestine missions to supply the French Resistance
Mar 5, 1944	Operation *Thursday*, insertion and ongoing supply of US and British commandos in the Burma campaign
June 6, 1944	Operation *Overlord* begins, the invasion of Normandy
June 6, 1944	Operations *Detroit* and *Chicago*
June 7, 1944	Operations *Hackensack* and *Galveston*
Aug 2, 1944	Operation *Halyard* begins. By December, 12,000 sorties brought supplies, weapons, and rescue Yugoslavia resistance fighters and civilians
Aug 15, 1944	Operation *Dragoon*, the invasion of southern France
Sept 17, 1944	Operation *Market Garden* begins, the invasion of Holland
Dec 16, 1944	Battle of the Bulge begins
Mar 24, 1945	Operation *Varsity*: Allied troops cross the Rhine River into Germany; the Flying Pipeline supplies ground forces and ultimately flies 233,000 liberated POWs from Germany to freedom
May 8, 1945	Germany surrenders
Aug 1945	C-47 crews fly 1,118 sorties over the Himalayas, delivering 5,327 tons of supplies
Sept 2, 1945	Japan surrenders

PART ONE

Liberating Europe

A Feasible Proposition

As long as they could remember, their boyhood dreams had soared with naïve abandon when they had looked to the sky.

But as war loomed over the horizon, those boys stood on the brink of manhood, their futures as uncertain as their families farms' harvests next year. Or whether a letter in next week's mail would read, "Having submitted yourself ... for the purpose of determining your availability for training and service in the land or naval forces of the United States ... you are hereby notified that you have now been selected for training and service therein."

Richard Kraemer had been fascinated by flying from the day in 1927 when he sat on a fifth-floor window ledge to watch the ticker-tape parade for Charles Lindbergh. After a "roller coaster" flight in a Stinson Reliant monoplane a few years later, he was hooked. So much so that after graduating high school in 1938, he took a mail clerk job at Eastern Airlines. In 1939, he borrowed $600 from his father to pay for remedial math and science classes so he could enlist in the Army Air Corps.

Goldie Goldman was a prankster. Although too small for his school's basketball team in central Texas, he could see himself locking his fighter's bullseye onto an enemy aircraft. He figured he would find a way, despite eyesight that was less than the required 20/20. Knowing he was about to receive his draft notice, James Ferrin saddled "Old Red" to ride across the Arizona desert to the local army recruiting office so he, too, could shoot the enemy out of the sky as cleanly as a clay pigeon.

Alan Boyd had grown up in a town of 700 residents surrounded by corn and cotton fields near the Georgia border where "the social hierarchy in town was dictated by skin color [and] there were unwritten rules of conduct for both sides." Black people stepped off sidewalks when any white person approached. The local Ku Klux Klan's mission was to "maintain appropriate social behavior."[1]

On December 8, 1941, he was accepted for pilot training only due to a loophole. Acceptance required two years of college at the time. He had attended the University of Florida, but following his sophomore year when he failed two classes the school's dean had informed him, "I am confident that the university is sufficiently strong that it can survive without you. Good luck, and don't come back." The enlistment qualifications did not require *passing* two years' worth of college classes.[2]

John Hoye had grown up in a small Wisconsin lumber town watching black-and-white wartime movies – *Hell's Angels, Dawn Patrol,* and *Young Eagles* – at the town hall above a saloon. A twenty-minute plane ride at a nearby air show sold him on becoming an aviator. A few years later, savings from a part-time job made flight lessons possible.

They all dreamed of someday sitting in the pilot's seat of a fighter or bomber. Hundreds of thousands of applicants would be necessary to produce 85,000 wartime pilots annually.[3] No one could predict how many would never return to their families.

While America drifted closer to the brink of war, close to 3,000 British airmen had already tasted blood in the air. Only twenty years of age on average, more than 540 had died and almost 425 had been wounded in the four-month Battle of Britain in 1940, a ghastly toll, the victory of which forced Germany's Adolf Hitler to cancel plans to invade Britain.

Prime Minister Winston Churchill's observation in the midst of his nation's battle for survival would prove prescient later in World War II when Allied aircrews fought a few hundred yards above the battlefield. "Never in the field of human conflict has so much been owed by so many to so few."[4]

British families had said goodbye to thousands more who had enlisted long before Britain had declared war on Germany on September 3, 1939. Arthur Clowes had joined the Royal Air Force (RAF) in 1929. He had shot down eight German aircraft over France prior to the Battle of Britain and had earned the Distinguished Flying Medal. American Geoffrey Allard, who also had enlisted in the RAF in 1929, earned the same medal. He had flown multiple missions each day over France until exhaustion forced him to return to England where he earned the Distinguished Flying Cross in the Battle of Britain.[5] Elsewhere, David Lord had entered the RAF training program in 1938. Barely a year later, he was flying supply missions in India. He had given up a boyhood aspiration to become a priest and had worked as a chemist's assistant and freelance journalist before enlisting.

The fledgling aviators who followed them would see their dreams recast and their fates charted by three men. A military officer who believed dropping infantry from biplanes behind enemy lines made strategic sense; a general who had been the second choice of West Point admission personnel; and a prime minister who had finally passed his officer training entrance exam on his third attempt.

> I did not care for the idea of keeping my head above the trench and looking for beastly Germans; however it had to be done. It was quite uncanny to watch the enemy trench which appeared somewhat like a black wave and only sixty yards in front, then you would suddenly see the flash of their rifles and machine guns immediately after would come the report and nasty thuds on the sandbags which you might be resting against.[6]

Private Edward Stewart and Brigadier General Billy Mitchell hated the paralyzing horrors of World War I's trenches. In just four years, British, Irish, and American troops had suffered close to 1.5 million casualties. Stagnation fused with relentless enemy fire, disease, and shell shock gutted legions of soldiers mired across 475 miles of trenches.

Mitchell, the Chief of Air Service, First Army in Europe with 1,500 aircraft under his command, had an idea. But getting it off the ground required authorization from General John Pershing, the commanding officer of the American Expeditionary Forces.

> If we could have only got [sic] ten percent [of dropped para-troopers] in action against the enemy's rear, we should have been successful. One machine gun, properly placed, can hold up a battalion at times … I proposed [to Pershing] that we should arm the men with a great number of machine guns and train them to go over the front in our large airplanes … We could equip each man with a parachute … Then we could attack the Germans from the rear, aided by an attack from our army on the front … this was a perfectly feasible proposition.[7]

Only twenty-five days after General Pershing had authorized Mitchell to develop the concept further, the end of World War I shot down his vision of airborne combat. A vision at a time when pilots sitting in open-air cockpits still ruled the battlefield's sky.

Two decades passed before suitable aircraft of substantial power and payload would become operational and, equally importantly, before biplane pilots could mature into multi-engine aviators commanding aircrews flying through artillery onslaughts. Thousands of young men, most in their early twenties, would be trained as pilots, navigators, radio operators, and crew chiefs with the guts to fly perhaps the most daring missions of World War II. They would carry Mitchell's vision into combat.

"I cannot even look at a machine in the air, without feeling that some accident is going to happen to it," the young aviator wrote not long after graduating West Point in 1907, sixty-sixth in a class of 111.[8] Pranks, demerits, a middling attitude, and missing his gradu-ation ceremony due to all three marked his college record. In fact, acceptance arrived only because another applicant had decided to attend college elsewhere. Fellow cadets considered Henry "Hap"

Arnold a likeable, largely forgettable, and a minimal effort student, characterizations he never disputed. Short of six feet tall and an average 180 pounds, Hap Arnold excelled neither in athletics nor academics.

His prospects were far from bright a few years after graduation, at least in the eyes of his commanding officers. One labeled him untrustworthy and short on common sense despite above-average intelligence. Not particularly promising for a young Army officer.

After failing an ordnance school admission test, he considered a new program operated by the Signal Corps. *Maybe aviation?* Arnold entered the program in 1911, the first year Congress funded an Army airfield at Simms Field in Dayton, Ohio. He and 2nd Lieutenant Thomas Milling were the only students, reflecting widespread speculation about the risks of learning to fly. Arnold needed only two-and-a-half hours of solo flights that averaged about eight minutes each and less than two hours of additional flight time to earn his aviator's wings.

With only two aircraft in the inventory, Arnold became a flight instructor on a crash course to prepare for a deadly profession. Aircraft sometimes dove toward the ground instead of gaining altitude when applying power. When flimsy biplanes occasionally flipped over, their pilots fell to their death. It spooked the man whose family once thought he would become a minister.

Arnold wondered if there was "an unseen hand that reaches out and turns the machines over in the air for there have been so many accidents that have never been explained," he wrote in a letter to his fiancée.[9] Yet Arnold became an innovative aviator, setting an altitude record, pioneering the use of goggles, and directing artillery fire from the air.

But when his aircraft suddenly made a gut-wrenching turn toward the ground, almost ending Arnold's aviation career, it cemented a fear of flying so profound that the Signal Corps considered relieving him from aviation duty. Arnold landed at a desk in Washington, DC, as assistant director of military aviation at thirty-one years of age.

Arnold's career took off in the 1920s. He became known as an aviation officer with a penchant for aircraft research and development. Senior officer evaluations of his performance bore no resemblance to those not too many years earlier. Two brigadier generals characterized him as inspirational, cheerful, tireless, magnetic, and a natural leader who had a pleasing manner and plenty of common sense.

In 1936, Arnold became the assistant chief of the Army Air Corps on the strength of his skills as an aviator; the ability to overcome disastrous evaluations early in his career; talent as an organizational leader; and his pioneering aviation research. Equally important, early in his career he had built friendships with a handful of influential officers who were on the rise within the Army. Past postings in Washington, DC, also had taught him the intricacies of navigating political skirmishes between senior military officers, War Department officials, the commander in chief, and Congress. He knew how to skirt strict lines of authority in the military and to encourage input by qualified civilians in the interest of results.

It would not be long before the parents of Paul Gale, Roger Airgood, George Merz, Bill Frye, and thousands of others would rely on the instincts and judgments of "Hap" when he trained them to fly and on those of General Dwight Eisenhower who would then send them into combat, often in defenseless aircraft with modest fighter support at best and rarely armed with the element of surprise.

As World War II approached, the Army Air Corps was not yet ready to commit to inserting troops into enemy territory by air. Opinion remained divided among the Air Corps' seniormost officers on the notion of paratrooper combat. The Chief of Infantry, Major George Lynch, was a fan of the concept. In his view, paratroopers could be sent on specific missions; conduct reconnaissance; hold a key position if at battalion strength; or together with mechanized forces mount an effective fighting force far from the front line. But after becoming Chief of the Air Corps in 1938, Arnold was not ready to commit to the airborne, instead ordering another study of the concept (despite previous studies years earlier). He made it clear that his inventory of transport aircraft likely could not support the concept and noted he was saddled with a host of competing priorities for money, focus, infrastructure, and strategy.

That changed a year later when World War II erupted in Europe, including the use of Russian paratroopers in Finland. The American air infantry concept was now firmly on a front burner. Challenges abounded.

First, troops needed a new parachute that did not rely on a free fall as required by parachutes at that time. A combat parachute would have to open quickly and reliably, almost immediately when the paratrooper jumped at an impossibly low altitude as low as 300 feet. Within a few months, paratrooper warfare took its first step when a parachute connected to a static line inside the aircraft passed its tests and a secondary parachute, worn on the front of the paratrooper who opened it with a ripcord, passed muster.[10] Paratroopers' lives would be dependent on a bloom of silk, or one they manually opened to release a slightly smaller savior. But only after aircrews delivered paratroopers into torrents of crossfire.

Volunteers in a "test platoon" assessed the use and viability of parachutes at Fort Benning. Techniques evolved and improved, such as counting to three and then pulling their emergency chute ripcord (only about five seconds before hitting the ground) if their primary chute had not opened. By November 1940, the War Department planned to have four parachute infantry battalions established a year later. That was less than a sliver of the airborne warfare fighting capability General Arnold would have to develop. Even more daunting, there was no US aircraft specifically designed to carry paratroopers or to tow gliders over the battlefield. Likewise, a US combat glider aircraft remained only a vision.

Arnold and President Franklin Delano Roosevelt meanwhile had been plotting a massive buildup of the Army Air Corps for several years. In a meeting on November 14, 1938, the president envisioned an Army Air Corps of 20,000 aircraft, reinforced by 2,000 additional planes per month. That lofty goal would never pass Congress, so the War Department's plan was trimmed to 10,000 aircraft and 10,000 more per year, roughly half of what the president wanted. Arnold was even more realistic when his staff produced a plan for 5,500 aircraft and increasing pilot training from 300 to 4,500 men annually. Even that might be considered aggressive, since Arnold had only 1,600 aircraft under his control at the time. The Army Air Corps had been so neglected in the 1930s that he had only 22,287 personnel, only twice the strength of the cavalry.[11]

Momentum toward war escalated in 1940 when US Army chief of staff General George Marshall ordered a study of Army Air Corps needs. The following year, several commands consolidated under Arnold's control when the Army Air Corps was renamed the Army Air Forces (AAF) on June 20, 1941.

Within a week in 1941 after Arnold had asked for a follow-up needs assessment, his air staff produced "Munitions Requirements of the AAF for the Defeat of Our Potential Enemies." It became the playbook for an arms race to prepare for war in the air, calling for 2.1 million men and almost 63,500 aircraft. It also illustrated just how much a skeletal AAF had to develop. Arnold's initial air force numbered only about 6,800 planes, only half of which were combat aircraft. Many of his 1,000 bombers were obsolete.[12]

Meanwhile, Britain had been at war with Germany for about a year when Churchill called for a parachute corps. In a letter to his joint chiefs of staff, he wanted "specially trained troops of the hunter class who can develop a reign of terror down the enemy coasts … measures for vigorous enterprise and ceaseless offensive against the whole German-occupied coastline …" A week earlier, he had written "We ought to have a corps of at least 5,000 parachute troops … advantage of the summer must be taken to train these forces … Pray let me have a note from the War Office on the subject."[13]

On May 31, 1941, his chiefs of staff authorized two paratrooper brigades and a glider force capable of delivering 10,000 troops in a single lift to the battlefield. A lofty goal when British combat gliders, the Airspeed Horsa and the larger GAL Hamilcar, were still in development. Some of the bombers already waging war against the Germans needed modifications to deliver paratroopers, supplies, and tow gliders. Like the US, an entire airborne corps, including ground personnel, would have to be organized and trained.

A year after Churchill had asked for paratroops, Britain's 1st Airborne Division became operational in November 1941. The division's 1st Parachute Brigade and (glider-borne) 1st Airlanding Brigade were entrusted to a decorated World War I soldier who later had competed in the Olympics.

Like Arnold in the US, Major General Frederick Browning had barely met Royal Military College admission requirements and had been an average student who was well-liked. But he also was an accomplished athlete, having competed in the 1928 Olympics as a member of the British bobsleigh team.

In World War I as a lieutenant he had taken command of three depleted companies and successfully thwarted a German counter-attack. Horrendous casualties would plague the recipient of the Distinguished Service Order (for bravery "beyond all praise") in later years as he developed a reputation as a superb administrator.

Unlike a few US airborne division commanders who would jump with their troops, Browning best led from off the battlefield. He shattered both legs in parachute training and then became qualified as a glider pilot at forty-six years of age. Ramrod-straight posture with hands clasped behind his back, his hair slicked back, and a trimmed mustache precisely the width of his upper lip perfectly fit an opinionated, outspoken, and aloof demeanor that irked many senior US officers.

A month later on December 27, 1941, planning began to establish a Glider Pilot Regiment. With British paratrooper and glider pilot training in place and the US identifying its wartime airborne needs, deployment to the battlefield would first hinge on powered aircraft. Britain would turn to its bomber fleet and glider designers while the US would rely on the world's most successful commercial airliner while stumbling toward a combat glider design.

Like the US, Britain's bomber fleet was old and tired. The existing twin-engine Armstrong Whitworth Whitley bomber had entered service in 1938, and already was outdated, slow, and vulnerable.

With modifications it could carry only ten paratroopers or tow a single glider.

The 1940 arrival of the four-engine Handley Page Halifax heavy bomber had limited paratrooper capacity due to its design, but its size and power would enable it to tow the larger, eighteen-ton GAL Hamilcar glider whose first combat mission would be over Normandy in 1944. The Short Stirling, another four-engine bomber, featured a pre-war design, a 1941 debut, and its low service ceiling would make it best suitable for towing Horsa gliders in the war.

A proven aircraft whose design that would specifically meet Allied paratrooper warfare needs did not exist. Perhaps the plane that dominated the commercial airline industry might be a candidate. But it would have to be redesigned to withstand the rigors and realities of airborne combat that had not yet been waged. And it was an aircraft that Donald Douglas did not want to build. His assembly lines at Douglas Aircraft facilities were at capacity, building the popular DC-2 aircraft that had dominated the commercial airline industry since its debut in 1934.

Square faced, short, heavily lidded, and favoring a pipe, Douglas had a mature look that belied his youth as he had migrated through a number of aviation jobs, including one with the Army's Signal Corps. (Later in life he would travel little, live a modest lifestyle, cherish his four daughters, and become something of a recluse despite being the well-known and highly regarded founder of one of aviation's most influential aviation design and manufacturing conglomerates.)

Then Cyrus Smith, the newly installed president of American Airlines at the age of thirty-five, called Douglas. Smith wanted a luxury "sleeper plane" for night routes. It would require major changes to the DC-2, or perhaps a new version, called the "Douglas Sleeper Transport" (DST). *A lot of effort for a small market*, thought Douglas, even if a daytime, twenty-one-passenger DC-3 version could become an offshoot of the DST notion.

But when Smith assured Douglas that he would have a $4.5 million federal loan to finance purchasing twenty aircraft, the deal became real. Douglas ultimately committed 400 engineers who produced 3,500 drawings to design a new generation of night-and-day aircraft.

On June 26, 1936, the DST joined American Airlines' "Flagship Service" fleet, ready to ferry fourteen passengers across America in unimagined luxury. Cocktails, a choice of three entrees, fine chinaware and silverware, curtained berths, goose down comforters, feather mattresses, the pilot mingling with the passengers, air conditioning, and a soundproofed cabin so conversations did not require yelling now defined airborne luxury. Three months later, the DC-3 went into daytime service, cutting the cross-country flight time from thirty-three to twenty-five hours with far fewer stops and no need for connecting night rail service.

Without intending to, Douglas engineers designed DC-3 features that would make it an ideal wartime aircraft to deliver paratroopers and gliders to the battlefield and to become an around-the-clock combat cargo transport and battlefield resupply aircraft.

At sixty-four feet in length with a ninety-five-foot wingspan, the military C-47 version of the DST had a top speed of 230 miles per hour. Powered by two 1,200-horsepower engines, it carried a payload of close to 8,000 pounds with a range of 1,600 miles. An engine-powered hydraulics system strengthened the landing gear. It raised and lowered the gear in seven seconds, compared to the previous sixty or more seconds via a hand pump. Its wings could flex as much as five degrees and it was the first aircraft without struts or wires. Corrugated sheeting on the wing's top skin strengthened compression resistance. Wing-mounted lights improved visibility for pilots. Redesigned propeller blade pitch reduced demands on engine performance. Hydraulically powered rear wing flaps improved lift at takeoff and the ability to reduce speed.

The C-47 design also enabled two mechanics to change an engine in only three hours, provided greater cargo storage capacity, and had strategically located access panels for fuselage and wing maintenance.

Twenty-eight passenger capacity. Simplified maintenance procedures. More efficient propellers. Improved engine performance. Stronger wings and landing gear. Increased pilot visibility in bad weather. Greater speed control for low altitude approaches and landing. All were ideal characteristics for the combat troop carrier and glider "tug" plane the US and Britain soon would need by the thousands.

Called the "Dakota" by the British, the C-47 Skytrain would define vertical envelopment and resupply operations from Europe to the far side of the Himalayas.

But that would only be possible if enough young men stepped forward to become aircrews despite a collective fate none could possibly imagine. Future aviators like Charles Power who would survive a night floating at sea after ditching in the English Channel; Robert Nelson who would coax his wounded aircraft back to England, saving the lives of four crew members who had been wounded; Stan Fishel who would become a prisoner of war after completing his mission; Frederick Hale who would fly in the dreaded "Tail End Charlie" position; Gerald Hamilton who would be saddled with the C-46 variant that became known as a firetrap; and thousands of others on both sides of the Atlantic.

Young men who would first heed a siren's call.

2

Combat Beckoned

This is where you'll serve America best. Young men of America, your future is in the sky. Your wings are waiting!

Actor Jimmy Stewart's eighteen-minute AAF recruiting video had all the hallmarks of a movie in 1942, filled with drama, daring, enemies, showdowns, patriotism, heartbreak, and victors' glory. Young men's pulses quickened in theaters across America as Stewart tapped into their most deep-rooted boyhood dreams. The allure was irresistible.

> You'll hit 'em hard and you'll hit 'em fast on this All-American team. You'll be flying and fighting in planes that were built to scorch the sky. You'll wear a pair of silver wings. And, brother, to win those wings you've got to be good!
>
> Maybe you'll be the pilot. You'll fly a big, powerful Fortress or Liberator … a fast medium bomber … or hard-hitting fighter. The US Army needs thousands of young men to apply each month for the world's greatest aviation training as aviation cadets – to become bombardiers, navigators, and pilots.
>
> Pilot – Navigator – Bombardier – The Three Musketeers of the Army Air Forces! Each of the three is a member of a keen, hard-fighting team, relentless against America's enemies!

USAAF advertisements swamped magazines and newspapers extolling the virtues, even the moral obligations, of serving and sacrificing for America in the sky. Radio stations aired public service announcements; newspapers ran features on local young men's exploits in the AAF; and store owners taped posters on their front windows.

There was almost no mention of the thousands of pilots – along with co-pilots, navigators, radio operators and crew chiefs – who would brave enemy fire only a few hundred feet off the ground, crossing enemy territory in aircraft filled with paratroopers or towing gliders overloaded with explosive ordnance. Or of the flight officers at the controls of those gliders.

War had been pummeling Britain for three years before Stewart filmed his sales pitch. Newsreels shown in British theaters a year following its declaration of war featured combat footage, staged closeups, and a somber tone. As ground crews inspected bullet holes in a pilot's plane the narrator solemnly noted "the inference being that he's a bad pilot for allowing himself to be shot up. When you read your morning newspaper that our fighters have brought down ten or twenty aircraft, visualize what you've seen today [in the newsreel] wish them luck, happy landings, and a good rest after labor."[1] In another, "Glory of the RAF," a breathless narrator extolled "… appeals for [RAF] recruits! The training organization has been expanded as loyal young men are wanted to fly … The Royal Air Force deserves the best of men and women … if you have the qualifications, the Royal Air Force wants you!"[2]

Finally in late 1942, enough American aircraft began rolling off assembly lines, along with British bombers modified to tow gliders and Horsas, to begin meeting the training needs of thousands of Allied power aircraft aircrews, paratroopers, glider pilots, glider infantry, and ground personnel.

For both US high school or college graduates, the flight path for young men eager to realize their fighter or bomber pilot dreams began with a visit to a local examining board for an aviation cadet qualifying examination, both physical and mental, a process that spanned a week.

Frank Hansley hailed from an Ohio village that once was a Native American maple sugar camp where two rivers converged. After leaving Heidelberg College to enlist, his physical examination was worthy of bidders eyeing a prize steer at the county fair. Measurements and evaluations included his height, stature, visual acuity, color blindness, dentition, health, and blood pressure. Two days of psychomotor testing measured hand–eye coordination, finger dexterity, divided attention, steadiness under pressure, and the ability to react quickly.

Frank Bibas had studied chemical engineering at Brown University and then law at Columbia University. At twenty-four years of age, he faced the same aptitude testing as Hansley which consumed another two days. Although written examinations underwent several modifications, they focused on resourcefulness, the ability to read and understand tables, graphs, and charts, vocabulary, reading comprehension, practical judgment, mathematics, and awareness of recent developments. All were multiple choice.

Pyrotechnic signals make use of ...
The general effect of clouds on the flight of a balloon is to ...
 A solitary driver is on an urgent mission in a small scout car. In the car are an axe, spade, spare can of gasoline, and 10 feet of 1-inch rope. The driver comes to a big tree which has fallen down from a cliff and is lying directly across the road. The trunk of the tree is 4 feet in diameter and rests directly on the gravel roadbed. On one side is the cliff, the other a river, so that the driver cannot drive around the fallen tree. In such circumstances, his best procedure would be to ...
 If a motor makes 2,000 revolutions per minute, the number of revolutions it can make in 2/3 of an hour is ...
 The chief reason for recent efforts to increase the use of plastics is to ...

If they passed the physical and mental exams with a score of at least 90 out of 150, applicants learned where and when to next report. Sidney Wettstein and the others faced about two weeks' wait for their classification based on their composite testing results, called a "stanine score." For many, the two weeks' waiting reeked with dread. Evaluators could classify them as pilot cadets or candidates for navigator or bombardier training, ending with specialized combat aircrew training. Or if candidates fell short of all three, send them to aviation technical training.[3]

"We're going to turn you into a military aviator."

Those were the most welcome words Dick Welter could hear when he arrived for nine weeks of pre-flight training. He did not know that about two-thirds of the curriculum would focus on military training and physical fitness, rather than flight training. Inspections, close order drills, ceremonies, military customs, and courtesies. Worse, struggling students faced remedial classes in mathematics, physics, and the ability to read maps and charts.

Aircraft and vessel identification, as well as radio code instruction, were closer to the life of an aviator, but due to a shortage of instructors, civilian college and high school teachers were hired, even though they had almost no knowledge of the subjects they taught. Teaching the teachers as well as the students became a challenge in pre-flight training.

Some aspects of physical conditioning were specific to pilots, such as exercises to strengthen arm and shoulder muscles for long flights. Even neck muscles required strengthening. "A pilot is constantly on the alert looking up and around as he flies … [when the pilot's] muscles are developed by simple exercises of turning the head … and looking over the shoulder and up into the sky … he is better able to withstand the strain," according to one pre-flight school manual.[4]

For Hansley and others who passed pre-flight, excitement blossomed in primary flight training at the next school. That whirlwind nine-week course gave aspiring pilots their first taste of flying, usually at the controls of a Stearman PT-13. It had debuted in 1935, featuring wood-framed wings, a fabric-covered fuselage, and a top speed of 125 miles per hour.

The two-seater biplane was ideal for a new pilot: rugged and easy to fly. Its bright yellow wings became a familiar sight over training facilities. More than 3,500 flown by cadets in 1940 acquired the nicknames "Yellow Peril" and "Pilot Maker."

Students faced several phases in primary flight training. Everett Reed and others from towns known only by their neighbors – Bradford, Kaufman, Sparta, Poplar Bluff – became acquainted with the general operation of an aircraft while flying with an instructor in the other seat who provided play-by-play commentary.

"Not so steep. Take it easy."
"Do you want to stall this crate?"
"Left wing too low, pull 'er nose up."
"Watch that tachometer, she's revving too high."
"Ease back on the throttle."
"Hold a little right rudder."[5]

With one instructor for every five students, sixty hours of flight time were achievable in five weeks, about half with instructors and half on solo flights where more than a few students struggled with the vacant front seat of their Stearman.

Priorities included forced landings and recovery from stalls and spins. The next phase focused on control and precision by flying 8s, lazy 8s, pylon 8s and chandelles. Then came an emphasis on landing approaches and landings.

Just as importantly, Robert Stuck and others had to prove they could solo within eight to thirteen hours of flight instruction. Upon completion of his first solo flight, a student could wear goggles on his forehead instead of around his neck when he went to the mess hall for a meal.

It was at this stage where many students "washed out." James Ferrin's instructor concluded he "is not well coordinated, and is occasionally dangerous in the air, not only to himself but also to others. It is recommended that he does not continue as a flying cadet." Ferrin received transfer orders to a radio operator school and then to an air base in central Texas, a posting Ferrin grew to hate.[6]

The others moved on to basic flying schools where the instruction began to prepare them for the realities of combat missions over Normandy, Holland, and into Germany.

Bill Frye had left the mining backwoods of West Virginia where the Cacapon River met Trout Run. A year of college, work as a clerk, and living at home at the age of twenty-one offered a modest future. He was among thousands of young men who had faced similar prospects when he volunteered for the AAF in 1942.

At the controls of larger and more complex aircraft, he learned to fly by instruments at night, in formation, and cross country. Precision and smooth-flying skills were just as critical. While some students wrestled with the more powerful, 450-horsepower Stearman models they flew, others found their calling.

> On solo flights I always felt a oneness with the aircraft, and a closeness to God … Aloft, surrounded by blue skies by day and starlit skies at night, flying over, under and around billowing white clouds, life took on a unifying sacredness, an awesome aura, if you will, of power and glory …[7]

Those who mastered them all then faced the second fork in their military pilot careers: selection for either single- or twin-engine advanced training. The decisions were out of the students' control. While their preference was a factor early in the war, the AAF's personnel needs, each student's inherent abilities, and his physical measurements all factored into whether he was sent on a course toward dogfights, bombing missions, and stateside cargo hauling, or one toward depositing paratroopers and glider pilots in enemy territory.

In advanced training, pilot candidates strapped into a Beech Aircraft AT-10 or would "meet the "Jeep," the AAF's designation for the Curtiss-Wright AT-9. The hump-backed, small airframe made its engines look oversized and the aircraft out of proportion. It had debuted only a year earlier and became the principal aircraft in advanced training, along with stripped-down DC-3 commercial airliners until enough C-47s arrived to carry the training load.

With each hour in the air, future C-47 pilots honed their battlefield-flying skills in their faster and heavier "ship." Howard Wank and Lawrence McMahon learned how to manage retractable landing gear and hydraulic flaps. Maintaining constant speeds on longer cross-country trips at night was as critical as flying at higher altitudes while using oxygen and discovering the different aircraft flight characteristics of lighter air. Their pilotage responsibilities now included propeller pitch controls, retractable landing gear controls, handles for wing flaps, carburetor heat control, and hydraulic gauges. Developing an intimacy that enabled the pilot to locate any of them only by memory and touch was paramount.

Flying about seventy-five hours in sixty days, they developed the fundamental package of skills they would need in combat: day-and-night takeoffs, navigation and landings, engine procedures, flight emergency protocols, and instrument and formation flying.

Following about nine months of increasingly intense training, aviators who graduated from advanced training earned their commission, a set of silver wings, and had reached another fork in their route to the battlefield. Each received orders for transition training specific to the aircraft they would fly in combat.

Dreams of fighter or bomber pilot glory disappeared in their boyhood's wake for those assigned to a troop carrier group (TCG) of mostly C-47s.

> Of course, we all wanted to be fighter pilots. The next best thing was to be a bomber pilot, the way we were thinking back then. I'd never even heard of troop carrier and didn't even put it down on my application ... I ended up with about 3,500 hours flying that thing [C-47]. They'll never build another airplane that good.[8]

Transition training began with shock. The C-47 was enormous, compared to the aircraft the cadets had flown.

Richard Wilson looked up at a cockpit that was close to twelve feet off the ground, at the head of a fuselage that sloped thirteen degrees downward to the tail. Two spaces for the navigator and radio operator, each about the size of a phone booth, separated the cockpit from the main cabin.

The C-47 pilots would be flying an oversized pipeline into battle. Along the length of the fuselage's main cabin, a metal floor a little below the centerline supported two facing metal benches, about four feet apart and stamped with side-by-side square indentations about sixteen inches square for paratroopers, where they would buckle in shoulder to shoulder. The C-47's slope up toward the cockpit would force most paratroopers to lean a little toward the cockpit, up against the man alongside, legs splayed into the narrow aisle.

The flying pipe was ribbed about every twenty-three inches. In between, shrapnel would tear through sheet metal about the thickness of a coffee can as easily as a key cutting through a can of Chase & Sanborn coffee. Near the radio operator's station, a four-inch black alarm bell hung mute. Alongside the cargo door aft, separate red and green lights would signal arrival over drop zones. Near the tail, past eight feet of cargo space, a lidless toilet and narrow window in a shoulder-width latrine offered modest relief behind a metal door.

Up front, the view from the pilot's seat was overwhelming. The complexity of dials, buttons, toggle switches, level switches, status and warning lights, throttles, and other indicators surrounded him on three sides, along with additional pedals, levers, and handles on the floor.

When the two massive engines grumbled to life the first time, Wilson could feel sound waves pounding his chest as they settled into a steady, thunderous rumble. He marveled at the view through the sliding window off his left shoulder as a forty-foot wing trembled during warm-up. He knew it held fuel and could become the source of his death when he flew through tracers and shrapnel in a few months. He was twenty-one years old.

Cross-country training became a greater priority for pilots in activated, new troop carrier groups, or as replacement pilots for established groups. C-47 and Dakota pilots would be departing from Allied bases in North Africa or Britain and set a course for drop zones as far as 1,100 miles away. Mission accomplishment could rest on the navigation skills of aircrews as they crossed channels and oceans, flew through storm fronts and around cloud banks, changed course to avoid thunderstorms, and took evasive action when possible.

In transition training, ripple and wave patterns on the surface of water revealed critical wind information, as did dust patterns over farm fields. Dead reckoning skills (navigation only by calculating, speed, direction, time, and wind drift) would prove even more critical in the absence of navigators in many aircrews.

In Britain, RAF cadets followed a similar route to their wings, starting with Ground School, then Elementary Training School and Service Training School, totaling thirty-four weeks of instruction. On average, a cadet had flown between 200 and 300 hours over eighteen to twenty-four months by the time he earned his aviator wings. Once commissioned, six weeks' operational training followed.

The risks of formation flying over long distances and in uncertain weather became real when pilots and passengers died while still training in the US. In October 1942, a C-47 filled with students crashed when its carburetor iced while approaching Midway Airport in Chicago, killing everyone aboard. One day after two C-47s collided during formation flying practice, C-47 instructor Charles Young glimpsed "a transport just as it disappeared behind the trees, going straight down. Almost immediately a column of vicious blowing smoke erupted straight up." When he reached the site, "Trees were burned and scorched white for fifty feet around … A man digging in the junk reached down and picked up a shoe. There was a foot in it. I saw a hand lying within the wreckage. There was a wedding ring on the third finger."[9]

Power pilot and aircrew training proved equally dangerous in Britain. One night at a training center in central Britain, a crew on a night navigation exercise broadcast an SOS from over the Irish Sea. They were never heard from again. The next day, an engine fire erupted twenty minutes after takeoff. Three Australian crew members were injured in the following crash and one died. Four months later, a crew was lost to suspected enemy action and the following day five crewmen were injured on a cross-country night exercise. That year, sixteen accidents just at one school, RAF Lichfield, killed forty-eight crewmen and injured thirty-two.[10]

Thousands of other young men had dreamed of joining the "fly boy" ranks but had failed to meet pilot-training requirements or eventually washed out of early training. Becoming transport pilots might not carry the allure of a fighter pilot, but at least they would be flying. Some would tow glider pilots, a rarely recognized cadre that became the stepchildren of the air forces in World War II.

General Arnold's aviation arms race in the months following Pearl Harbor included orders for 4,500 gliders by mid-1943 along with 4,200 glider pilots. Specialized pilots whose mission had not been fully developed for an aircraft that had not yet been invented on December 7, 1941.

Initially, the goal had been for 4,000 power pilots to voluntarily transfer to the glider program.

Of those accepted, two glider training programs were established. Fledgling combat pilots with previous flying experience would spend four weeks at a preliminary school, in part learning how to land light aircraft with no engine power, called "dead stick" training. Dead stick training was critical to the future role of the glider. Once released from his tow plane, the pilot would control the direction and descent of his glider with "s" turns and slips (moving forward and to the side simultaneously) in making his landing approach. Day and night, the students practiced the landing technique at altitudes from 500 to 3,000 feet.

Young men who had never flown a plane faced forty hours of basic training, followed by fifteen hours of dead stick training.

By the end of 1942, a network of twenty preliminary glider training schools had been established, mostly operated by civilian contractors across the US. Schools in Wisconsin, North Dakota, and Minnesota surely would close with the first heavy winter snow (as early as October), while others in California (average January daytime temperature in Twentynine Palms, 64° Fahrenheit) and Texas would become year-round operations. Unlike power pilot schools at or near airports, several glider pilot schools had all the sophistication and amenities of a gold rush mining camp.

Like many students, Don Manke had loved the idea of flying from the time he had tried to build an airplane as a boy on his Wisconsin family farm. His introduction to flying was in Fort Sumner, New Mexico, where "it hasn't rained here for six months [and is] a place where you can see for fifty miles and see nothing."[11] Thunderstorms turned student tents' dirt floors to mud and it soon acquired the nickname "Little Valley Forge" when heavy snows collapsed tents and wicked winds threatened to destroy those still upright.

Texas would become the center of preliminary-advanced training for the pilots learning to fly an aircraft whose nicknames would include "Flying Coffin," "Purple Heart Box," "Tow Target," "Flak Bait," and "Death Crate." According to military historian Charles Day, gliders were "low performance trailers that had to be towed by C-47s to a point almost directly over the landing area, and once over the designated spot, the real piloting skills necessary to reach the ground quickly in one piece took over."[12]

Meanwhile, hundreds of RAF cadets had been learning to fly in the US since mid-1941.

After almost two years of war, Britain needed pilots, in a country, the climate of which limited year-round training and that lived with the threat of German attack. Despite the training program in Britain, the need had become critical following combat losses and the increasing inventory of aircraft requiring aircrews.

The vast American sunbelt stretching from California to Florida became the solution. The US Lend-Lease Act of 1941 authorized funds to build six training centers dedicated to RAF cadets. Each would be staffed with civilian instructors using an RAF curriculum and be supervised by RAF officers. The program spanned primary through advanced instruction over twenty-eight weeks at each school. General Arnold authorized nearly 550 aircraft trainers

(Stearmans, Vultees BT-13s, and North American Harvards) for the schools in Texas, California, Oklahoma, Arizona, and Florida.

The two principal American aircraft that would deliver troop and weaponry to the battlefield could not have taken more divergent paths from America's manufacturing mobilization, what President Roosevelt called "the arsenal of democracy," to enemy territory. While the DC-3 would become known as the C-47, "the workhorse of the Army Air Forces," the CG-4A glider was not on the drawing board at the start of World War II.

Three months after the president called for America's industrial mobilization in 1940, Douglas Aircraft Company began constructing a massive manufacturing plant in Long Beach, California, adjacent to the city airport. Eighteen buildings spanned 2.8 million square feet where 43,000 employees ultimately produced a C-47 or bomber every ninety minutes. Just seven months later and sixteen days after the attack at Pearl Harbor, the C-47 made its initial test flight. It was the first of 9,441 produced for the AAF by Douglas for the US and more than 1,900 for Britain.[13]

The British, meanwhile, would rely primarily on modified two- and four-engine bombers along with a limited number of C-47s from America.

Meanwhile, the drive to invent and test a battleworthy US combat glider towable by C-47s stumbled through a host of pratfalls and blunders. It had taken almost a year, but on June 20, 1942, the AAF found its glider when a fifteen-passenger prototype completed a trip from Wright Field in Ohio to Chanute Army Field in Illinois and back, a flight of 220 miles.

Designed by the Weaver Aircraft Company ("Waco"), the CG-4A was a distant relative of the Eiffel Tower. The glider's lead designer was Francis Arcier, who had studied aeronautics from Eiffel Tower designer Gustave Eiffel. After immigrating to the US, Arcier had designed one of the first all-metal airplanes in 1930, itself a distant cousin of the pioneering DC-2 that debuted only four years later.

Just who would manufacture the gliders was anyone's guess, including the Army. The AAF took no chances by awarding sixteen contracts to manufacture the Waco design, including those to companies unqualified to build any combat aircraft. Only four had any related experience and only two, Ford Motor Company and Cessna Aircraft, possessed manufacturing facilities.

The manufacturers relied on a network of subcontractors cobbled together in hopes their backgrounds in steel tubing, wood, and fabric could be adapted to war. A casket company fabricated metal fittings. Steinway & Sons would build wire-controlled tail and wing assemblies. A wood product company in Minnesota produced surprisingly complex flooring to support heavy glider cargo loads.

Only Ford Motor Company met the AAF's production goals, by retrofitting a station wagon plant into a wartime aircraft production facility. No stranger to high-volume production, its engineers pioneered a method that reduced the time to dry glue from up to eight hours to ten minutes by utilizing the plant's waste steam.[14]

Authentic, combat-relevant flying experience began to mount for both tow aircrews and glider pilots. In less than a year, the tandems would be flying hundreds of miles from air bases in England to the Continent's battlefields, through clouds and fog, deep into enemy territory, descending to 600 feet through enemy fire, and then releasing their laden "box kites." Then turn, drop their tow ropes over a designated location, and make the return trip, often again through the enemy's gauntlet.

The CG-4A glider resembled a mutant dragonfly with a large, squared head (cockpit) in front of fuselage more than forty-eight feet long that tapered to a large tail. Its strut-based wings spanned eighty-four feet. Covered in doped cotton fabric, painted, and wrapped around a tubular steel frame, a few glider pilots likened it to a box kite with all the finesse of a boy's entry in the Soap Box Derby. To others, it looked like what a handyman might build in his barn.

The glider's crude appearance belied its 70,000 parts, including a sophisticated honeycomb wood floor that increased its payload. Fully loaded at 3.7 tons, each glider carried up to thirteen glider infantry or a combination of 37mm or 75mm artillery, medical supplies, jeep, trailer, ammunition, ordnance, and explosives. Twelve infantry sat shoulder to shoulder on two facing benches, a thirteenth on a small seat near the exit door. Small portholes on each side proved ineffective against airsickness.

The British glider version, called the "Horsa," would dwarf the Americans' CG-4A. It carried twenty-eight passengers or more than 7,000 pounds of cargo. Constructed primarily with plywood, Horsas were as long as an American heavy bomber. Approximately 3,800 Horsas would be built by a network of subcontractors similar to the US approach. Predictably, RAF pilots generally preferred the Horsas while American pilots considered them more ponderous compared with their slightly nimbler CG-4As. Truth told, both had little more agility than a snow sled.

The Allied airborne combat arsenal took shape in 1942. Britain had established its 1st Airborne Division and Glider Pilot Regiment earlier and the US activated its 82nd and 101st Airborne Divisions in mid-August. C-47 aircrews, glider pilots, RAF cadets, and paratroopers were training over deserts, prairies, and farmland at dozens of bases from Georgia to California. In Britain, Operational Training Units for Dakota and Horsa flight personnel had been established at RAF Bramcote, RAF Crosby-on-Eden, and RAF Wymeswold.

Douglas C-47s began arriving in significant numbers. Of the more than 10,000 that were ultimately manufactured, aircrews began ferrying the first of nearly 2,000 C-47s destined for the British RAF under the Lend-Lease program. The RAF's modified Halifax bomber had entered service in 1940, the Short Sterling the next year, and the Armstrong Whitworth Albemarle would join the fleet in 1943. The British Horsa had made its first flight in late 1941, the Hamilcar followed in March 1942, and the American CG-4A was authorized for production three months later. The Allied fleet of gliders that would ultimately total approximately 18,000 finally took shape. While the US C-47 Skytrains and British C-47 Dakotas would tow the bulk of gliders into war, the British Stirlings, Halifaxes, and Albemarles also would tow gliders into combat and drop paratroopers to a limited degree, despite their bomber designs and defensive machine gun stations.[15]

Previews of mission airborne triumph and tragedy had marked 1942 as well. In February, a 120-paratrooper RAF raid on a German early-warning radar outpost near Le Havre on the English Channel had been successful. British commandos captured vital equipment, intelligence, and a radar operator had been taken prisoner for interrogation in England. Half of Operation *Biting*'s force assigned to secure the beach had been dropped more than a mile from its assigned drop zone, however, a precursor of future missions.

In November, a two-glider RAF mission to attack a German heavy-water production plant in Norway failed miserably. Ice accumulation broke one glider's tow rope. It crashed into a Norwegian mountainside as its Halifax returned to England. Half the personnel died in the crash and the others were killed by the Germans. The second Halifax in Operation *Freshman* crashed, killing the aircrew. Its glider survivors were shot within a few hours of capture.

US recruiting had been so successful by the end of the year that the AAF had a surplus of power pilot applicants and had assigned 93,000 to inactive reserve pools. Another 9,000 volunteers were training to become combat glider pilots.[16]

C-47 aircrews meanwhile developed the fine touch of inching the throttle forward to straighten a tow rope, gently applying forward pressure to increase their speed enough that their glider lifted off the ground first and held steady, then added more throttle, more speed, and finally pulling back on their control yoke to lift the C-47's nose and begin a long, shallow climb. Before running out of runway and plowing into a cotton field or barn.

Some men in training experienced firsthand how a routine flight could become as disastrous as a direct hit taken in battle. Glider pilots died when tow ropes broke at low altitude, forcing one glider crew to crash into a stand of cottonwoods at night and another to slam into a cinderblock building, the only obstacle for miles in the prairie's expanse. In Britain one night, a Stirling flew low and hit a tree not far from Warnford Park. The glider it towed crashed, killing the two pilots and twenty-four paratroopers.[17]

Long before approaching the shores of Europe, they had learned how a quirk, odd circumstance, or bad luck in training would bring a messenger's knock on the front door back home.

> Vision that morning was bad. Lots of fog and several layers of clouds … when that plane was making a left turn the pilot saw another plane coming at him in the opposite direction, about to drop a tow rope. To avoid the tow rope, the shuttle plane made a very steep climb, but he began to stall out … We saw it make almost a full nose-up stall, then slide backward and fall off on the right-wing side about 1,200 to 1,500 feet. As it started to dive the pilot had full emergency power on, trying to pull it out. But he never could get the nose up and it went almost straight down in a swamp near us. The plane's impact was so violent that we found the melted engines maybe twenty-five feet down through the mulch and the earth under that swamp.[18]

Meanwhile, combat beckoned. On missions of extraordinary aircrew vulnerability. In an aircraft powered by two 1,200-horse-power radial engines five feet wide and four feet long, each only about fifteen feet from the pilot and co-pilot. Twelve-foot propellers spinning at forty-two revolutions per second. Strapped into a cockpit with a single overhead escape hatch and with their parachutes hanging from a hook. Surrounded by control panels nearly chin high limiting visibility to narrow, horizontal windows. Sitting atop a labyrinth of twelve connected fuel tanks. With no guns. *At least bombers have machine guns,* some pilots mused.

In only seven months, British paratroopers and glider pilots, American glider pilots, and C-47 aircrews all would meet over Sicily.

Too Good to be Wasted

We should not permit transport pilots to carry well-trained American soldiers with the same nonchalance that routine cargo is flown on a freight line. Unless the parachutists and troop carrier personnel have an opportunity to work together and understand the other's problems the best planned operation may fail due to lack of good teamwork and cooperation.[1]

Anger had gnawed at American navigator Paul Gale when he boarded his C-47 in Tunisia late on July 9, 1943, a night that had turned angry. The unexpected storm's wind gusts told him his aircrew's flight while towing a glider across the Mediterranean in a few hours would not be smooth. Crew chiefs were starting the engines of 143 other C-47s, the aircrews of which would fly the same turbulent route toward Malta and then north to Sicily.

Where are the new coordinates? Releasing a combat glider was a precise business, based on a specific longitude, latitude, and altitude. Carefully calculated by factoring a loaded glider's weight, glide slope, and environmental factors. Gale had received release data premised on less than ten-knot winds or calm conditions. But now it was obvious gale-force winds would batter the C-47s that later were estimated to approach forty-five miles per hour a few hundred feet above the ocean.

A shortage of navigators in part had led to the decision that only one navigator would be assigned to each four aircraft. Serials (groups) of C-47 pilots would follow their leader, based largely on his navigator's directions. Worse, there had been minimal glider-towing training at night for the airborne's role in Operation *Husky*, the Allies' first major airborne assault of World War II. Gale had participated in only two daytime training missions with gliders.

Not long after takeoff as they headed out into the Mediterranean, RAF glider pilots Lieutenant Walter Carn, Sergeant Edward Garratt, Staff Sergeant John Ainsworth, Captain Thomas McMillen, and others wrestled to control their bucking gliders above the churning whitecaps, so low that the waves' sea spray plus squalls generated by the tugs' propellers blurred their visibility. The gliders were flying almost sightless into battle.

Eighteen months had passed since the Japanese attack at Pearl Harbor and almost four years since Hitler had invaded Poland. In early 1943, the Allies finally stood ready to wage war in Europe. President Roosevelt and Prime Minister Churchill had decided at their Casablanca Conference in mid-January that Sicily would be the springboard to the European Theater of Operations (ETO). Its thirty airfields two miles off Italy's southern coast had plagued the Allies for three years in North Africa and now would be key to invading Italy and possibly taking the Italians out of the war.

A linchpin of Operation *Husky*'s amphibious landing would be major airborne paratrooper and infantry support, a war strategy not yet tested by the enemy. A strategy that demanded training in simulated combat conditions; large-scale rehearsals; intricate coordination between the air forces, infantry, and navies; and communication that could withstand the bedlam of combat. Preparation, teamwork, and cooperation. The keys to defeating the enemy and limiting personnel and aircraft losses to "acceptable."

A landing delivered by more than 2,500 ships, Operation *Husky* would be a one-two punch attack against an enemy force estimated to number 230,000. Like a straight cross to the enemy's chin, General George Patton's Seventh Army would land on the south coast and advance northward across the island toward

Palermo. A right hook by General Bernard Montgomery's Eighth Army's amphibious landing would come on Sicily's east coast south of Syracuse, its initial objective to the north. Once Patton reached Palermo, he would turn his troops east to link up with Montgomery near Messina at the northeastern tip of the country. The pincer would herd surviving enemy forces into a desperate, battered evacuation to Italy.

Four airborne paratrooper and glider infantry missions on three nights would support Operation *Husky*, comprised of mostly C-47s (60th, 61st, 62nd, 64th, 313th, 314th, and 316th TCGs), American CG-4A gliders, and a few British Albemarles and Halifaxes. The aircrews would deliver the American 82nd Airborne Division's 505th and 504th Parachute Infantry Regiments and the British 1st Airlanding Brigade and 1st Parachute Brigade, beginning just after midnight on July 9, followed by July 11 and 13 drops. Four waves were sequentially codenamed Operations *Ladbroke*, *Husky I*, *Husky II*, and *Fustian*.

Only hours before the troops came ashore before dawn on the 10th, Paul Gale's aircraft was part of Operation *Ladbroke*, mostly C-47 aircrews from two troop carrier groups tasked with towing 144 gliders carrying 1,700 infantry to three landing zones near Syracuse on the east coast. Their objective was to capture the Ponte Grande canal bridge in support of the British Eighth Army coming ashore a few hours later.

Simultaneously in *Husky I*, 226 aircrews from four troop carrier groups carrying more than 3,400 505th Parachute Infantry Regiment paratroopers would arrive over their drop zones on both sides of midnight near the port of Gela on the southern coast, only about two hours ahead of General Patton's troops wading ashore.

Operation *Husky II*, delayed a day to July 11, would put 144 aircraft into the air, headed for an abandoned airfield near Gela on the south coast with the 82nd's 504th Parachute Infantry Regiment.

In Operation *Fustian* two nights later on July 13, 135 aircraft would deliver 1,856 paratroopers (and 286 parapacks) of the British Parachute Brigade north of Syracuse to take the Primosole bridge. Nineteen Albemarles and Halifaxes would tow gliders filled with members of the 1st Airlanding Anti-tank Battery Royal Artillery and their heavy equipment. The paratroopers and gliders would use the same drop and landing zones.

Four airborne missions on three nights to buttress two beachheads, seize key objectives, and clear routes inland. On each mission, the aircrews' orders were to fly in formation, at night, approximately 450 miles from the far side of the Mediterranean. They would be making endless small corrections in airspeed, power, and altitude to stay in position as they crossed over Allied ship convoys; penetrated the Germans' anti-aircraft defenses; and reached their landing or drop zones on time and on target. Coordination would be vital. They would not have the element of surprise, however.

A month earlier, one of Hitler's most respected and experienced airborne commanding officers, General Kurt Student, had predicted many of the key elements of Operation *Husky*.[2] He anticipated two main assaults (near the ports of Syracuse and Gela); aircrews would arrive from North Africa; they would most likely arrive between midnight and 0200 hours; and they would engage German positions on the ports' landward sides.[3] All were spot on.

More alarming than Student's instincts was the lack of Allied preparation prior to the invasion. One historian concluded Operation *Husky* "lost its logic" when General Montgomery decided not long before Sicily's D-Day that Operation *Ladbroke*'s British glider mission would take place at night. That compounded an earlier decision that had assigned the glider mission to the 51st Troop Carrier Wing which had no significant glider towing experience. That placed a premium on preparation, but the gilders' arrival was delayed and sometimes delivered to the wrong North African bases. Unlucky American and British glider pilots were assigned to glider assembly. By the time enough were finally assembled, the training calendar had been strangled.

Due to a British pilot shortage, inexperienced C-47 aircrews would tow American gliders piloted by British glider pilots largely unfamiliar with the CG-4As. They had accumulated an average of only 4.5 hours' training (only 1.2 hours of it at night) and approximately sixteen landings apiece. A large-scale rehearsal was out of the question. Twenty-two American glider pilots would fly as volunteer co-pilots in Operation *Ladbroke* and four more in the follow-up Operation *Fustian*.

The battle began long before the gliders reached Malta. Blustering winds rocked every aircraft, particularly the gliders that weighed only about one-third that of a loaded C-47. Paratroopers and glider infantry discovered their paper bags sagged and then split under the weight of vomit. After several hours' flight, some C-47 aircrews missed the navigation beacon on Malta, others began overtaking their flight leaders, some began to lag, and others were pushed off course. Wicked weather and limited navigation capability had already made a carefully orchestrated glider arrival impossible when a wall of searchlights and anti-aircraft artillery bursts, called "black roses" by some aircrews, appeared dead ahead.

Orders required the tow pilots to release their gliders 3,000 yards from shore to stay outside the range of the enemy's artillery barrages. *How the devil do you know when you are 3,000 yards from shore at night without any instrumentation?* Navigator Gale and others recalculated and adjusted their final approach, the flight plan be damned.

"What do you want me to do?" asked the pilot.
  "You have to move up."
  "Well, I can't move up. There are planes over me, there are planes under me, there are planes alongside of me."
  "If you move up, they will move up because everybody is flying on everybody else. Otherwise, cut it [the glider] loose here. We might as well drown here if we are going to drown."[4]

Desperate to accomplish their mission in a hail of artillery fire, many aircrews made repeated runs to get to their designated release points, then turned back into oncoming aircraft. Others took evasive action with what they wished could be sharp turns and sudden dives. But a C-47 flew "in slow motion" compared to their boyhood dreams of piloting a fighter. In some ways, their turns without power steering resembled the handling of a twenty-ton, fully loaded Mack truck. Maddeningly slowly when under enemy fire.

Communication proved haphazard as about one in three communication cables wrapped around the tow ropes between the planes and gliders failed. Some conceded victory to the wind by releasing their gliders well beyond the 3,000-yard mark. The gliders' release often came with no warning. A few had a second's warning.

"Glider from your tow ship. You are opposite your point of release. Goodbye and good luck."[5]

"You see those fireworks up ahead? I believe you're close enough."[6]

Operation *Ladbroke* turned tragic as glider after glider crashed into the sea. Hitting hard, some bouncing, before the cockpits plowed into the sea, suddenly stopping as if stuck in wet concrete. A few shot down by enemy fire, many from release too far from shore. *How many had made it to shore? Any? Anywhere near their landing zones?* No one could be sure as the formation had disintegrated as mauled C-47s flying closer to shore turned, dropped their tow ropes, and headed back toward Tunisia on solo missions of survival.

Not far away, 226 aircraft carrying 3,405 paratroopers of the 505th Parachute Infantry Regiment had flown across the Mediterranean at times as low as 200 feet to avoid enemy radar, a vast force spread across 100 miles of ocean. Near-zero storm visibility, sea spray, radio silence, and howling wind had created the same havoc as that endured by the glider force. The steady drum beat of windshield wipers and howling wind marked their odyssey into battle.

Whether over a drop zone or several ridges away, the enemy was everywhere. Aircrews ducked and weaved as they looked ahead for a potential drop area so they could settle at 500 feet on a straight line for their paratroopers, the enemy's artillery and small arms fire be damned. For some aircrews, death came in a second while others found themselves alongside their paratroopers and the enemy on the ground.

Captain Lawrence D. Lichliter's aircraft was one of many modified with external bomb racks attached to its belly to carry parapacks that could be dropped with critically-needed battle supplies. Direct hits on engines and gas tanks often started a fire or a more localized explosion, barely piercing the howl of combat. In a split second, his C-47 disappeared in a fireball. Fellow pilots believed Lichliter's parapacks held ammunition, the cause of the massive explosion, instantly killing the aircrew.

His left engine afire was costing 2nd Lieutenant Ernest Terry power and altitude after he had dropped his paratroopers. Nose down and heading toward the sea, any hope of saving his crew rested on his ability to turn and land his C-47. If possible, as close to one of the drop zones and hopefully near American troops. Just as glider pilots were learning elsewhere on Sicily, exiting their crashed aircraft and finding cover as quickly as possible was paramount in enemy territory where aircrews often became surrounded if they survived the crash. Shortly after landing, Terry and his radio operator, Corporal Felix Pientka, were killed by a German machine gunner while 2nd Lieutenant Clyde Casey and crew chief Charles Power lay in a ditch, pinned down most of the night until paratroopers neutralized the enemy threat.

Decisions confronted aircrews throughout the night as floating C-47s began taking on water or smoldered ashore. *Do we swim for the beach? What about the wounded guys? Which way is the tide going? Is this ditch deep enough for us? Should we head for those trees? Where's that shooting coming from? Anybody got a first aid kit? How much longer before daylight?*

Warrant Officer Bob Uhrig recorded aircrews' chatter following the *Husky I* mission. Responsible for a smooth-running airplane on each mission, crew chiefs typically stood behind the pilot and co-pilot to monitor the instruments during takeoff, route of flight, and landing. Then, as an aircrew approached a DZ (drop zone) or LZ (landing zone), they climbed a ladder up to peer out the clear, bubble-shaped astrodome in the top of the fuselage behind the cockpit to watch for visual signals from other aircraft or to pass along visual signals. Crew chiefs and sometimes pilots were in unique positions to witness aircrews' carnage, bravery, and sacrifice as *Husky I* unfolded.

> We had an equipment pack ready to throw out [the door] when there was a terrific explosion, and debris flew into the ship and into our faces. We found out later that it was a ship in front of us that had blown up … I watched this until she hit the ground and then there was a terrific explosion which lit up the whole sky.[7]

> We were flying along at about 850 feet above the ground just over the target when we were caught in the beam of a searchlight which they kept on us for about one-and-a-half minutes, but it felt like hours. The next thing I knew they shot the ship down that was flying in back of us and I saw him blow up and crash.[8]

Operations *Ladbroke* and *Husky I* failed miserably to meet their combat objectives. Only twelve gliders reached their landing zones while sixty-nine crashed at sea. More than 600 men died, half by drowning. Fewer than one in six *Husky I* paratroopers reached the vicinity of their drop zones, scattered across 1,000 square miles of southeastern Sicily. Six loads of paratroopers remained unaccounted a month later, although many engaged the enemy as smaller units until they consolidated.[9] Colonel James M. Gavin, a regiment commander in the 82nd Airborne, landed twenty-five miles east of his drop zone, so far off the mark the bursting shells to the west reassured him that he was in Sicily. A small victory in an airborne disaster that would ripple far beyond the C-47s floating offshore. A disaster that would reach Bayard, Iowa.

Second Lieutenant Jack Stiles had held steady in the last element of his formation as the enemy's artillery shells punctured the sky with red and white bursts. Shock waves and shrapnel had pounded fuselages, shattered cockpit windows, and sliced through young men about to jump into the chaos.

Seconds after the last paratrooper jumped from his plane, Stiles nosed into a controlled dive "down to the deck" to get under the enemy's artillery. It was the last time he was seen as each pilot on the mission, once free of the paratroopers he had delivered, turned away and charted an individual course back to his base in Tunisia.

Stiles had earned his wings less than two years earlier. He had graduated Bayard High School in Iowa in 1937 and had taken classes at Drake University in Des Moines to meet the pilot training qualifications. Athletic and studious, he had married Virginia Doty from Amarillo in a ceremony while training in Missouri.

Shortly after the Sicily campaign a telegram arrived in Bayard. Stiles was missing in action. A telegram with no specifics and only a vague promise that updates would arrive "when more information becomes available." After only six months' marriage, Virginia might already be a widow.

Two nights later, the 144-aircrew from four troop carrier groups (61st, 313th, 314th, and 316th) carrying the 504th Parachute Infantry expected a "milk run" under a quarter moon on July 11. Allied troops had stormed ashore more than thirty hours earlier. A day's delay from July 10 due to uncertain battlefield conditions had provided more time for preparation and better communication in Operation *Husky II*. The weather had settled over the Mediterranean, enabling steady formation flying until the airborne fleet would set its course on its final leg along a corridor about two miles wide and extending two miles inland toward the drop zones near an abandoned airfield east of Gela in support of the American 1st Division.

Mission completed, they would turn parallel to the coast, remain inland for several miles, and then turn toward the sea and back across the Mediterranean. The route would avoid any friendly fire from the 3,000 ships and 150,000 troops, most of which had reached Sicily's coast.

The route proved deadly. Coordination and communication crumbled as the aircraft approached Sicily's coast.

> ... one .50 caliber machine gun, situated in the sand dunes
> several hundred yards from shore, opened fire. As soon as this

firing began, guns along the coast as far as we could see toward
Punta Socca opened fire and the naval craft lying off the shore …
began firing anti-aircraft guns.[10]

Husky II disintegrated against a wall of enemy and friendly fire
both at sea and over land. Improvisation by pilots on their first
combat mission trumped routines learned in training. Impromptu
combat tactics that had been impossible to realistically teach over
Nebraska. "The airplane spun at a right angle and nearly pulled the
controls out of my grasp. For a second, I didn't realize what had
happened. Then finding myself out of formation I began a violent
evasive reaction. I saw three planes burning on the ground and red
tracers everywhere as machine gunners sprayed us as if potting a
flight of ducks," recalled one C-47 pilot.[11]

Other aircraft, mortally wounded, fell out of formation as well,
including Flight Officer John Uphouse's plane that streamed flames
as it plunged toward the sea. Their mission had morphed: "have a
plan and work through the panic," they had learned in training.
The aircrew enabled their paratroopers to exit before friendly fire
had scored several direct hits. Uphouse's C-47 hit the water a few
hundred yards offshore. Days passed before it surfaced along with
the dead aircrew. Uphouse had grown up in the Pacific Northwest
wearing the uniform of the Wolf Club. Similar to the Boy Scouts,
he had spent his childhood in uniform, marching in parades,
bugling, singing, and appearing on a local radio station. He would
never complete his first combat mission.

Snap decisions by some pilots offered their paratroopers a
chance at survival, an opportunity later cruelly extinguished.
One pilot gave his jumpmaster twenty minutes' warning. Later,
the red light illuminated. Four minutes to go. Only one minute
later, green. "Go!" The paratroopers jumped into a stream of
friendly fire from troops on the ground. Some had not gotten the
word that American paratroopers were inbound that night and
assumed they were German.[12] Infantry from the 45th Division
killed three in the air, and another died when he failed to give the
correct password.

Options were few for the aircrews when Allied ships pounded their aircraft along with American troops ashore taking aim as they approached. Aircrews flashed their red recognition lights to stem friendly fire. Sergeant John Hoye and other pilots ordered their crew to fire flares. They were red, leading to speculation later that perhaps the surface ship crews thought the flares to be enemy fire. Their return fire intensified, the sound of shrapnel clanking off Hoye's plane sounding like hail pelting a metal shed. Hoye struggled to stay in formation when shrapnel cut through his face and arm. A bullet found his mouth, splintering three teeth and part of his upper jaw. He and his crew held a steady course as his paratroopers jumped. His plane now ablaze, he managed to successfully crash land, his descent so horrific that personnel first listed him as missing in action for fear of a fatal crash.

Second Lieutenant George Merz had insisted on a ditching rehearsal in Tunisia. Now on his approach to the DZ, his flight leader's formation lights disappeared as anti-aircraft fire erupted. *Stay the course. Now, the red light.* His paratroopers stood, hooked their chutes to the static line and waited. *Almost there.*

The mid-air collision felt like a gut punch. Somehow, his flight leader's plane had collided with Merz. His right elevator and the lower half of his rudder control surface gone, Merz could feel the wobbled C-47's immediate loss in altitude. He had to find a "safe" place to land. He turned toward the sea as the crippled C-47 drained more altitude.

"Prepare for landing."

His crew chief and paratroopers pushed the two small howitzers he was carrying out the cargo door before impact. His paratroopers, though, would ride with him into the sea. *Sit down, buckle up, and hold on.*

"Landing lights."

"Half flaps."

Only seconds now, as Merz killed the power to both engines. The C-47 plowed into the water, sending one paratrooper crashing into the cockpit's control console before the plane settled, nose down, and water began to fill the cabin. "Everybody out!"

For the second consecutive airborne mission, the results of *Husky II* would nettle not only senior officers up the chain of command to General Dwight Eisenhower, but dozens of devastated families back home. Twenty-three C-47 aircrews had crashed due to friendly fire and thirty-seven others had limped back across the Mediterranean in severely battered aircraft. A loss ratio of sixteen percent was intolerable. A handful of pilots had returned with their paratroopers, saying it would have been suicide to have them jump into the crossfire. Others had braved as many as three passes over their DZ, hoping to illuminate their green light to drop their paratroopers into the maelstrom.

According to one historian, "the legend of a navy which shot from the hip without distinguishing friend from foe spread widely and lingered long among the troop carrier units."[13] Surely such fratricide would never occur again.

The last airborne support mission for Operation *Husky* was Operation *Fustian* on July 13. More than 130 aircrews flying C-47s would deliver paratrooper and glider reinforcements.

Aircrews from three American TCGs (60th, 62nd, and 64th) and British pilots flying a few Albemarles and Halifaxes would fly the same route from Tunisia to Malta as previous missions and then turn north to make a run up the east coast to DZs and LZs several miles north of *Husky II*'s destination two nights earlier. The route would take them over forty miles of Allied convoys and warships. Incredibly, across forty miles of friendly fire again, this time initiated by a transport ship crew that had not been informed of the airborne mission. C-47 aircrews pressed ahead, into a mirror image of *Husky II*.

German bombers had attacked the Allied fleet shortly before the C-47s arrived. The ships' gunners might have mistaken the silhouetted parapacks on the C-47s' bellies for German torpedo bomb racks. While the lead aircrews in the 60th TCG reached their DZs unscathed, the remainder endured murderous Allied salvos.

First Lieutenant Lee Carr figured he was in for it, flying far from the front of the airborne assault and with no hope of being overlooked.

Yet the first convoy he overflew remained dormant. But another convoy near Syracuse opened fire, even after Carr illuminated his red identification lights under his fuselage. *The lights are enabling those guys below to be more accurate.* Soon a river appeared, a marker for this final approach to his DZ. He dropped down and flew along the river before making his final turn and pulling his nose up to reach the prescribed drop altitude.

At 350 feet, a searchlight found him and seemed to lock on as tightly as a movie's closeup. So did enemy artillery. The C-47 took several hits, body blows that vibrated through its airframe. Seconds later, his paratroops saw the green light. No more than five exited before Carr's evasive piloting threw the rest to the deck. More direct hits ripped off a small cargo door and pounded the tail. Piece by piece, shrapnel gashed the plane, dismembering it with each thud.

He dove back to the treetops and exited the area until he was out of the enemy's range so his crew could reorganize for a second run to the DZ. *Round two,* it seemed. Again, spotlights stuck to the C-47, as if on cue for the enemy fire's barrage to hit the plane's belly with its red tracers, cutting through the fuselage. Even as the aircraft rocked from the punches, more paratroopers jumped as the crew chief, Staff Sergeant John Wallace, was accidently pushed out the door (he was wearing a parachute). Then back to treetop level to depart, circle to regroup, and turn back for round three. The remaining paratroops jumped this time, even though static lines tangled. Carr's crew had fought as long as possible. It was time to head home, to the far side of the Mediterranean.

Like a punch-drunk fighter, the aircraft's controls had become sluggish, the plane heavy as it slowed. The impact with the sea tore away the right engine. The plane bounced, as if trying to get off the mat, but settled. The C-47 finally stayed down, about two miles offshore. Carr and his crew swam back to Sicily and eventually contacted friendly forces for evacuation. They reached their base a week later.[14]

Each crash landing in the sea started a new battle, the chaos of getting out. *Get the life rafts out the exit. Get 'em inflated. Help the injured paratroopers remove their gear and get into the raft. Did we*

get everybody out? Keep sending the distress signal before the plane
sinks. Be sure the maps and photographs are secured so they go down
with the plane.[15]

Allied fire forced Staff Sergeant Robert Wellingham and his
co-pilot, 1st Lieutenant Robert Cristina, off their course. They
headed out to sea and then turned to make a run toward their DZ,
flying so low the C-47's propellers trimmed two haystacks. When
their right engine exploded, there was only one choice. Pull back,
gain altitude to 400 feet, and bail out. In seconds, flames reached
the cockpit, burning Cristina on his arm and face. As the plane
nosed over, Cristina and the rest of the aircrew scrambled toward
the door at the rear, climbing over the bodies of dead paratroopers.

His parachute barely opened before Cristina hit the ground, the
C-47 crashing so closely in a mangled metal pyre of death that
he could feel its heat. Cristina and another airman later captured
a group of Italian soldiers before reaching a British outpost and
returning to his base a week later.[16]

A nightmare awaited the few British glider pilots who reached
land. Many were horrified at the mission's landing zones filled with
obstacles. Captain Thomas McMillen and Lieutenant Walter Carn
both suffered shattered ankles in hard landings. McMillen landed
his glider only a few hundred yards from the Ponte Grande Bridge.
Riding side saddle on a bicycle, McMillen led his men under fire
toward the bridge, ultimately capturing it with others. Cut off
from ground troops, his men carried Carn to a farmhouse where
he directed his men's attacks for fifteen hours behind enemy lines
until united with friendly forces. Both earned the Military Cross
for their heroism.

Individual gallantry surfaced throughout the night. Staff
Sergeant John Ainsworth successfully landed his glider at sea. Once
he ensured his men had escaped and wore life jackets, he swam
three miles to shore armed with only a knife and engaged enemy
troops. After surviving his glider's crash inland and getting clear,
Sergeant Edward Garratt returned to evacuate his troops still inside
who were too injured to run, limp, or crawl to cover. Detonating
ammunition almost severed one of his arms as he helped his men to

safety. He remained with them without food for the next thirty-six hours. The following day, his arm was amputated.

Ainsworth received the Military Medal and Garratt the Distinguished Conduct Medal.

The results of Operation *Fustian* eerily mimicked *Husky II*. About ten percent of the total airborne force had been shot down. Thirty-four aircraft were heavily damaged. Twenty-five returned to Tunisia with their paratroopers after evading enemy and Allied fire or had been unable to locate navigational landmarks obscured by smoke and battle flames. Only four of the sixteen gliders that had left Tunisia played a meaningful combat role that night and the paratroopers again found themselves widely dispersed.[17]

Although the Allies captured Sicily about eight weeks later when they drove the German and Italian troops off the island, recriminations and ramifications rippled across Allied command. A host of British glider pilots considered the American C-47 aircrews cowards for releasing their gliders too far at sea in Operation *Ladbroke*. (Those returning to Africa with planeloads of paratroopers in *Fustian* reinforced that perception.)

Yet the aircrews' orders were not to fly over land; to release their gliders 1.7 miles from shore to stay outside the range of enemy anti-aircraft artillery; not to wait for the glider pilots to release; and had received inconsistent orders on the proper altitude to release their gliders.

Meanwhile, friendly fire and dispersal across a broad swath of Sicily had decimated paratrooper personnel and significantly compromised their combat value.

Operations *Ladbroke*, *Husky I* and *II*, and *Fustian* were Pyrrhic victories by all measures. A company of 120 British troops had orders to take the Ponte Grande bridge and hold it until reinforcements arrived. But they were so dispersed that only a platoon of thirty was in position to accomplish the mission. No more than eighty-seven of 1,730 men defended Ponte Grande bridge at the height of the battle. Similarly in Operation *Fustian*, a paltry 295 men were able to assemble at their respective rendezvous points out of a force of 1,855. Paratroopers discovered they were spread across thirty miles on Sicily, to say nothing of the hundreds who never made it ashore.[18]

Yet in Operation *Husky*'s aftermath, the 82nd's command-ing officer, General Matthew Ridgway, remained a supporter of airborne troop missions by issuing six tactical principles for their continued use: night operations are most likely to be successful, routes should be based on the best obtainable intelligence, daytime operations require air support, use of airborne divisions in airborne operations is not warranted until adequate aircraft are available, airborne division usage should be limited until larger ETO opera-tions develop, and their training should be as light infantry and be used for shorter periods to provide combat experience.

Major General Joseph M. Swing, an Allied airborne advisor, cited five factors that led to the disastrous airborne results: poor route coordination; reliance on a complicated route; a trigger-happy Navy; coincidental enemy bombing raids; and poor communication with anti-aircraft crews. Neither questioned the American aircrews' nor the British glider pilots' devotion to their mission orders or courage.

Similarly, the Fifth Army Airborne Training Center issued a stinging analysis: "Training was, in general, inadequate. Combat efficiency for night glider operations was practically zero. The combined force of [82nd] Airborne Division and troop carrier units was extremely deficient."

Dismay matched anger in notable post-mission British reports.

"Of the 72 gliders [carrying 796 men] … 44 came down in
the sea, 20 in Sicily, 7 in Africa and 1 in Malta. On a personnel
basis, this meant that 64% of the [Battalion] came down in
the sea, 25% in Sicily, and 11% in Africa and Malta. The
[195 men] who came down in Sicily suffered 18% casualties in
landing, chiefly from handcarts which broke away from their
lashing-points, and 12% casualties in action, a total of 30%.
Of the 28 officers and 478 [others] who landed in the sea, 19%
reached Sicily by swimming and then joined the land party,

suffering casualties in action on a similar scale; 23% have been reported drowned, missing believed drowned, or missing; 1% were killed or wounded by enemy action at sea; and 57% were picked up in the sea, and returned to base via Malta, Algiers, Alexandria, and Suez. Most of those drowned managed to get out of the gliders but then sank before freeing themselves of their equipment and climbing onto the [gliders]."[19]

Despite his last-minute changes in his ambitious and untested air plan, tardy gliders that crippled training plans, and a night mission with inadequate training, General Montgomery pulled no punches in his diary. "The big lesson is that we must not be dependent on American transport aircraft, with pilots that are inexperienced in operational flying. Our airborne troops are too good and too scarce to be wasted."[20]

General Eisenhower had become an airborne division skeptic. Smaller, self-contained units could be inserted into enemy territory from the air. More on a guerrilla basis, he suspected, than a massive assault force. Otherwise, airborne division-sized operations were too complex; required too many resources; had proven to be too vulnerable; and would be excessively unreliable in view of the risk.[21]

American navigator Gale agreed with Eisenhower's operational cynicism:

That was the most grievous mission in military history. I had sixty-four missions before I finished the war, and that was the one that disturbed me the most.[22]

The troop carrier pilots, co-pilots, navigators, radio operators, and crew chiefs flying nearly 650 sorties over Sicily had been dealt a bad hand. Their first time in combat, they had been given orders from senior officers equally inexperienced in massive airborne operations against an entrenched enemy. By any measure, the aircrews were test pilots flying unprotected in aircraft on enormously high-risk missions. Yet they pressed ahead, flying through unimaginable crossfire.

The cost in blood for the airborne combat's maiden mission was unsustainable as the invasion of the European continent loomed. The human cost, especially at the hands of fellow infantry, ships' crews, and their officers, gnawed at enlisted and officers alike. A cost that never surfaced in *Stars and Stripes* news reports at the time.

Furthermore, several contributing factors would echo in future airborne assaults. Out-of-date intelligence. Poorly selected landing and drop zones. Inadequate use of pathfinders and their limited ability to communicate with the incoming airborne force. The limited capacity of the CG-4A and the relative fragility of the Horsa.[23] The attendant loss of heavy support weaponry from crashes and scattered parapack drops.

If they were to play a significant role in Normandy, pathfinders marking DZs and LZs before sunrise would be necessary, far stricter flying corridors would be critical, and there would be no flights at night over Allied anti-aircraft emplacements, including the Navy.

"Friendly fire." Operation *Husky* demonstrated it was perhaps the greatest and the deadliest misnomer of World War II.

Granted that every war is madness ... fratricide ... is the worst of all; it reaches deeper into ugliness, cruelty, and absurdity.[24]

4

Get 'em Out!

The main thing we're interested in tonight, even above our
own safety – repeat – even above our own safety, is to put a
closed-up, intact formation over our assigned DZ at the
proper time so these paratroopers of ours can get on
the ground in the best possible fighting condition. Each
pilot among you is charged with the direct responsibility of
delivering his troops to the assigned DZ. Their work is only
beginning when you push down that switch for the green light.
Remember that.

A barnstorming pilot before he enlisted, Lieutenant Colonel
Charles Young, stood before a map of Normandy on June 5, 1944,
that stretched toward the ceiling. Dozens of aircrews sat before him,
some bare-headed, others wearing helmets, and several hunched
forward, chins resting on open hands or clenched fists. Now the
commanding officer of the 439th Troop Carrier Group, he scanned
the taut faces of young men who had trained for almost two years
to fly into combat. On the signature airborne mission of World
War II. D-Day at Normandy. "If we can give the airborne the best
drop in a practice session, I have every reason to believe we can do
it on the real thing."[1]

The deepest fears of the pilots seated before him were as visible
as a Times Square scrolling sign.

The Allied invasion of Europe, Operation *Overlord*, was hardly a secret in early 1944, but where? Surely it would come from England, but on the shortest route to Calais or 175 miles away at Normandy? The 2,400-mile German defensive line on the north coast of Europe had been fortified for years following Germany's invasion of France. Thousands of concrete bunkers were bolstered by a reported 6 million mines and clusters of heavy artillery emplacements. Forty-two infantry and panzer divisions bivouacked in the area, although not fully manned. Fifty thousand Germans had dug in to defend Cherbourg's deep water port on the Cotentin Peninsula, a sliver of land only twenty-three miles wide. The Germans had concentrated artillery in the area, flooded dozens of fields, and studded others with stripped, upright tree trunks about thirty yards apart and connected by wired mines (called "Rommel's Asparagus"). They could become a random collection of Allied tombstones if gliders plowed into them, fileting C-47s' fuel-filled wings, or if paratroopers drifted onto the mines' trip wires.

Submerged inshore barricades and mines were no less daunting for the 150,000 American, British, and Canadian troops bound for five beaches on more than 5,000 ships in Operation *Neptune*, the naval and airborne part of *Overlord*. The Americans would land at beaches codenamed "Utah" and "Omaha," British forces at "Gold" and "Sword," and Canadians at "Juno."

The assemblage of aircrews was unprecedented. Squadrons from fourteen US troop carrier groups from three air wings (50th, 52nd, and 53rd) would coordinate with fifteen squadrons from the British No. 38 Group and No. 46 Group RAF.

In addition to the two-pronged amphibious assault, more than 13,000 paratroopers of the 82nd and 101st Airborne Divisions and more than 500 American and British gliders would land or drop onto nine zones clustered around Ste-Mere-Eglise at a strategic crossroad six miles inland from Utah beach.

At the same time to the east, the RAF's 6th Airborne Division would be supporting approximately 8,000 men in the 2nd British Army's I Corps coming ashore. The British amphibious force included Canadian, New Zealand, and Australian personnel as well.

The 3rd and 5th Parachute Brigades and the 6th Airlanding Brigade would drop and land about five miles inland from the beaches, midway between the coast and Caen.

They all would rely on Allied aircrews flying more than 1,000 C-47, Dakota, fighter, bomber, and subsequent resupply sorties across the English Channel, praying Sicily's friendly fire nightmare would not be repeated, yet inevitably enduring enemy fire tearing into their aircraft as they descended to make their final runs. Then spotting their designated drop and landing zones on their first pass.

Operation *Overlord* could not succeed without the airborne troops achieving their tactical objectives in Operation *Neptune*. The American 4th Division on the right flank risked stagnation and annihilation if paratroopers and glider infantry failed to clear routes inland from the beach. The 82nd and 101st Airborne Divisions had to block German reinforcements from moving forward once the amphibious landings were under way. Equally important, disrupting enemy communications behind the frontline would buy valuable time for Allied troops to establish a beachhead with adequate manpower and firepower. The British assault formed the easternmost flank of *Overlord*. The 6th Airborne's inland battlefield objectives were to capture two bridges at Benouville and Ranville to thwart German counterattacks, destroy four other bridges on two nearby rivers, destroy a heavily fortified German artillery installation threatening Allied ships offshore, and occupy a ridge near Ranville to block enemy troop movement.

If all went well to the east, British commando units at the forefront of the troops wading ashore would link up with the 6th Airborne's force by the end of D-Day.

Multiple pre-dawn waves of C-47s and modified British bomber aircrews would arrive over Normandy on D-Day. Several hours before sunrise the Americans would fly Operations *Boston*, *Detroit*, and *Chicago*. Their target areas were about twenty miles from RAF aircrews flying Operation *Tonga*. Both would deliver pathfinders, followed by their main force, and then gliders with reinforcements and equipment. Shortly before sunset, the British would fly

Operation *Mallard* while the Americans flew Operations *Keokuk* and *Elmira*.

Mission accomplishment would rely on aircrews surviving the battering by enemy fire while staying on course to fields and pastures surrounded by the enemy. Flying through curtains of high-explosive and armor-piercing ordnance from the Germans' concentrated 88mm *Flak* 36 emplacements firing thirty-four pound shells every four seconds and 20mm *Flak* 38 autocannons unleashing torrents of searing fire at 220 rounds per minute. Shredding, slashing, rupturing.

First Lieutenant Louis Emerson, Jr, would have to stay focused on his mission as a pilot after writing farewell letters to his wife, Marilyn, his unborn son, and to his parents before he climbed aboard and took off. Elmer Wisherd could not worry about his family back home or wonder if his father had bagged a deer or two for the family freezer. An attorney before he enlisted, Mitchell Woods would have to concentrate on his radio gear. Thoughts of family and his father's law practice had been stowed when he had climbed aboard hours earlier.

For many British officers, D-Day's Operation *Neptune* had become real a week before takeoff. RAF Lieutenant Richard Todd sat among thirty officers in a briefing for the first time on D-Day's assault plan. Hundreds of aircrews would soon receive similar briefings. Sergeant Clifford Bevan, a bomb aimer; Pilot Officer Joseph Smith, a rear gunner; and Flying Officers Albert Barton and Richard Watkins were among those whose dread of being shot down while staring at oversized maps later might become shock at survival. All would fly toward a baptism of horror.

The aircrews' mission accomplished, the paratroopers and glider infantry then would have to fight for time once they landed. Although one paratrooper considered himself "a loaded ammunition dump" as he had climbed aboard, most carried only enough ammo and combat supplies for two or three days and there was no assurance the supply parapacks and bundles later dropped by their aircrews would land in friendly territory. Reinforcement missions later on D-Day and D+1 (Operations *Freeport, Memphis, Mallard, Rob Roy* and others) could become lifesavers if the enemy kept the airborne troops from linking up with the Americans' 4th Division or the British I Corps.

The largest airborne mission to date was dangerous, but not the house of cards that Sicily had become. This time, the English Channel crossing would be on a clear, moonlit night with sparse clouds. Bold black-and-white identification stripes on every plane's wings and rear fuselage would help avoid the sins of "friendly fire." A surfaced British submarine's navigation light would be one of the more prominent landmark beacons this time. The US and British aircrews flying generally parallel routes would cross the Channel as low as 500 feet, rise to 1,500 when passing over the French coast, and then descend to make their final run. Trailblazing pathfinders would mark drop and landing zones. The lessons of Operation *Husky* remained fresh among mission planners.

Despite Young's confidence in his men, at least one senior officer considered Operation *Neptune* almost a suicide mission. RAF Air Marshal Sir Trafford Leigh-Mallory, the commanding officer of *Neptune*, envisioned devastating losses. In a memorandum to General Eisenhower a week before D-Day, Leigh-Mallory feared losses could reach half of the 82nd and 101st paratroopers and seventy percent of the gliders. He likened the plan to "throwing away" the two airborne divisions over the course of five waves. First US Army Corps General Omar Bradley argued that, despite the risks, the airborne mission was critical to the success of his amphibious assault plan.

More than 1,200 troop transports, 1,000 CG-4A gliders, 300 Horsa and Hamilcar gliders, and thousands of aircrews and glider pilots stood ready to deliver the paratroopers and glider infantry in less than twenty hours on D-Day. One pilot likened England to a huge aircraft carrier as American troop carrier groups, 38 Group RAF, and 46 Group RAF would depart from more than twenty airfields.[2]

More than 400 aircraft would deliver the 101st in Operation *Albany*. Another 369 aircrews would fly in the troops of the 82nd in Operation Boston. Both would jump at about 0130 hours, shortly after the pathfinder teams had marked the drop zones. Not far behind, more than 100 aircrews would tow gliders in Operations *Chicago* and *Detroit* to support both divisions. The gliders would release at about 0400 hours. All would converge on nine target zones, some of which overlapped one another, before sunrise.

Similarly, British aircrews would fly C-47 Dakotas amounting to nearly half the 11,600 aircraft assigned to the invasion as well as Albermarle, Stirling, and Halifax aircraft. The bombers were armed with three manned gun turrets and bomb bays. Some aircrews would combine a bombing assignment with their paratrooper or glider mission. The Dakota aircrews were as defenseless as geese flying in a staggered head-to-tail formation.

Two hours before midnight on June 5 in Operation *Tonga*, approximately 275 British aircrews would take off with pathfinders to mark and light DZs and then about thirty minutes later the main body of paratroopers would arrive. Two hours later, a glider force of more than thirty aircrews followed, towing Horsas and Hamilcars loaded with engineers, paratroopers, heavy equipment, and tanks. Operation *Tonga* would be only the opening act of D-Day for the 6th Airborne, for which several squadrons had been training for two years.

Only fifteen hours after RAF aircrews had taken off the night before, many would sit in their idling aircraft waiting for the signal to begin their takeoff with a glider on their second mission of the day. More than 300 gliders in Operation *Mallard* would reach Normandy in the last wisps of daylight on June 6. A few hours' sleep, a midday briefing, aircraft refueling, necessary repairs, and marshalling into position for takeoff had been completed by 1700 hours. By 2100, the gliders would circle and descend toward their landing zones as aircrews again turned for home.

A second American glider wave, Operations *Keokuk* and *Elmira*, also would arrive at about 2100 hours on D-Day, just before sunset on British Double Summertime.[3]

Collectively, airborne troops all would land in a glider or on their feet in a thirty-six-square-mile patch of hedgerows. About every 200 yards, centuries-old parallel embankments covered in impenetrable brambles and mature trees hid paths that separated the hodgepodge of fields. Large enough for enemy troops, vehicles, and light artillery to defend, ambush, and reposition under cover. Operation *Neptune* troops would fight on a chessboard of isolated battles separated by the equivalent of honeycombed above-ground tunnels, one tree line to the next, often requiring a day to advance one mile.

Detailed Allied briefings, by group and by squadron, had accompanied senior officers' motivational speeches. Operations laid out mission objectives and reviewed landmark and topographical features on sand tables and easels; Navigation charted courses, beacons, turning points, and destinations; Communications rolled through frequency monitoring; and Weather talked of clearing skies, a full moon, and scattered clouds on the western approach to the DZs and LZs. A 1,500-foot-thick fog bank (as low as 500 feet) over the Cotentin Peninsula went unnoticed.

There would be no weather planes flying in advance of the invasion and aircrews would follow strict "radio silence" orders. The airborne invasion plan had been calculated down to thirty-minute increments following a two-hour flight across the English Channel. If the pathfinders could successfully reach their drop zones and set up their radio-transmitting "Eurekas" only about one-half hour in advance of the paratroopers, the "Rebecca" receivers aboard the lead aircraft might have a path through the cloud bank. If not, American and British pilots, co-pilots, and navigators would have to make sudden decisions and calculated guesses when they went "feet dry" over France.

The sheer scale of Normandy airborne missions had required months of practice in English skies, simply learning how to efficiently marshal hundreds of aircraft into the proper sequence and separation long before they reached the battlefield. Thousands of hours practicing in the air had been necessary if each aircrew was to be in a precise position hours after takeoff to drop men or release gliders over a few farm fields hundreds of miles away.

The first fatality of Operation *Neptune* on the eve of D-Day was time.

We waited … I realized that the die was cast and that I would
shortly be facing death for the first time in my life … I kept
wanting the signal to start engines to be given. The longer the
wait the greater the anxiety. Suddenly, there was a flare shot
from a jeep beside the runway … the signal to start engines …
at exactly 2300 hours, there was another flare and the lead ship
started moving.

For more than an hour before takeoff, 1st Lieutenant Louis
Emerson, other C-47 pilots, paratroopers, glider pilots, and their
glider infantry had mingled among the aircraft and gliders. Taking
photos. Checking their aircraft. Smoking. Chatting. Playing cards.
Writing letters. Dozing. Praying. Again, checking their aircraft.
Small groups lingered outside while others climbed aboard as they
tossed Woodbine or Lucky Strike cigarette stubs aside. A few wrote
messages on the fuselages, often in a weak attempt at humor or a
vulgar note to Hitler that left no doubt.

Many paratroopers had been eager for a ray of optimism from
their pilot when the aircrew arrived, even though their questions
repeated training lessons and mission briefings. "How high will
we be when we jump?" "What will your speed be?" "Will there be
planes behind us?" Perhaps confirmation would breed confidence
just before takeoff.

It also had been a moment of intense reflection before the engines
started. Chaplains made their rounds among the aircraft and after
the paratroopers had settled onto their fuselage benches. "I made my
way from plane to plane. I went down the long line of paratroopers …
I tried to touch their hands and often gave them a pat on the head.
I missed one lad and he seriously said, 'Chaplin, lay your hand on
my head.' I did, too, and no one laughed. The grips of the hands of
the [air]crews and the pilots were especially long and hard. To them
I said, 'I can't run your ships, but I will pray.' Their response was an
emotional 'Thanks, Chaplain' or 'Thanks for coming.'"[4]

The RAF's D-Day "stand to" order also arrived on June 5, after
several days of air testing the squadrons' aircraft one last time. For
most paratroopers and aircrews, a hot midday meal started the

final countdown at airfields assigned to the two RAF groups. Then to the airfields where they examined aircraft once more, checked equipment, adjusted harnesses, and where several aircrews met each other for the first time. Late afternoon naps were an option, but few were taken.

Before takeoff, squadron chaplains gathered their men into a semi-circle for a field service. Standing on an ammunition box, one offered his perspective, faith, solace, and inspiration to an audience that mostly stared straight ahead, faces smeared with black cream, weapons laid across their helmets on the ground. Two hymns, "Onward Christian Soldiers" and "Abide With Me," marked the time to assemble at each plane in jumping order. Lieutenant Todd stood at the head of his line as his pilot, 1st Lieutenant Gordon Thring, and the remaining members of his Stirling aircrew settled into their positions. Hundreds of aircrews and their paratroopers did the same at eight British airfields.

Takeoff sequences began playing out every few seconds across southern England on either side of midnight on June 5. One engine, then the other, awakened, turning over slowly before the propellers erupted into a blur. Pulsating vibrations spread into the cockpit and fuselage, up through the pilots' padded seats and across the shallow, metal paratroopers' bucketed benches. The planes began to rock gently as the engines' revolutions per minute (rpms) increased as if they were floating on a calm sea, the propellers now invisible.

First at 1,000 rpms to warm up, then faster to make sure dials and gauges remained "in the green." Louder and louder as exhaust heated the fuselages' paper-thin skin. Fumes – a mixture of wood shavings, metal, hot grease, and oil – somehow seeped into the main cabin. The cacophony outside took an angry tone, muting conversations. The planes quivered just short of takeoff power, as if anxious to start a run. It was time to go to war.

Everyone checked and tugged their seatbelts. In the cockpit, some pilots prayed, unaware that their breathing had turned shallow. After takeoff checklists had been reviewed and switches tested, cockpit lights were doused when pilots donned wrap-around red glasses for fifteen minutes to adjust their eyes to the darkness that would blanket every man on his way to the battlefield.

The prop wash buffeted fabric-covered and mostly plywood gliders from cockpit to fuselage where the glider infantry waited, staring across the main cabin at one another. In most cases, aircraft towing gliders waited along the runways' edge, wingtips close to touching, with the gliders aligned on the centerline. Occasionally, the C-47s were on the centerline with the gliders staged at a forward-facing angle along the runways' edge. Ground crews had already connected each to its tug aircraft using a 350-foot nylon rope less than one inch thick and wrapped with a communications cable. They had staged all aircraft nose to tail, as tightly packed as a marching band waiting for its cue to step out.

Finally,

> "I looked left and saw another big group [of aircraft] ...
> Another fleet of airplanes was moving in from the right
> and pulling into the line we were in. Further back behind
> this group was another convoy of airplanes, joining us in
> an ever-growing show of force. It was a sight that I've never
> forgotten. The timing was so good, and the preparations were
> so good, that all of these airplanes could come in and line up,"
> recalled one crew chief.[5]

When the takeoff signal finally appeared, the lead C-47s and Dakotas inched forward, then rolled and built speed. Each following pilot watched the airfield's aircraft controller, up ahead and standing off to the side, for the signal to follow. A two-arm gesture as if pulling the plane forward, then a sweeping motion of the controller's arm as he turned toward the end of the runway – as if he were starting a car race – spurred each aircraft from its creeping start.

Slowly at first and then "pouring on the coal" to reach takeoff speed. At sixty-five miles per hour the plane leveled when the tail rose. More speed as each plane swayed a little. As the speed mounted, rudders and ailerons became responsive. Then, at ninety-five miles per hour, those with paratroopers left the ground. Unsteady air bounced the planes, leaving no doubt among the paratroopers that they were airborne. For those towing gliders, the gliders first broke free of the ground and then held steady, slightly above their tow planes. After months of training, the tug pilots could feel their gliders' lift on the taut tow rope, as if a catfish had mouthed the bait and was moving off. To some, it felt like a bus slowly pulling away from a stop and building speed. At some airstrips, buddies briefly ran alongside the runway, waving or pointing with extended thumbs up. Seconds later, each tug plane rose, often with precious little runway to spare.

One trailed another as quickly as every ten or fifteen seconds. Yet it could take as long as an hour for a squadron to become airborne and then assemble into formation before heading toward France. *We're under way.* Two turns on the way to the assigned altitudes were accompanied by slight power reductions from takeoff speed. As the aircrews adjusted flight controls for maximum flight efficiency, each plane "settled in," like a horse finding its natural pace. The engines' racket, no longer sounding as if each was straining to become airborne, settled into an almost soothing rumble.

The spectacle roused English families for miles around, drawing them outside.

"I ... gaze[d], awestruck at the constellation of their red, green, and yellow lights, which rode across the heavens and streamed southward toward the sea. It seemed as if every aircraft in the world was in flight as we followed wave after wave without intermission. Dim disciples of darkness became black plasmas of the clouds, which the moon had not yet risen to illuminate. The element of noise in which they swam became solid, filling our ears, entering our lungs, and beating the ground beneath our feet like the relentless surge of an ocean swell," recalled one lad.[6]

Simply reaching the battlefield required pilots to trust each other as they flew in formation across the English Channel, flying only two hundred feet apart at close to 140 miles per hour. In back, after two C-47 rides in training, paratroopers were riding to war. Most were silent, even the jokers in the group, as the engines' hypnotic roar was interrupted only by the clicks of cigarette lighters if the smoking lamp was illuminated.

Hundreds of pilots turned off their red and green navigation lights as they assembled over their bases before heading toward the enemy. Downward recognition lights were extinguished later after they passed over the bulk of the Allied fleet and as they approached the French coast, leaving only the blue formation lights atop the wings and fuselage to avoid midair collisions. Some paratroopers began muttering "Hail Mary, full of grace ..." Soon shrapnel, sounding like rocks hitting a tin roof, pounded home certainty.

For those in the rear of serials, each pilot flew by "follow the leader," locking onto the formation lights and the glow of exhaust stacks and flame dampeners of the plane directly ahead. The airborne armada's lights resembled a "lit highway," according to one pilot when he turned at an English Channel navigation beacon and looked back at a parade that stretched back to London and beyond.

Operation *Neptune* had gone "too smoothly" across the English Channel. Enemy artillery on coastal islands had fallen short and the aircraft had avoided German radar. Then, only ten to twelve minutes before reaching the drop zones, the fog bank appeared in the Americans' path. A thick, ominous wall with no way of knowing how far it extended inland. Flying mostly at 700 feet, most pilots opted to head straight into it.

American combat formation flying was based on "Vs of Vs" of nine aircraft, a lead group of three closely trailed by three on each side. The flight leader of each nine carried additional responsibilities for his flock as the trailing aircrews knew to follow his airborne cues. Dropping down through the cloud bank might not leave enough altitude for a drop once they cleared it. *Will the following pilots be able to maintain visual contact as they descend? Will the group drift off course only minutes before reaching the DZ by flying through the clouds? Or better to go over the top and bet there will be enough time and distance left once we clear them?*

Making a "dead run" by staying in the clouds would force pilots to fly without visual cues or landmarks, relying only on their artificial horizon indicator, tachometer, airspeed, and manifold pressure gauges. When flight leaders disappeared in the gray blanket, some trailing pilots instead pulled hard for more altitude before breaking clear at almost 2,000 feet while others headed for the treetops to avoid midair collisions, risking enemy artillery flak from the 88mm guns that could fire almost horizontally to rip through wings and the fuselage, if necessary.

Either way, fog had transformed five major practice missions involving all the groups a month earlier into a beehive of smaller missions with fates likely dictated by those sitting in the cockpits. *Will the drop zone be clear? Can I hold steady low and long enough for the paratroopers in back to jump? Too low, though, to give my crew a chance to bail out afterward if we're hit? How much longer can I stay at this altitude? "How's our oil and hydraulics look?" Keep checking my gauges in this soup. "How's it going back there?"*

Luck, though, could trump pilots' skills, instincts, and training.

On his way to *Albany*'s drop zones, as 2nd Lieutenant Marvin Muir approached the French coast, his plane took a direct hit in its belly, just behind the cockpit. Pilots flying on his wing saw flames erupt inside the fuselage, trapping Muir and his co-pilot. They could not be sure about the navigator and radio operator just aft of the cockpit. Muir held his course as his paratroopers jumped in a matter of seconds. *Now what?*

Muir fought a dying plane as it nosed upward, perhaps as he tried to avoid the rest of the formation, and then stalled and fell onto its left wing, then to the right. He fought to regain control as fire engulfed the main cabin and at least one engine. Dropping fast, other C-47s pulled away to avoid a collision as Muir's speed increased, past 150 miles per hour, much too fast for a controlled landing. Now in a thirty-degree dive, his crew sat helpless as the ground rushed up. Everyone died on impact, ending a nightmare than had lasted less than sixty seconds.

Muir had enlisted in 1941. The Indiana native was twenty-four years old. His parents would receive a killed in action notice, and news later that he had been posthumously awarded the Distinguished Service Cross for his "selfless, courageous actions and extraordinary heroism … at the cost of his life."

As aircrews trained together they grew as close as brothers at home. Yet now they were flying in a cloud of uncertainty, not knowing who would return to their airfield. Not knowing whose bunks would be empty.

As the fog draped their cockpit, 1st Lieutenant William Hitztaler and 2nd Lieutenant Stanley Edwards lost contact with their formation. While still at 1,000 feet, eighteen 82nd paratroopers jumped as the aircraft absorbed dastardly accurate enemy fire. Shrapnel hammered the aircraft just behind the cockpit, destroying the control panel and wounding Staff Sergeant Orlo Montgomery, the radio operator. He fell off his seat, clutching the legs of the navigator, 2nd Lieutenant John Hendry, who stood next him. As his blood stained the deck, Montgomery lost consciousness.

The spreading fire in the left engine and along the trailing edge of the left wing could trigger an explosion at any second in an uncontrollable aircraft. Except for Montgomery and a wounded paratrooper, the aircrew bailed out. Their fates would be as diverse as their boyhood paths that had led them to an airstrip in England months earlier. Hitztaler's wife and Hendry's father later welcomed William and John home, thanks to French families who risked their lives hiding them after they had parachuted to relative safety.[7] The mother of crew chief Alvin Vezina and Stanley Edwards' father would have to wait. Both spent the rest of the war in a German prisoner of war camp. Bernadine Montgomery later learned that she had become a widow on D-Day. Her husband's remains were never recovered. Decades later, he remained listed on the Tablets of the Missing at the Normandy American Cemetery in France.

Five crewmen had spent months together in the air, training, trusting, and developing a sense of teamwork. A brotherhood as tight as a fraternity. Like all aircrews, wondering what fate awaited when the day came to fly toward France and the enemy. Only minutes apart, two were rescued by the French Resistance, two became prisoners of war, and one died.

Major Campbell Smith held his aircraft steady, flipping the main cabin's green light as he broke free of the clouds with *Boston's* drop zones fast approaching. It cast a "ghastly glow" on the face of paratrooper Eugene Hetland, first in line and standing at the open door, according to Technical Sergeant Winfield Wood. William Streiter and George Shenkle standing close behind did not look any better.

"Get 'em out!"

The crew chief tapped the paratrooper's shoulder. He yelled, jumped, and the others followed in seconds, each yell quickly swamped by the engines' and war's cacophony.

"All clear!"

In less than a minute, eighteen paratroopers had jumped and Wood had pushed four bundles containing more than 1,000 pounds of ammunition, demolitions, and a 60mm mortar out the door. As Wood gathered the static lines, without warning, the plane lurched downward and almost onto its left side, an evasive maneuver to gain speed and fly under enemy fire. *Have we been hit? Do I jump?* Wood couldn't be sure. The wings leveled as Smith pushed the throttle "to the stops" for even more speed. Then he turned for England.

They had dropped their troops spot on at 0206 hours, right on time, in a black sky filled with the reddish-black bursts, engines flaming yellow, and aircraft sinking out of formation as the remainder headed for England.

As the Allied aircrews fought their war over their drop zones, the paratroopers' war began, sometimes before they jumped, dove out the cargo door, or stepped into a bomber's jump hole. "The plane was going down. I moved as fast as I could to get out and, after bailing out, saw the plane go up in a ball of flame." "As I stood near the door, a shell exploded under the left wing, and the ol' 47 did a handstand on the right wing tip, and I was thrown back across the cabin. There was a mad scramble to get out the door, but I was able to get there first so I didn't get tangled in any static lines." "Just as I approached the door, the top of the airplane opened up. It had been hit by some type of explosive shell. As I turned into the doorway, the plane started a right wing dip going into its death spiral. It took everything I had to get over the [jump door] threshold. It seemed to me the threshold was just a little more than chest high as I rolled over and got out. I was the last man out of the plane." "I pitched down through a wild Fourth of July. Fire licked through the sky and blazed around the transports heaving high overhead. I saw some of them go plunging down in flames."[8]

Aircrews that survived crashes joined paratroopers and glider crews on the ground. Not long after releasing his glider, 2nd Lieutenant Floyd Bennett tilted his head just slightly and looked down toward a wing. The right engine didn't sound quite right to the co-pilot.

"Feather right engine," ordered the pilot, 2nd Lieutenant Samuel S. Cromie, as he powered the left engine. It sputtered, then gagged. Yellow daggers erupted from the shredded right engine. The crash became as certain as falling rotted tree fruit with no hope of a soft landing.

"Get ready to crash!" The navigator, crew chief, and radio operator ran back to the main cabin. Their plan was to lay down and press feet hard against a bulkhead. They did not make it. They hit and caromed off trees before stopping. Daylight poured in from the rear. The tail was gone. The right wing was missing. So, too, was much of the left wing.

All that remained was to destroy equipment and materials in the dismembered hulk, stay out of the snipers' line of fire, and hope nearby paratroopers could direct the aircrew to a command post.

Meanwhile, RAF takeoffs were as organized as the Americans', flying a more southerly route from west of London to the Caen area while the IX Troop Carrier Command had approached from the northwest. Yet over France they shared the same horror, unexpected enemies of survival, and fates that could be as unpredictable as many were heartbreaking.

A Nightmare

Enemies abounded as Operation *Tonga*'s RAF aircrews approached France before dawn and then near sunset on Operation *Mallard*. Drifting cloud patches had forced several aircrews below their prescribed altitudes for their glider's release. Haze dimmed the moon. Although fog had thickened to the northwest on the Americans' route, wind and foul weather also had dispersed the RAF aircrews into approaches from every direction toward target zones.

Later in the day with the enemy fully alert and zeroed in, RAF aircrews' fates hinged on skill and the enemy's aim dosed with luck.

Survival in war can be cruelly fickle when surprise evaporates. When Flying Officer Richard Watkins and his aircrew were shot down, most appeared to have survived the crash. But they had come to a stop in the midst of an entrenched enemy. German machine gun fire killed the navigator and most of Watkins's aircrew and their paratroopers before they could exit the aircraft. Not far away, Flying Officer Albert Barton, a former policeman, carried an entire platoon in his Dakota when enemy fire brought down his aircraft. In a split second, his aircrew of six and the nineteen paratroopers trapped back in the fuselage perished on impact. An entire platoon gone in a second. A single piece of shrapnel found Sergeant Clifford Bevan, a bomb aimer, over Normandy. He suffered for at least two hours on the return flight England. He died shortly thereafter. His gravestone reads, "Not gone but waiting ahead, his duty done. God's greatest gift, remembrance."

Flying Officer Gordon Wilson's mission had been almost as routine as a training exercise. At 0105 hours near Caen, the Canadian flying with the RAF and his Albemarle crew dropped nine paratroopers, six kitbags, and six containers. The aircrew had returned to its Portsmouth airbase at 0246 hours. Nineteen hours later, the same crew in the same aircraft took off on its second mission, towing a glider. This time, they did not return.

Two minutes after glider release, enemy flak set their Albemarle on fire at less than 200 feet off the ground. Wilson pulled hard on his yoke. When he reached 1,100 feet he ordered his crew to "abandon ship." What had been a crew of strangers months earlier, a former college student, clerk, railroad porter, and self-professed "traveler," bailed out. No one saw the rear gunner, Pilot Officer Joseph Smith, exit the aircraft.

Wilson slammed into a roof while his three crewmen landed either in fields or hung from trees before cutting themselves free. In each case, French villagers guided them to Allied units and escape back to the beach.

Wilson's navigator, Flight Lieutenant J. K. Maxwell, had spotted a burning aircraft shortly after he had cut loose from his parachute in a tree. *Is that our plane?* As he approached the scattered wreckage, burning flesh and smoldering hair grabbed his throat. Already too charred to immediately identify, Pilot Officer Joseph Smith, the rear gunner, later was listed as killed in action.

Approaching from the northwest, 1st Lieutenant Robert Nelsen and his co-pilot, 1st Lieutenant Joseph Denson, had crossed the width of the Contentin Peninsula in less than eleven minutes while looking for his drop zone in the absence of a pathfinders' radio signal. When he reached the English Channel, the crew realized "we had gone a beach too far." A sharp right turn brought them back westward for a second pass and another barrage of enemy machine gun fire. It could have been from the Germans' 20mm autocannons or a MG-42 machine gun that was lethal at Nelsen's altitude and could fire more than 1,000 rounds per minute.

This time, it raked the length of the fuselage. The aircraft lurched briefly, power returned, and the paratroopers jumped. Their chutes swung only twice before hitting the ground. Hard.

Four of his five aircrew members lay or sat bleeding. Splinters had peppered Staff Sergeant William Aldridge's face when an enemy bullet decimated navigator Walter Connors' wooden table. Shrapnel had hit the second lieutenant in the buttocks.

Up front, Nelsen sat bleeding as Denson took control of the aircraft. His wounded aircrew pulled Nelsen out of the cockpit toward the paratroopers' bench seats for a dose of morphine. Nelsen started sweating. Profusely. A hard turn put the flying aid station on a course for England and an emergency landing strip. The only good news was confirming the C-47 was not bleeding oil or fuel and that Denson flew unharmed. The crew fired a red flare to alert ground crews that medical attention was necessary upon landing. At 0430 hours, personnel cleaned Nelsen's wound in an emergency room. He survived his shattered leg wound.

Denson was the only crewman not sent to the hospital. "The British doctors gave me a few swigs of scotch, and later a bottle of gin," he recalled.

To the north, 2nd Lieutenant Robert Airgood smelled gasoline only seconds after he had dropped his paratroopers near his designated DZ. Chaos and confusion had marked the route through the fog bank, following the cues of the flight leader who slowed at the last second to jumping speed, too fast, forcing Airgood to cut power and push his nose up to avoid over-running his flight leader and then mainline a blast of power to avoid a stall. *There's the landmark. The church steeple.* The green light spewed paratroopers out the door in the midst of added power. Not what they had practiced. Then a steep dive to 100 feet and a turn toward home. The gasoline smell now put the aircrew on a different alert. *Where? How?*

Midair damage control was not practical, other than not lighting any cigarettes on the way back to England. As soon as the C-47 braked to a stop, the aircrew hustled to a spot 100 feet away in the grass, just to be safe. No smoke, no fire. *There.* Gasoline flowed out of the tail. A wing's trailing edge, too. A single machine gun bullet had punctured a fuel tank. Miraculously, it had only sprung a leak.

Responsibility for mission accomplishment and survival extended beyond the aircrews. The ground crews at the air bases were as nervous as new fathers, waiting for "their" planes to return from combat, anxious to see the aircrews disembark and to learn how the aircraft functioned and what needed immediate attention. Like a hospital waiting room, ground crews on D-Day stayed vigilant for hours, some pacing, others scanning the sky or looking for distractions until the first American and British planes appeared far off in the distance. Sometimes, it was sole aircraft, barely visible. *There he is. How's he look? Right altitude out there? Stable approach? Any smoke? He doesn't sound right.*

Once a plane landed and personnel removed the dead and wounded, the repair and refueling deadline loomed, as fixed as a morning newspaper's first edition. First, assess any aircraft for the damage the plane had suffered. Then triage the repairs necessary for combat readiness on the next day's mission. *Replace an engine? Hydraulic system repairs? Aileron? Rudder? Flaps? Electrical systems? Fuel system? Any skin that needs patching?* Personnel in two squadrons in 38 Group RAF watched twenty-seven aircraft limp home, heavily damaged and barely flyable. By the following morning, all but two were ready to take off on their next mission.

Each aircraft's wounds and sometimes the blood inside told the story of what an aircrew had endured on its return to its airfield. Scrubbing clear coagulated blood pools, splatters, and smears, as well as vomit, was just as vital to aircrew confidence and morale as replacing a shredded hydraulic line.

Others who had trained for months – some for years – who had sat through briefings, and had sung hymns before boarding their aircraft, met destinies as different as their life's journey toward war and an unknown fate.

His Dakota was a tight fit for Flying Officer Harvey Jones. So tall that he ducked through doorways, the former Niagara Falls tour guide had studied business at the University of Toronto before the war. Now he steadied his aircraft filled with paratroopers after it had burst into flames.

He ordered everyone to jump and most did. But his radio operator, Cobby Engelberg, lay injured behind Jones. *Maybe I can land this thing.* It was more crash than landing, killing Jones on impact. Engelberg somehow survived despite a skull fracture when a French farming family rescued him. An act of sacrifice that would transcend future generations. (After the war, Engelberg named his son "Harvey" after Jones. Decades later, Harvey Engelberg traveled to France to see where his father had been saved and his namesake had died, where he had been buried with a simple cross stating "Died for France, Long Live England." He also was given a few small pieces of the Dakota that had been saved by French farmers for more than seventy-five years.)

First Lieutenant John Devitt was a cool, calculating pilot. After a cup of Red Cross coffee, he had reported to his Operation *Chicago* aircraft at 0119 hours, a plane that had been assigned to him months earlier. Like many pilots, he had developed a sense of responsibility – even kinship – for the C-47 that he now considered his "personal property." When he had boarded, he found his co-pilot on one knee praying in the fuselage. Devitt did not join him, figuring the odds of not surviving the mission were between five and fifteen percent. On the positive side, his survival odds were somewhere between 20:1 and 16:1. The odds held. He survived.

But another mission loomed on D-Day. Another two-and-a-half-hour flight, this time towing one of the ungainly British Horsa gliders, laden with seven men from the 101st, a truck, 37mm field gun, radio batteries, ammunition, fuel, and the glider's crew. Although his mission was successful, for years afterward Devitt remained haunted by the sight of a Horsa that had been splintered into kindling by machine gun fire as it had landed earlier in the day.

Unlike C-47s and Dakotas that could withstand artillery shells' ten-inch entry wounds and a shotgun's worth of shrapnel exit wounds, the Horsa sometimes suffered structural failures and its size was an inviting target.

War can become unimaginably small and intimate in foxholes, trenches, and at the end of a tow rope. After returning from Operation *Detroit* on D-Day, an officer cut Captain Louis Emerson's nap short. "You're flying another mission today. Get up." He would be towing Flight Officer Glen McPherren in a glider carrying a 105mm howitzer at 1600 hours. McPherren had served as best man in Emerson's wedding.

A few hours later as they approached the French coast, McPherren watched an artillery shell explode almost next to Emerson's right engine, killing it. The engine's fire extinguisher failed as the engine's fire burned so fiercely that the C-47's fuselage windows began to melt.

Every combat pilot had trained for one-engine flight. Emerson and his co-pilot first triaged the dead engine by throttling it back, adjusting the fuel mixture, and pushing the overhead switch to feather (stop) the propeller. Then shutting down relevant engine systems. Almost at the same time, turning their attention to their remaining good engine by applying any necessary power and aileron and rudder pressure to keep the C-47 steady and straight.

The "six pack" in the cockpit would dictate the odds of their survival: airspeed, heading, altitude, oil pressure, temperature, and manifold pressure. Even if they had suffered damage to their hydraulic and electrical systems.

Flying on one engine miles from his LZ, Emerson faced a decision every pilot dreaded. *If we cut [McPherren] loose too soon, he would land in the water and sink like a rock. We can probably make it to the LZ and still have about 300 feet altitude. With a little luck we could then get back to the coast, ditch beside a ship, and if I do a good ditching job we might not even get our feet wet.*

Emerson cut his best man loose over land and then turned hard toward his good engine to head back over the English Channel. Straight toward two German machine gunners whose aim was uncanny. One burst peeled away an engine's cowling. The next knocked the cylinder heads off and a third destroyed the propeller's dome. Now uncontrolled by the cockpit, the engine "ran away," broke down, and stopped, as if committing suicide. Emerson now sat at the controls of a critically wounded nine-ton glider. With only one chance at survival. Trees.

"Flaps! Landing gear!"

Neither functioned. He dropped below the treetops, hoping his wings shattering limbs would slow him. Not much.

"Prepare for crash landing!"

Emerson bounced the C-47 hard off the ground, dragged the right wing tip to "steer" toward a gap in the trees ahead and plowed through, the trees and wings taking the brunt of the impact. The nose reared like a wild horse and the sounds of crushing metal sucked the breath out of Emerson. Then silence. Emerson had broken his ribs and his co-pilot was knocked unconscious while suffering a compound fracture of his left arm.

Fire engulfed the right side of an aircraft that had been broken in half, the tail askew from the fuselage. Emerson and his crew managed to pull themselves clear, hunker down in a ditch, and wait for darkness. At about 0300 hours, they crossed paths with a paratrooper standing sentry duty and were taken to a nearby barn where a group of paratroopers and a medic hid. They would survive.

Watching a man, perhaps a friend, die stuck with others long after the war.

Only two minutes after he had released his glider near Caen, his blazing starboard engine gave RAF Flight Officer Jack Le Huray one option following the cluster of direct hits. Order his crew to bail out. Two crew members, Flying Officer Bill Woodcock and Sergeant Charlie Carr, jumped as the aircraft hemorrhaged altitude. Up in the cockpit, Le Huray and his second pilot, Flying Officer Linn Farrell, could only ride the Dakota into the ground. They survived the crash that broke Farrell's leg in two places. *Where are Woodcock and Carr?*

After he landed and shed his parachute, Woodcock spotted Carr struggling in the Caen Canal. "Hang on!" Woodcock yelled as he swam toward Carr. But Carr's parachute pulled him under the water's surface. He was never seen again. He drowned in a stretch of water only two hundred feet wide, a few miles from the English Channel for which Carr and the crew had rehearsed ditching procedures for weeks.

American and British resupply missions following D-Day were critical to strengthening the Allies' beachhead and fueling their advances inland. None were immune from loss.

Radio operator Mitchell Bacon was a busy man. The former lawyer would be flying a supply mission on D+1, yet unfinished work remained the night before. He was sorting various personal items on his bed when the others noticed him.

"What's up?"

He was preparing for death. The bespectacled staff sergeant was sure he would die on the next morning's mission. Better to separate military-issue gear from his personal belongings before shipment back home to his uncle who had raised him.

"You can't possibly know that."

"You shouldn't even be thinking that."

"You're crazy, Mitch. Forget all that stuff."

"Come on, man, get that out of your head."

The next morning after breakfast at 0300 hours, he looked at a friend. "I just want to tell you goodbye. I am certain I won't be returning from this mission."

He had flown earlier on D-Day, but somehow the West Virginia lawyer knew that later in the day his mission would be different.

As most are, the resupply flight was routine until it wasn't. When Captain Howard Sass' C-47 crossed the French coast, enemy gunners immediately locked on. A direct hit, perhaps by the enemy's high explosive incendiary ordnance, ignited parapacks under the fuselage.

A "sheet of fire" visible through the open cargo door horrified his wingmen. They watched the plane fall out of formation and bundles tumble out the door as they screamed "Bail out! Bail out!" over their radios.

No parachutes appeared before the plane hit the ground hard, slid into a hedgerow, and exploded into a yellowish-orange ball of death. It did not take long to clear Mitchell Bacon's belongings from his barrack's bunk before his replacement arrived.[1]

First Lieutenant David Mondt had noticed his leg was damp as his aircraft returned to England. He reached down. Not blood, hydraulic fluid. A single rifle bullet that had missed pilot Glenn Grimes and found the hydraulic system, the life blood of the plane. It had disabled the brakes, flaps, and landing gear. The co-pilot recalled his training. "On combat flights, don't use the cabin heater. It might have a hole in it and you could become asphyxiated. If you lose your hydraulics, get the gear down and the safety pin in, any way you can. Three point that and gear will find and hold." It did, resulting in a successful landing in England.[2]

The giddiness of survival often surfaced the moment the aircrew touched down back in England. Equally relieved, ground crews slapped backs and threw playful punches as the aircrews walked into operations rooms for a debrief, sandwiches, coffee, tea, and a double shot of Old Rye Overholt dispensed by flight surgeons.

In Operation *Neptune*'s aftermath, several American squadron after-action reports crafted a glowing view of mission success. "The mission was a success – all planes dropped on or near the 'T' and there was very little opposition – some small arms fire and almost no flak," according to one report.[3]

Although understated in general, British after-action reports (commonly referred to as "War Diaries") generally were more forthcoming and consistent with analyses that followed Operation *Neptune*.

"The drop was not entirely a success as navigational difficulties resulted in a large part of the force being mistakenly dropped at another zone near Ranville, four miles to the north, and as a consequence more than a third of the 8th Battalion's aircraft dropped their paratroopers there instead."[4]

"Due to poor weather conditions complicating navigation, and the pathfinders who were to illuminate the drop zone with their beacons landing astray, the drop was badly scattered and only threadbare elements of both battalions were able to form up and go about their business."[5]

In the absence of weather recon aircraft, the undiscovered fog bank decimated the Americans' tight, dimmed, and radio-silent formations long before dawn. Only two in five aircrews included a navigator on the night missions. When the formations broke apart, more than half the aircrews could barely use "dead reckoning" when fog shrouded landmarks below. Instincts were the final option as the pilots approached their DZs at two miles per minute. Overloaded C-47s and unexpectedly stiff wind (reportedly up to twenty knots per hour) also conspired to push aircraft off course.

Only one pathfinder team each for the 82nd and 101st hit its DZ. When other pathfinders landed too far from their DZs, many opted not to use their guidance equipment and risk misleading the following aircrews. British pathfinders were equally dispersed and landing only thirty minutes ahead of the main force proved insufficient. A handful of British aircrews found it difficult to distinguish between two key canals the width of rivers as navigation landmarks in their sector. In the meantime, the radio operators' Rebecca-Eureka technology proved vulnerable to margins of error, miscalculations, and became overwhelmed when employed by too many navigators simultaneously.

As a result, "a map of the drops looks as though a pepper shaker had been waved three or four times over each zone," according to one American analysis. By the end of the first day, forty percent (8,000 men) from the 82nd and 101st remained unaccounted. The notion of inserting a concentrated force of firepower at the enemy's back had proved folly. Only ten percent dropped on their DZs, up to thirty percent were within a mile, and twenty percent were within one to two miles.[6]

One in ten paratroopers were more than ten miles from their DZs, the equivalent of aiming for the New York City area and landing in Newark, New Jersey. Yet the wide dispersal enabled troops to engage across a broader expanse to sever German communications, leading the enemy to think they were a larger force. The 82nd successfully captured the town of Ste-Mere-Eglise the morning of the drops and later secured several key German approaches to the beaches. Meanwhile, fifty percent of the artillery delivered by the glider pilots within two miles of their LZs was useable and ninety percent of the glider infantry assembled within a few hours after landing.

American airborne supported the 23,000 troops coming ashore on Utah Beach who suffered fewer than 200 casualties, despite the dispersed drops of paratroopers. By contrast, without airborne support a bloodied Omaha Beach saw more than 2,370 men killed, wounded, or missing.[7] While myriad factors inevitably power every victory or defeat on the battlefield, the role and contributions of the airborne's vertical envelopment among the hedgerows was clear.

To the east, the RAF glider missions were far more accurate than the paratrooper flights across the twenty-four square miles assigned to the 6th Airborne. Similar to the US airborne dispersal, only twenty-five percent of the 3rd Parachute Brigade initially assembled at its rendezvous point. About sixty percent of the 5th Parachute Brigade initially reached its assembly point. Just 150 paratroopers in the 9th Parachute Battalion landed close enough to attack their Merville artillery objective. Though successful, the intrepid force suffered sixty-five casualties.

Regardless, the 6th Airborne achieved all its first-day objectives on D-Day.

Overall, Allied aircrews delivered more than 24,000 paratroopers into enemy territory on June 6, 1944. Waves of silhouetted aircraft flew close enough to firefights on the ground that "an endless skytrain ... stopped the fighting in some sectors as men looked skyward with unbelieving eyes."[8]

Yet Louis Emerson, Harvey Jones, Campbell Smith, Robert Nelsen, Gordon Wilson, and hundreds of others remained tactical test pilots. The Germans quickly learned to concentrate their 88mm and 20mm artillery and machine gun fire most effectively over the landing and drop zones. One pilot called it "curtains of artillery," prompting aircrews to sometimes ignore orders prohibiting evasive action.[9]

Hundreds of well-trained but green-to-combat Allied aircrews had met the savagery of war over Normandy. Staff Sergeant Alan Boyd and other pilots had flown their missions with one hand on the wheel, the other on the throttle for hours. Although exhausted upon their return, for many sleep proved elusive.

That night the barracks felt empty and eerie. More pilots had been shot down, and most of the glider pilots were gone. I tried to fall asleep but couldn't. I thought of lost friends, crashed gliders, and the poor men on the ground. A nearby pilot's crying and moaning kept me awake. He was having a nightmare.[10]

On future missions over the next nine months, hundreds more would benefit from and sometimes too often share Normandy's scars and nightmares. Only after the war did one pilot realize his Normandy mission amounted to a drop exercise over Nebraska compared to what he and fellow pilots would face three months later over Holland.

But first American transport aircrews would head south to Italian airfields. Several would be flying repaired and replacement C-47s only six weeks after their missions in Normandy. In a few weeks, they would converge on DZs and LZs in vineyards where tugs with American and Horsa gliders would be "as thick as flies around a dead road rabbit" and where doomed aircraft would "whistle in at about 100 miles per hour, hook a wing, and go cartwheeling down the field like a cheerleader at a football game."

6

A Silver Ribbon of Road

... partially obstructed by rows of trees or vines, approximately ten feet high ... crossed by a roadway and irrigation ditch ... deep stream bed ... high house, farm building, and trees ... probably a drainage ditch ... it is believed feasible ... east end of field completely blocked by large farmhouse, farm buildings, and sixty-foot trees ...[1]

The French Riviera's terrain analysis four days in advance of Operation *Dragoon*, set for August 15, 1944, looked ominous to Colonels Charles Young, Frank Krebs, Theodore Kershaw, and Charles Smith. The Normandy veterans respectively had led the 439th, 440th, 441st, and 442nd Troop Carrier Groups.

The lessons of Normandy remained painful. Operation *Neptune's* photo reconnaissance and terrain analysis had failed to highlight flooded landing zones, hedgerow barricades, Rommel's Asparagus, and towering trees. Glider pilots and paratroopers in particular had paid a steep price.[2] Two months later, the combined *Dragoon* drop and landing zones – as small as 200 feet wide by 625 feet long – would be a tough proposition for glider pilots releasing from their tugs that had slowed to 110 miles an hour, while paratroopers would be floating through and onto an obstacle course.

Among the glider pilots now assigned to the *Dragoon* mission, Normandy veterans Jack Merrick, Solomon Belinky, and John Hanscom knew that after release they might have forty-five seconds or less to choose a spot and then another forty-five seconds to decrease their gliders' speed to seventy miles per hour as they made their descent, perhaps toward a farmer's furrowed field bordered by stone walls or another featuring a farmhouse. Having survived *Ladbroke*'s disaster in Sicily, RAF Staff Sergeant Tom Tillies of the 1st Independent Glider Pilot Squadron could only hope his Horsa would be released within range of his landing zone this time, and over an LZ large enough for a Horsa.

Operation *Dragoon*'s terrain analysis of fields about fifteen miles inland from the Riviera coast resembled slalom courses rather than landing and drop zones. If they were accurate. *And how current are they?* Second Lieutenant Jack Merrick knew that, for all the advance planning, improvisation became the flight plan once he had cut off from his C-47. Perhaps selecting a field with obstacles might reduce the competition from other glider pilots. In southern France, there would be no shortage of fields pockmarked with obstacles.

Although more detailed maps were available for this mission, recon photography taken at an oblique angle revealing obstacle height would not be available until the day before takeoff and be of little use. Aircrews and glider pilots would have to rely on weeks' old photos, with no way of knowing if new hazards had appeared in the interim.

The opening paratrooper wave would fly in the dark of the moon, with a high-pressure weather system that "might produce fog in the early morning," but pilots should expect two-to-three-mile visibility. Their departing airfields in Italy would remain hot and dry.[3] *Could this be the "milk run" that proved elusive over Normandy?*

In only six weeks following *Overlord*, thirty-six American divisions had come ashore. Two million men required more than twenty tons of supplies daily, making a second major port, Marseille, vital to ETO objectives. Comprising more than 2,500 vessels, Operation *Dragoon* would deliver 94,000 men along a forty-five-mile stretch along the Cote d'Azur on the French Riviera, only sixty miles from Marseille. Once a beachhead took hold, the 3rd, 36th, and 45th

Infantry Divisions also would advance north up the Rhone River valley, creating a pincer attack (with Normandy Allied forces advancing down from the north) that could push the Germans back to the Rhine River and perhaps trap German units attempting to retreat from western France.

The Allied 1st Airborne Task Force organized specifically for *Dragoon* would rely on an American inventory of 471 C-aircrews, and ground personnel at ten Italian airfields under the command of a Stanford University alumnus who held a Bachelor of Arts degree and then had enlisted the year he graduated. Brigadier General Paul Williams, commanding officer of the IX Troop Carrier Command, was serious, studious, and a highly regarded tactician with twenty-seven years' experience.

Similar to Normandy's two-pronged D-Day airlift, pathfinders, paratroopers, and gliders would arrive before dawn with a second wave arriving in late afternoon. And like Sicily, American aircrews would be responsible for delivering the 1st Airborne, a prospect that worried many British officers. *Would the Americans' navigation and widely dispersed drops be as dicky as over Sicily?* several wondered.

One hour after pathfinders had dropped, beginning at 0423 hours in Operation *Albatross,* almost 400 C-47s would deliver the British 2nd Independent Parachute Brigade, the 509th Parachute Infantry Battalion, the 517th Parachute Combat Team, the 550th Glider Infantry Battalion, and the 551st Parachute Infantry Battalion to the area surrounding Le Muy, an unlikely region of rocky foothills and Maritime Alps Mountains.[4] It sat at the intersection of four highways, the Argens River, and a railroad line. One (LZ-C) would be a paratrooper drop zone, the others (LZ-A and LZ-O) designated as joint drop and landing zones.

Glider-towing Operation *Bluebird* would follow about an hour later, releasing a glider force of British Horsas and American CG-4As at 0815 hours.

Then in a second wave, paratrooper reinforcements would arrive at about 1800 hours in Operation *Canary*, followed by the main glider force in Operation *Dove* arriving an hour later. Leading aircrews would fly a morning paratrooper mission beginning with take-offs at 0200 hours and then return to the combat landing zones towing a glider nineteen hours later.[5]

Operation *Dragoon* had hardly been a secret. In fact, planners changed its name from *Anvil* due to security concerns.[6] Yet intelligence briefings had painted a generally feeble, beleaguered German force waiting for the Allies in southern France. German General Friedrich Wiese had taken command of the Nineteenth Army only a few months earlier with unachievable orders. Seven undermanned divisions filled with boys, decrepit veterans, and POWs from the Eastern Front would defend 400 miles of the southern France coastline. One in three under his command did not speak German. Regardless, hundreds of concrete bunkers had been carved into hillsides, thousands of mines had been planted, anti-aircraft emplacements had been established, and crossfire emplacements had been positioned to defend beaches. While recognizing the capture of Marseille and advancing northward along the Rhone River were the obvious Allied objectives, a critical fuel shortage and some units' reliance on horse-drawn carts, wagons, and bicycles further hobbled Wiese.

Memories of *Husky* had remained fresh in operational planning for Operation *Dragoon*. About a two-hour flight stretched ahead for aircrews, north to the island of Elba off Italy, then west-northwest over the tip of Corsica on a straight line to the Riveria. Their route kept them at least twenty miles to the north and parallel to the amphibious convoy's course to the beach on a starry night with a sliver of the moon low in the west, and a sea "as calm as a mill pond." Radio beacon and rescue ships lined the route and the pathfinders would mark the target zones with fluorescent and smoke markers as well as Eureka homing beacons.

Nine C-47s shattered the Italian night in the first hour of August 15. Thundering down mostly dirt runways with unseen roiled dust blossoming behind them as they lifted, a British pathfinder team for each of the three drop zones turned toward France. Comforted by an umbrella of fighter escorts, a few fuzzy shoreline lights appeared as they approached France. The dim apparitions brought chills. Fog again awaited the aircrews leading the Allies' second major airborne invasion. A fog bank that might hang over the French Riveria or extend inland for miles. With no way to gauge its depth or proximity to the hilly ground inland, the nine aircrews pressed ahead, soon recognizing that the low overcast would shroud their inland destination, muddling the first flight of *Dragoon*'s airborne support.

Normandy had proven the critical need for pathfinders to reliably mark the drop and landing zones for the hundreds of aircrews who were only about one hour behind them. *Now what?* The pathfinder aircrews circled over the fog bank, waiting, hoping it would thin so the they could spot landmarks to confirm their locations. But dawn and the sun's warmth were hours away. Meanwhile, the fog bank remained anchored in the valleys between the foothills as the paratroopers were crossing the Gulf of Genoa. The hour's separation between the pathfinders' holding pattern and the inbound paratroopers shrank as inevitably as an incoming tide. The pathfinders could not wait any longer. Either by order of the pilot or jumpmaster, each of the three teams leaped into the gray blanket, hoping their aircrew's dead reckoning route calculations had been accurate.

Their parachutes snapped open, slowing their descent to about sixteen miles per hour. Down through the fog until farm fields, orchards, vineyards, and cobbled hillsides appeared through the haze. They looked nothing like the drop zones shown in their briefings. One team landed more than three miles from its drop zone. Another, more than ten miles off target. Only one, LZ-O's pathfinders, was successful when it landed only a few football fields off the mark.

Hours earlier in Italy, paratrooper Captain Ernest Siegel had walked up to Colonel Charles Smith with a single question on his mind as Smith's aircrew assembled at the 442nd TCG lead aircraft. Siegel had been the captain of his youth hockey team and later a New York state trooper before he enlisted in 1940. He would be the paratroopers' jumpmaster on Smith's plane.

"Yep, I'll land you next to the woodshed." Just where Siegel intended to establish his company's first headquarters. Others were not so sure.

The British paratrooper and glider infantry wounds remained raw from Operation *Husky* only thirteen months earlier. Most held the American pilots responsible for premature glider releases into a deadly sea and dispersed paratrooper drops so profound that a few worried they had missed Sicily entirely. British Major Richard Hargreaves of the 4th Parachute Battalion considered the Americans' navigation skills "appalling" on that mission. Now, once again, they would be relying on American aircrews to deliver them onto specific fields at choreographed intervals after a 250-to-400-mile flight in the dark from Italy.

Captain Geoffrey Mortimer in the 4th Battalion shared the same concerns about the American pilots' reliability. "Before we flew off from Rome I had a 'friendly word' with the US pilot ... to reassure myself that [my] seventeen passengers were going to be dropped at the right place." The pilot pulled out a note card on which he had sketched his flight route and pointed to a dotted line. "I reckon we fly right along that line." Mortimer was hardly satisfied, noting the moon should illuminate a road "like a silver ribbon" inland from the coast and that the pathfinders' alert light should go on precisely at eight-and-a-half minutes after crossing the beach. The pilot's reply, "Geez, what do you know about that!" rattled Mortimer into wondering what kind of briefings the US aircrews had received.[7]

C-47 aircrews from three US air wings, the 50th, 51st, and 53rd, carrying 5,600 paratroopers, artillerymen, and 150 pieces of artillery had taken off from Italy not long after the pathfinders had departed. Operation *Albatross'* effectiveness as a fighting force – and even survival – would heavily depend on reaching their drop zones accurately, on time, and at the proper altitude.

The paratrooper aircraft fleet spanned 100 miles across the sea, in groups of approximately thirty-eight planes. After they had assembled over Elba, by 0343 hours the flight serials had turned toward the Riviera at intervals of five minutes. Only one troop carrier group had stumbled, the 441st, when it failed to link up with the leader, the 442nd, over Elba.

All aircraft now featured Normandy's recognition stripes and the Rebecca wayfinding receivers, but only for use by each flight's lead ship. One in three radio operators tuned into the mission's command radio frequency. Stragglers flew with orders to proceed to their objective regardless of any delays and all pilots were prohibited from taking evasive action.

Colonel Young led his 439th TCG toward southern France. After graduating from Phillips University in Oklahoma, he had bought a biplane with two friends for $350 and began barnstorming towns and airshows in the Midwest before his career as a commercial airline pilot. After leading their TCGs over Normandy, *Albatross* was shaping up to be a "milk run" at 3,000 feet and 140 miles per hour on a direct route with only a few clouds in a black sky. As routine as one of Young's prewar commercial Midwest flights from Kansas City to St Louis and smooth enough that some paratroopers nodded off on their way to battle.[8]

But as the troop carrier groups approached France, alarm grew. At fifty miles from the beach, the majority of their radio operators' Rebecca short-wave receivers remained dormant. No pathfinder navigation signals registered from two of the three DZs. Those pathfinder teams were still traipsing through the unfamiliar countryside.

Minutes later, a familiar glow appeared in the distance. One that the pilots had regularly seen when training in England and that had chafed the pilots who had flown Normandy missions. Fog. Low and heavy, perhaps 1,000 feet thick. If it extended along the pilots' final twenty-minute approach inland to Le Muy, there would be no signal ground panels and no smoke pots revealing wind direction. Hundreds of aircrews would be flying as if they were wearing blinders.

The gray blanket below hid every feature and landmark as the night sky began to fade at the first hint of dawn. Direction, speed, distance, time spent, their briefings, and a microwave navigation scanner in the aircraft that could identify shorelines, rivers, and cities up to ninety miles away would dictate airborne success or failure. Based mostly on his navigation radar, Colonel Young's navigator convinced him to reluctantly alter his course. During his turn, one of Young's trailing pilots collected tree branches in an engine. Much too low and not at all what they had been briefed to expect.

Pilots only had a few minutes' flying time from the coast – if they could see the beach as they passed over – to their target zones. There would be no leeway if they changed their course at the last minute. Young stayed on his navigator's course, leading the 439th to drop its paratroopers as far as twelve miles from their DZ. The other aircrews faced similar decisions as they followed their flight leaders, looked down, and saw fog. After the 441st had been unable to link up with the 442nd near Elba, it became lost in the absence of signals from pathfinders at its DZ destination. Its paratroopers jumped around the wrong town, ten miles from their DZ.

"On your feet! Hook up! Sound off!"

The red light near a C-47's door had awakened. Finally, only four minutes to the jump.

The engines' growl through the open jump door filled the fuselage as the laden paratroopers stood and stretched cramps and stiffness as best they could, and sorted into jumping order like a hand's dealt cards. *Snap the parachute line to the overhead cable. Check the gear on the man in front of me. Give him an "okay" slap on his rump. Wait. One minute.*

"Stand in the door!" The paratroopers squeezed toward the rear, a hand on the man's shoulder ahead. Perhaps only a few more seconds before the green light wakened. *Faster, faster,* some silently pleaded, anxious to get out the door.

The aircraft's landing horn began blaring, telling the paratroopers the C-47 had slowed close to jumping speed, flying below 1,000 feet, and its landing gear was engaged. Up in the cockpit, the co-pilot's hand hovered near the green light switch. *Now!*

The cockpit crew in one plane could feel Anthony Dorsa, Marvin Gillman, Ira Butler, Eugene Beckner, and thirteen others leap in less than a minute. They jumped into the sea. Close to twenty miles short of its DZ, the aircraft had not yet crossed the beach. Dorsa, Gillman, Butler, and Beckner already had earned battlefield Bronze and Silver Stars. The entire stick of paratroopers vanished.

Confusion washed over British paratroopers as they approached their drop zones. The gray, featureless view out the jump door looked nothing like what the paratroopers had trained for. *The red light's on and we're still over the ocean?*

Only twenty years old, Captain Anthony Farrar-Hockley in the 6th Parachute Battalion was the last paratrooper in his aircraft to jump. For a split second, he hesitated. "I saw below that was, to all appearances, the sea and I was seriously concerned about this grey shimmering mass some way below me, to the point that I got out the mouthpiece of my inflatable life jacket ... it proved to be a layer of cloud. I was scarcely through that by more than four or five seconds when I hit the ground."[9]

Major Richard Hargreaves in the 4th Parachute Battalion was so shocked when the jump's green light illuminated that he warned his men, "watch it, I think it's water." He and his men jumped and plowed through the cloud layer with no clue where they might land. In Hargreaves' case, it was in the top of a fir tree.

Colonel Smith's 442nd TCG held an ace. His aircrews' briefings had included a three-dimensional sand table that depicted the hills, ridges, and mountaintops near DZ-A. As the 442nd flew inland, several mountaintops appeared above the fog bank, unique landmarks that enabled Smith's navigator to pinpoint the otherwise invisible drop zone at 0400 hours. Most were dropped within one-half mile of the DZ. "No other group in the course of the war made so accurate a drop under such difficult conditions," noted one postwar analysis.[10]

"China Boy, LZ covered with ground fog. Return gliders land in Corsica if necessary. Williams China Boy." "China Boy" was the code for recalling Operation *Bluebird's* gliders. "Williams" told the aircrafts' radio operators the message had come from General Williams in Italy.

The radio transmission shocked C-47 radio operators Eugene Millard, John Hudson, and Sebastiano Gattinella shortly after their aircraft had passed Corsica. Their squadron was towing thirty-five Horsa gliders less than an hour behind the paratroopers. The fog would make a Horsa landing impossible from 1,500 feet. The amount of fuel American planes needed to haul the larger Horsas made delays and holding patterns impossible. The aircraft towing Horsas returned to Italy while those hauling the CG-4As opted for a holding pattern.

First Lieutenant Eugene Waterfill was a pure Kentuckian, having attended one-room schools before graduating high school and then holding odd jobs until he had enlisted in 1942. He was a natural navigator, a veteran of Normandy, and had climbed aboard to organize his station just behind Smith in the cockpit. He, along with 1st Lieutenant Frank Rice and 2nd Lieutenant Cecil Barnes, charted a return course to Italy. The aircrews would follow their lead and disappointment.

Seventy-five C-47s had taken off on the heels of the paratroopers' Operation *Albatross*. As the Horsas headed back to Italy, forty aircraft towing American CG-4A gliders circled Corsica, since they required only a 1,000-foot ceiling for release. Maybe the fog would lift before their planes' fuel level became critical.

Then several minutes later, another message. "China Boy proceed to destination. Return gliders only if, repeat, if fuel insufficient." The C-47s reversed course a second time. But turning C-47s took time. An hour's flight time had disappeared, the gliders would be landing much closer to amphibious assault than planned, but at least the fog had burned off so they could release their gliders over their LZs.

One threat never materialized. German anti-aircraft fire throughout the day would be surprisingly light, nothing like what the Normandy veterans had experienced. Weather, mission planning, and even dusty conditions at Italian airfields would prove far more deadly than flak.

Losses, however, had already arisen. An aircrew flying the extremely reliable C-47 stood ready to execute a perfect mission, but could be crippled by an imperfect glider. In only their third airborne mission, American glider quality continued to be as unpredictable as a roulette wheel. Even after checking their glider before takeoff, a pilot and co-pilot could never be sure. Not far from Corsica, a glider's right wing separated from its fuselage. Like a beached whale, it laid over on its side, snapped its tow rope, and disintegrated as it nosed toward the sea. Nearby aircrews in the tight formation shuddered at the sight of shredded glider fabric dancing in the armada's turbulence. Flight Officers Robert Hardin and William Kern surely died on impact.

By afternoon, the pathfinders and paratroopers had seized control of the three drop zones, just in time for the largest *Dragoon* glider mission, Operation *Dove*, when the C-47 aircrews would fly over "fields cluttered with billowing parachutes that had been left where they lay by the jumpers who had landed before dawn."[11]

The American "follow the leader" principle of airborne mission planning would again prove disastrous. With the 442nd again in the lead, its flight leader released a glider near Corsica when its tail became unstable. When the aircrew turned to avoid a collision, the rest of the group followed their leader while the 441st passed nearby. By the time the 442nd returned to its original Riviera course, five troop carrier groups had overlapped each other. The nine-minute separation between them had already proven to be inadequate. The 1,000-foot intervals between troop carrier group elements were equally disastrous. A traffic jam developed over the Gulf of Genoa more than 100 miles from the Riviera shoreline.

Chaos reigned when the five TCGs arrived over the landing zones. C-47 pilots Herbert Vammen, Victor Armistead, William Ware, and Leo Kaffenberger were among those now flying solo missions, looking for new routes to avoid midair collisions, searching for fields not yet filled with wrecks, and holding at an altitude suitable for release and a fast descent to the vineyards and orchards below.

Several pilots climbed to 3,000 feet to avoid near collisions, three times the altitude prescribed in their flight plans. Many felt they had little choice other than to release their gliders at that altitude and hope the glider pilots could slalom their way down to a vine-yard and skid to a stop short of a stone wall. Freelancing decisions and luck ultimately would dictate casualty rates. "Christ, what a mess," one glider pilot reflected later.[12]

The aircrews in the final two serials stared down at a parking lot of gliders as if scattered by a giant hand. They sat cockeyed at crazy angles, missing wings, and some resting on top of one another. Rommel's Asparagus that the briefers had missed for lack of a recon flight just before the mission had snapped countless wings off fuselages.

Once aircrews released their gliders, they dropped tow ropes over a designated location away from the mayhem. It also gave radio operator Marty Wolfe a good look at what had become "more like a demolition derby than a milk run" across the patchwork of fields.[13] Glider pilot Richard Fort agreed.

> … the trees were really tall … the landing space too short … I'm too low! … the treetops are at my eye level … I pull back on the stick … slip left, full spoilers, level out, spoilers off … We drop into the row of vines, posts, wire, and our right wing hits the wing of another glider and is gone … sounds like an implosion of a giant wooden match box … the outer third of the left wing is gone, and the nose plows up dirt, buckles, then breaks … as we grind to a stop. I'm still gripping the stick.[14]

Six hours later, the C-47 aircrews had touched down back in Italy as thousands of paratroopers and glider pilots dug in for what would be a long night.

> Gunfire and other explosions ebbed and flowed all around us. We could identify the spatter and crackle of small arms fire and the heavier boom of artillery … We also listened to the whine of missile launchers and to men shouting at each other. The worst of all … was the horrible din … the sound of voices calling for medics …[15]

Operations *Albatross, Bluebird,* and *Dove* ended at 2138 hours when the last aircrew landed in Italy, the final link in a chain of 852 sorties.[16] Several aircrews had flown two missions in less than twenty hours, totaling 1,300 miles. Only one aircrew had failed to return when German artillery shot it down at sea while homeward bound. They survived. The aircrews suffered no casualties while thirteen glider pilots died, most from injuries suffered when landing.

They had delivered the equivalent of a division to southern France, along with 213 pieces of artillery, 221 vehicles, and 500 tons of supplies. Casualties amounted to only two percent of the paratroopers and four percent of the glider force.

Although several post-mission reports proved to be inaccurately positive, paratrooper dispersal through the fog bank in the morning echoed Normandy. A few groups landed fifteen miles from their DZ, two jumped into the sea, and out of 720 paratroopers in one TCG only 300 had assembled the following day. Overall in the first wave, two of seven battalions landed wide of the mark.

Analysists deemed fifty percent of the paratrooper drops as ineffective while the glider releases achieved ninety percent accuracy, although extracting the equipment from their mangled fuselages proved time consuming or impossible.

Despite the surprising lack of German resistance and remarkably low casualty rate, the C-47 aircrews had been ambushed by mission planning, briefing, and ill fortune. Ghosts of Normandy and Sicily, more than a few pilots later mused.

Briefing photos and descriptions of the drop and landing zones had again been outdated and disastrously misleading. The overhead photography was weeks old and failed to reveal the ground-level obstacles that destroyed gliders and cost glider pilot lives.[17] Like Normandy, fog had threatened the mission, a danger that a single advance weather aircraft would have revealed. Inadequate spacing between serials once again created airborne traffic jams that shredded flight plans. Striking a balance between delivering a concentrated fighting force quickly to the battlefield with an orderly and reliable flight remained elusive. The same held true for holding at the prescribed glider-release altitude, regardless of aircraft congestion or enemy fire. Most glider pilots gladly would have taken their chances with enemy fire in return for a lower release and a shorter descent to landing.

The demands placed on aircrews at times remained untenable. Limited training and rehearsals as well as the final "go decisions" coming practically on the mission's eve hampered both Sicily and southern France missions. A far more rigorous training regimen was needed, since months could pass between major invasions. As one military analyst noted, "It takes at least as much skill to drop paratroops accurately by night on fields as it does to drop bombs by day on factories."[18]

Yet Operation *Dragoon* was an unprecedented success. For the first time, troop carrier and airborne combat commanders worked together on mission planning. Four airlifts in fifteen hours brought 9,000 men ashore. The Allied force captured Marseille less than two weeks later after advancing 400 miles up the Rhone River. On September 12 Seventh Army infantry units linked up with units advancing southward from Normandy.

Their D-Day missions complete, the demands on Allied aircrews continued unabated. Paratroopers and glider infantry on the ground were always on the edge of combat starvation, requiring constant resupply flights to captured and temporary airstrips as they advanced. In fact, they needed about one-third as many aircrews to keep advancing as the number of aircrews necessary to deliver them to the battlefield at the outset.

Like Sicily and Normandy, Operation *Dragoon* again demonstrated that paratrooper and glider transport aircraft were extremely vulnerable, even though the Allied transports had yet to encounter significant German Luftwaffe attacks. A rubber plug in the C-47 and Dakota fuselage windows could be removed, enabling paratroopers to shove the barrels of their weapons out if they were attacked by enemy aircraft. But a handful of rifles or British Brens (light machine guns) hardly offered any real protection against enemy aircraft attacking at 350 miles per hour.

Like cavalry horses, the slow, unarmored, inflammable
planes of the troop carriers were very vulnerable to fire. For
this reason, a direct airborne attack, even after preliminary
bombardment, on any area strongly protected by antiaircraft
[fire] was considered suicidal as a cavalry charge over open
ground swept by enemy guns.[19]

In only six weeks, the airborne "cavalry" would mount another
charge. This time, flying five times farther over enemy territory
than on any previous mission with no hope of ambush. And once
again, without the benefit of a significant rehearsal in an Allied
quest for "a bridge too far."

7

Baptism of Fear

"Standing. Waiting. Staring at the back of the next man's helmet. Weighted down like a miner's mule. Waiting. A flickering red glow filled the cabin when the cargo door had been opened, evidence of the fires below in the aftermath of the Allied bombing runs. Those at the head of the line watched the enemy's tracers arc over and under the plane, wondering if fire might soon split the difference at their plane's altitude."[1]

The seconds before jumping into torrents of enemy fire were eerily familiar to the British and American paratroopers who had jumped twice into France as they reached their drop zones in Holland in Operation *Market Garden* on September 17, 1944.

The Allied fist had been crushing Hitler's Wehrmacht for weeks. Southern France's advance had almost reached Germany's border in only a month. The breakout from Normandy created a unified Allied front in the West. Italy was crumbling. Russia was pulverizing German troops in the East. With forty-eight divisions under his command, General Eisenhower stood ready to take aim at the Fatherland.

The largest airborne assault to date would mobilize from twenty-four English airfields. More than 1,500 aircrews would deliver more than 20,000 paratroopers of the British 1st Airborne at Arnhem and the US 82nd and 101st Airborne Divisions to their assigned sectors nearby. More than 1,000 fighters and fighter-bombers would provide air cover on D-Day alone. A vanguard of more than 800 bombers would drop more than 3,000 tons of ordnance on enemy 88mm and 20mm artillery targets, among others. A massive glider reinforcement mission would take place on D+1. All to open the "back door" from Holland into Germany.

Field Marshal Bernard Montgomery had sold Eisenhower on a strategy to flank the northern edge of the Germans' defensive Siegfried Line by capturing Arnhem, thereby opening an assault route into Germany's Ruhr industrial region. Destroying the steelworks and armament factories there would cripple Germany. Could the war in Europe be over by Christmas?

But all that would be possible only if the British could capture the 400-foot-long bridge across the Lower Rhine at Arnhem. That would enable the British Second Army's XXX Corps, commanded by Lieutenant General Brian Horrocks, to drive north from Belgium and link up with British paratroopers in Arnhem. That would open a route into Germany, only fifteen miles to the east.

Mission planners had dismissed reports of two German panzer divisions recently arriving in the Arnhem area as not credible.

Major General Maxwell Taylor, an intellectual multilingual risk taker, led the 101st. The 82nd's Brigadier General James Gavin was "the jumping general." Toughened by his Pennsylvania coal-country boyhood, he had joined his men in the airborne drops over Sicily. Major General Robert Urquhart, commanding officer of the British 1st Airborne Division, had no airborne experience, was susceptible to airsickness, but had earned his men's respect with his unpretentious leadership style. Lieutenant Colonel John Frost was Urquhart's British 2nd Parachute Battalion commanding officer whose core mission was to capture the bridge at Arnhem.

On D-Day, Dakotas, Albemarles, Stirlings, Halifaxes, Horsas, and Hamilcars would deliver 186 pathfinders, 2,283 men in the 1st Parachute Brigade, and the 1st Airlanding Brigade to the Arnhem area.

The British success would be possible only if a series of battle dominoes fell in unison along a fifty-mile stretch of Highway 69 to the south, a two-lane, elevated road from the Belgian border north to Arnhem, bordered by boggy terrain that would limit maneuverability. Worse, the invasion force would have to capture six river and canal crossings from Son (north of Eindhoven) to the Lower Rhine. If the Germans destroyed even one or two bridges, the assault could grind to a halt.

Ten miles from the Belgian border, Taylor's 101st had orders to secure fifteen miles of Highway 69 and its bridges from Eindhoven to Uden. To the north, Gavin's 82nd mission was to capture ten miles of the highway and secure bridges at Nijmegen and Grave. That would first require securing the Groesbeek Heights ridge to the east and establishing a defensive line along the nearby Reichswald, a broad forest ideal for hiding German tank units.

The fates of American and British pilots – 2nd Lieutenant Eugene Shauvin, 1st Lieutenant Donald Pahlow, and Pilot Officers Len Wilson and John Gilliard among others – hinged on a chain of decisions, offsprings of General Eisenhower's establishment of the 1st Allied Airborne Army under the command of Lieutenant General Lewis Brereton. It consolidated five US and British divisions.

Ten US Troop Carrier Groups were committed to the mission, along with ten squadrons of 38 Group RAF and six squadrons from 46 Group RAF within RAF Transport Command. The assault plan was so massive that IX Troop Carrier Command's Major General Paul Williams insisted that only one airborne lift per day was feasible based on his ground personnel capacity and due to limited recent combat flight training, given the demands of resupply missions. The fundamental battlefield principle of concentrating an overwhelming combat force at a decisive point in time and place would be compromised.

Instead, *Market Garden* would not be the one-day onslaught that had characterized *Husky*, *Dragoon*, and to a large extent, *Neptune*. Worse, Montgomery's belief the XXX Corps in Belgium could reach Arnhem in two days would prove to be ill-considered to the point of being naïve.

Based in part on the lessons and scars of earlier missions, General Brereton issued orders that recon photography be available at least seventy-two hours in advance so it could be distributed and reviewed at final mission briefings. Further, *Market Garden* would be a midday mission, with aircrews arriving over DZs and LZs at about 1300 hours. The daylight mission enabled planners to group serials even more tightly than those on previous missions, this time at four- and six-minute intervals, less than half the time allotted over Normandy. More than 1,000 aircrews would deliver paratroopers and gliders in only sixty-five minutes on D-Day, by far the most concentrated arrival of airborne firepower to date.

They would be arriving over Holland from two directions after flying in one of three designated "lanes," one-and-one-half miles apart, from England. The 101st would arrive from the south after crossing part of Belgium, a path that spanned forty miles of fortified German-held territory. The 82nd and 1st Airborne would arrive from the north, overflying eighty miles of what was considered to be less intense enemy anti-aircraft fire. Finally, for the first time there would be no Allied armada posing a threat of friendly fire on a major airborne mission.

Sicily, Normandy, and southern France aircrews had all suffered from unreliable and sometimes nonexistent navigation support en route to and over the DZs and LZs. This time, there would be Eureka marker boats in the English Channel, and if formations broke up, the aircrews could activate their Rebecca equipment.

Pathfinder teams were not considered a high priority on a daylight mission. Yet for the first time there would be extensive airborne combat experience flying in *Market Garden*, against an enemy that had dug in four years earlier.

But no mission plan is ever perfect. The aircrews would be flying planes not yet retrofitted with self-sealing gas tanks. Many gliders had not received a reinforced cockpit nose. Only about half the gliders had benefitted from parachuted speed arrestor installations. Once again, relevant photography and maps were in short supply. More alarming, there had been no mission-specific training, exercises, or rehearsal. For more than a month, command had thought the mission was only days away. The final decision had come only one week in advance of H-hour on September 17.

IX Troop Carrier Command forces would be shorthanded. The paratrooper, glider, and subsequent supply missions were so massive that nearly all glider pilots would fly without a trained co-pilot alongside. The gliders' co-pilot seat would be occupied by one of the glider infantrymen aboard. Perhaps ten minutes' orientation just before takeoff would have to suffice as training for a three-hour flight into combat.

Meanwhile, drop zones on previous Allied airborne missions had ranged from six to fifteen miles inland from troops coming ashore. In *Market Garden*, they would be spread out across twenty-five miles of highway, starting ten miles north of the XXX Corps at the Belgian border. Another twenty miles would separate the British 1st Airborne from the nearest American drop zones.

A standing order given to every pilot in Operation *Market Garden* was rooted from the day he had begun flight training. First your mission. Then the safety of your crew. Finally, your survival and getting your ship home.

Bomb blasts fractured the late summer Sunday morning across the Dutch countryside on September 17. Families at Sunday breakfast tables, others working turnip and sugar beet fields, and church service parishioners paused as an ominous growl swept across southern Holland. Allied bombs pounded German artillery emplacements in towns, forests, and haystacks. Not far behind, more than 400 aircraft approached from the south, headed toward Eindhoven carrying 6,700 paratroopers and two glider serials totaling 120 gliders. At serial intervals of only four minutes, the inbound parade stretched across eighty miles. As German artillery crews scrambled, families, farmers, and priests looked skyward with smiling faces and hearts filled with dread. The destructive price of liberation inevitably would be heartbreaking as German artillery units and ground troops mobilized.

First Lieutenants Robert Stoddart, Jr, and John Corsetti steadied their aircraft as they approached the drop zones while thousands of 101st paratroopers descended over Eindhoven, Son, and Veghel. Staying on course toward Eindhoven superseded personal safety as the enemy's artillery that somehow had survived Allied bombing seemed to lock onto their aircraft filled with paratroopers standing under their illuminated red light and poised to jump.

Their marksmanship found Corsetti's left engine west of Eindhoven. He held steady at 600 feet. First Lieutenant Arthur Harrington led sixteen paratroopers out the cargo door. Less than a minute later as Corsetti climbed, rapid-fire 40mm guns erupted, their shrapnel pummeling his right engine. The fire was immediate. He had lost all power and now was flying a dying glider.

"Get out!"

The immediate order gave his three crew members time to follow the paratroopers out the door. Alone in the cockpit, Corsetti had dropped to 1,000 feet when the plane leaned over onto its right side and dipped into a vertical dive. Now a flaming tiki torch, fire stretched upward from both engines and the fuselage.

About a week later, August Corsetti learned that his son had died in the crash. Corsetti's co-pilot, radio operator, and crew chief all returned to duty nine days later.

Not far away, Stoddart headed toward another drop zone north of Eindhoven. Enemy artillery fire butchered his aircraft. Everyone had to get out immediately, he knew, including his crew. His paratroopers were highly trained, but an aircrew jumping out of a mangled aircraft even at a decent altitude did not necessarily guarantee survival.

Second Lieutenant Raymond Flowers and Technical Sergeant Howard Wilson suffered injuries when they landed. Stoddart's crew chief, Technical Sergeant Ivan Thede, died after his parachute failed to open. "Streamered in," the paratroopers called it, when they helplessly watched a plummeting man's collapsed parachute fluttering above him. Visions of a quivering death pennant would stick with those who watched and others who later retrieved the broken body.

Stoddart's father received a telegram identical to the one delivered to August Corsetti. His namesake likely had died on impact before his plane melted into a charred skeleton in a tree stand at the edge of his drop zone.

More than seventy-five tow plane/glider tandems followed the 14,000 paratroopers to Eindhoven and Nijmegen, arriving at about

1400 hours. Battlefield mayhem greeted Captain Albert Waldon and the other glider pilots, just as it had met the paratroopers' arrival.

With a ringside seat to the enemy fire peppering their serial's C-47s, aircrews counted the seconds on their final approach to their LZs. The Germans had learned how to target the gliders by aiming about ten feet behind the tow plane and then "walking the aim" back along the tow rope to the glider. The C-47s were hardly immune, however. Captain Waldon sat powerless in his glider pilot's seat as one aircraft nearby turned away trailing smoke while another looped over Waldon before turning nose down. At the last second, a crewman jumped. His parachute failed to open as a fireball swallowed the C-47.

Evading enemy bombardment pounding their aircraft proved impossible for the parade of aircrews towing fully loaded gliders. It was a dicey proposition in the best conditions. The nylon tow ropes could break from evasive action, typically against orders. Artillery flak could cut through the ropes in an eye's blink. The communication wire wrapped around the tow ropes often malfunctioned. One pilot likened their plight to being as vulnerable as a covey of pheasants landing in a cornfield's stubble during hunting season. Another shared his sentiment that as battle neared, "I could feel a chill come over me. I felt like a sitting duck and wished we were at our drop zone."[2]

Staff Sergeant Don Bolce's aircraft towed one of those gliders to the Eindhoven area. The clear astrodome behind the cockpit gave him a front row balcony seat to the parade of C-47s and gliders bound for the landing zones as each C-47 and glider tandem fought its own war.

"Get out of there!"

The radio operator had spotted a bright glow bathing a trailing C-47. The glider pilot cut away and dropped toward his landing zone.

I kept my eyes focused on the burning aircraft as the fire raged, but still no parachutes. The C-47, almost completely engulfed in flames, started down toward the ground. Still no chutes! "Get out of there! Get out of there!" I screamed. The plane slammed into the ground with a tremendous explosion with orange flames and black smoke that seemed to have risen hundreds of feet almost instantly. The sight horribly shook me. I felt total sorrow and anguish for the poor men who were now dead, though I had no idea who they were. Our mission to deliver our glider was still ahead of us.

When Bolce put his headphones back on, radio silence had become a fond wish. Aircrews were yelling about which C-47s had been hit, which were losing altitude, pointing out burning wrecks below where only the aircrafts' vertical stabilizers were visible through the flames, and warning about the heavy flak up ahead.

Later on reflection, "*Market Garden* left its mark on all of us, whether aircrews, glider crews, paratroopers, or glider infantry. We will never forget our baptism of fear," he wrote.[3]

Whether on D-Day or the days that followed, threats other than enemy fire could likewise terrify veteran war correspondents amid the infernal chaos faced by aircrews and their glider pilots. American correspondent Walter Cronkite joined the 101st in Operation *Market Garden* on assignment. Previous rides in a bomber failed to prepare him for airborne glider warfare. After sitting in the glider, wondering if his tow plane's aircrew would survive their final approach, his glider's release brought new horror. Exploding artillery outside his glider sounded and felt as loud as a bass drum at a rock concert before his glider "dropped like a stone" when released from its tow plane.

"Weave, skipper, weave! ... Keep weaving! ... take a look at the port outer motor on fire ... Bail out!"

The radio call petrified *Daily Telegraph* correspondent Edmund Townshend as he sat in the co-pilot's seat on his first flight in an aircraft. Unlike Cronkite, his combat mission ended when Townshend dropped through the open floor hatch in his Stirling. "For minutes like hours, dreading attack by machine-gunners below, I swayed slowly to earth. Breathlessly I watched the Stirling roar away in flames, losing height. With relief I saw other para-chutes opening in its wake." With the help of Dutch Resistance,

Townshend evaded enemy patrols for four days before reaching a British unit.[4]

That same baptism took place about eight miles west of Arnhem when the 1st Airborne arrived at 1240 hours. Enemy artillery fire on their approach was surprisingly light and the landings so efficient that they required only one hour and fifteen minutes. Yet the promising start to *Market Garden* would prove illusory.

From the beginning, aircrew training had focused on efficient take-offs, tight formation flying, the approach, the drop or release, reversing the original course, and heading home. A single piece of shrapnel, concussive blast or red-hot bullet could cut any mission short. For aircrews on September 17, the enemy removed the last leg of the mission from the flight plan when some flights to the drop zones near Nijmegen became one-way missions. First Lieutenant Norman Baldwin, Jr, had not yet met his son when he took off on D-Day, his third combat flight mission of the war. He had missed Norman Baldwin III's birth by one week after he had hugged his wife, Clara, and deployed to Europe. The twenty-three-year-old had transferred to the AAF after serving in the army's cavalry for two years. After dropping sixteen 82nd paratroopers near Groesbeek, he initiated a broad left turn, the moment when C-47s were broadside and most vulnerable to gunfire that often felt inevitable.

The Germans' signature 88mm crews fired high-explosive shells with fuses timed to explode alongside or inside a fuselage, releasing a cloudburst of shrapnel that left gaping entry and exit wounds in men and aircraft. Their armor-piercing shells could penetrate armor a mile away. Armor-piercing ordnance exploding thirty feet away could bring down a plane and its men aboard.

The enemy's explosive shells found an engine.

Fire erupted from the main section of both wings, a fatal wound. As the aircraft seeped altitude, Baldwin's crew chief, Technical Sergeant George Harrison, and his radio operator, Corporal William Armstrong, strapped on parachutes and jumped. Flames had reached the co-pilot, 2nd Lieutenant Burton Squire, burning him severely. He would ride the C-47 to the ground alongside

Baldwin. Screams pierced the billowing smoke when the burning plane skidded to a stop in a field not yet cleared of the enemy.

Seriously burned on his head and arms, Squire squirmed out of the cockpit's shattered starboard window. Paratroopers who had witnessed the crash took him to a nearby first aid station. The next morning, a German counterattack overran the station, capturing Squire. Baldwin, meanwhile, had died in the crash.

Less than two miles away, Armstrong and Harrison had survived their low-altitude jump. *Should we take cover and wait for things to settle or head toward that town over there?* They opted for the latter, hoping to find members of the Dutch Resistance. Instead, a postal clerk spotted them, drew his pistol, and escorted both to German troops in nearby Kranenburg. They had survived, but their clouded future now matched the smoke rising from their aircraft's carcass in a burned cornfield.

"She's on fire, sir!"

First Lieutenant Stan Fishel didn't need the announcement from his crew chief, Charles Rosko, as "red lights flashed all over the instrument panel" and smoke filled his aircraft. His aircrew had completed an uneventful run to their DZ, only to be hammered by the Germans once they had made a U-turn to head back toward England. Fishel lost contact with his formation when he descended and "stayed on the deck, flying between the trees and windmills" while skirting small villages on his way to the English Channel.

Nearing the coast, "we ran out of trees" as the C-47 passed over the Scheldt River estuary northwest of Antwerp. As if the Germans had been waiting with their firepower, the aircraft suddenly, steadily, bled power.

It became clear Fishel's C-47 was going to hit the water in only minutes, maybe less, while the crew was still taking fire. Ditching procedures replaced the ad-lib flight plan back to base. His co-pilot, 2nd Lieutenant Fred Roth, transmitted a "Mayday" message three times, followed by the aircraft's call sign; then set the VHF to continual transmission; and finally turned to see if Fishel needed help with his belts and shoulder harness. Meanwhile, Sergeant Carmen Sanfilippo, the radio operator, tuned his IFF ("friend or foe identification" transmitter) to "Emergency" and transmitted "SOS" three times. In the main cabin, Fishel's crew chief, Sergeant Charles Rosko, battened down anything loose that could fly through the cabin, and then jettisoned everything not critical to their survival. "Less weight means longer float," they had learned in flight training. *Only seconds now.*

Ditching resembled a roll of the dice for American and British aircrews. Each crew member faced his fate differently, survival impossible to predict. The pilot and co-pilot sat in high-backed, deeply upholstered leather seats with stout safety belts. The radio operator sat on an aluminum swivel chair with a seat belt. The rest of the crew could only "hang on" and hope since there were no dedicated handholds. The navigator, crew chief, and cargo loader (a "despatcher" in British aircraft) simply sat on the cargo compartment's floor, their backs against the bulkhead, and imagined what it would be like to carom off the walls and floor at impact. Head, facial, and bone injuries among them were common.[5]

Up front, Fishel struggled to keep his wings level, flatten his approach as much as possible, check for retracted landing gear, slow to a near-stall, and come to a sliding stop on the water's surface. They called it "belly in" during training, much like what many youngsters called a "belly flop" in a swimming pool.

Training and discipline overcame fear as the plane settled. While Roth climbed through the eighteen-inch-square emergency hatch in the cockpit roof, Rosko deployed an emergency raft. After Roth, Rosko, and Sanfilippo had climbed in, Fishel took one last look inside the plane before joining them. Their aircraft refused to sink right away, as the aircrew marveled at a hole the size of a man's head in each engine.

Now what? They started rowing against a stubborn tide as their plane finally sank in their wake. If they could reach the English Channel, perhaps they would be rescued by an Allied ship before night descended? Small arms fire buzzing past their heads scuttled that plan. A white handkerchief tied to a raised oar signaled surrender as they dumped their weapons, escape kits, and personal items into the sea.

Stan Fishel had been the comptroller for his family's business before enlisting and then marrying Shirley four days before he was commissioned as a second lieutenant in 1943. Now, instead of returning to his squadron in Folkingham eight hours after he had taken off, Fishel and other British and American aircrewmen would embark on an 800-mile trek ending at the gates to a prisoner of war camp in Barth, Germany. The sign on his barracks door hinted at what lay ahead.

KNOCK
BE PREPARED TO TALK AS WELL AS LISTEN. WE
HAVE GALLANT MEN WHO HAVE BAILED OUT
OF EVERY TYPE OF SHIP UNDER EVERY TYPE OF
CIRCUMSTANCE WITH EVERY TYPE OF CHUTE
FROM EVERY ALTITUDE AND WITH ANY NUMBER
OF PROPS FEATHERED. WE HAVE EATEN BETTER
AND WORSE FOOD THAN YOU HAVE, KNOW
BETTER STORIES, MORE WOMEN, MORE GENERALS
AND CAN, UNDOUBTEDLY, HAVE GREATER
GASTRIC EXPLOSIONS THAN ANY FIFTY-SIX MEN IN
THE WHOLE CAMP.[6]

War breeds intimacy among strangers. Within aircrews, that bond was forged from shared experience, the threat of death or worse, and for the lucky ones, survival.

Pilots of C-47s, C-47 Dakotas, and the modified troop bombers all had limited options after taking a direct hit. Enemy volleys gave Pilot Officer John Gilliard, his RAF squadron's leader, only one option following a direct hit that crippled his Stirling bomber. *Stay steady so they can jump.* "Bail out!"

His bomb aimer, flight engineer, wireless operator, and squadron leader followed one another out in seconds as the Stirling lost power. With the lifeless bodies of two despatchers and his rear gunner in back, the plane sank too low for Gilliard to jump. Perhaps while attempting a belly landing, he died on impact, perhaps seconds earlier from wounds left by hailstorms of shrapnel. A veteran of missions over Malta and Tripoli, Gilliard had earned the Distinguished Flying Cross before dying on his forty-third mission. He was twenty-four years old.

Strangers sometimes made survival possible.

"Bail out! Bail out!"

The fire aboard 1st Lieutenant Donald Pahlow's aircraft threatened to engulf his C-47 after he and his crew had delivered eighteen 101st paratroopers to their drop zone near Boxtel. The German flak had found his plane's rear fuel tanks. Nearby aircrews turning for home spotted the burst of flames. Their shouts over the radio carried a frightening urgency. He agreed.

"Get ready to bail out!"

Just seconds earlier, co-pilot William Baker had watched a plane on his wing burst into flames and tracked two men who jumped out of the maimed fuselage. They fell straight into Boxtel, their parachutes – if they were wearing them – never opening. Now the second lieutenant scrambled to take off his flak jacket and snap on his parachute. Radio operator Rollin Ellis and crew chief Christopher Domitrovich did the same.

This flight also carried two strangers. Captain William Wade was an intelligence officer accompanying Corporal Thomas Hoge, who was covering the mission for *Stars and Stripes*. Neither was trained to bail out of a dying aircraft glowing an angry red. As smoke filled the cabin, the crew and Hoge headed out the door, while Pahlow helped Wade with his parachute. A kind gesture that cost both their lives when the plane crashed, exploding in another ball of flame.

The survivors' fates were as impossible to predict as it had been to imagine the terror of parachuting into enemy territory. Concealment and luck would define the odds of survival for Baker, Ellis, and Domitrovich. They landed far apart, each calculating a course of action that began with hiding from the enemy, waiting for dark, and staying vigilant. When the firefights ebbed, Baker walked up to a boy milking a cow. Two villagers approached Ellis. Another walked up to Domitrovich. Each offered his help.

All three had found members of the Dutch Resistance, remarkably brave Dutch residents who ultimately harbored hundreds of downed airmen, moving them from town to secluded forests and back for weeks until the British liberated the area and the fighting waned. Remarkably, the Dutch reunited the three crewmen at one of the network's hideouts.[7] About every week they were smuggled among barn lofts, farmhouses, churches, straw houses in the woods, and even a large hole in the Kampina Forest near Boxtel that had been covered with camouflage netting. Resistance fighters delivered food sometimes hidden in milk cans. Escape was frequently discussed, but a lack of identification papers and the inability to speak German confined the notion to fantasy.

As Operation *Market Garden* stretched over more than a week of combat, the refugees could only wonder if Pahlow, Wade, and Hoge also had survived.

Many C-47 and Dakota pilots looked to their commanding officers to lead from the front in their combat missions. They expected their squadron and troop carrier group leaders to earn their respect by confronting the same risks as the pilots and aircrews they commanded stateside and in Britain during mission training.

The 440th's commanding officer, Colonel Krebs, and his co-pilot, Lieutenant Colonel Howard Cannon, the 440th's operations officer, led forty-two aircraft toward Nijmegen. After flying together over Normandy, this time the enemy fire on their approach had been comparatively tame. But once they dropped their 82nd paratroopers, their left engine's propeller "walked through the fuselage, broke free and sliced the fuselage just behind the cockpit," as cleanly as a cheese knife through gouda.

Was that a direct hit? An unseen, sudden impact had severed the propeller from its engine, sending it into the fuselage, breaking the leg of radio operator Edward Sullivan, and severing hydraulic lines that splattered the main cabin and the crew. As the C-47 hemorrhaged hydraulic fluid, Krebs and Cannon strapped on their chutes and followed their crew out the door at about 800 feet, Krebs breaking his foot when he landed. Stranded on the ground with a broken leg, Sullivan was immediately taken prisoner.

As hundreds of other crewmen would experience in the coming days, taking cover in ditches or tree stands became the order of the day until a farmer, a young boy on a bicycle, or a priest dared approach them when out of sight from the enemy. Dutch residents had learned how to survive – and often fight back with the stealth of a mosquito – against the Germans following their invasion four years earlier.

Generally wary of large groups of downed airborne personnel, the Dutch Resistance paired Krebs and Cannon for protection. Relocating them every few days required enormous risks in daytime transport while sometimes crossing paths with unsuspecting German soldiers. Their first few nights were spent in a Dutch police station. Then nights in a shed, upstairs in a shuttered department store accessible only to the Germans occupiers, in the closets of several homes, under the floor of one Dutch residence, and in a small room concealed by a woodpile on the floor of a silo. From their last hideout, Krebs and Cannon heard the arrival of a German 88mm artillery crew and then several days of fevered barrages between the Allies and Germans.

The sophisticated nature of their odyssey astounded the Americans. The Dutch fabricated false identification papers complete with photo IDs and authentic official seals. Krebs and Cannon were passed off as policemen, farmers, a city clerk, and a schoolteacher. A *sub rosa* communications system enabled Krebs to connect with commanding officers of the approaching Allied infantry, reporting on the number of aircrews harbored by the Dutch as well as their locations. Meanwhile, periodic sweeps by German units in search of the Americans failed to uncover Krebs and Cannon.

Meanwhile, missing in action telegrams had only inflamed families' worries that had simmered since the pilots' deployment to Europe. As the weeks passed, they could only speculate. *If he hasn't been found, is he dead and buried somewhere? Could he possibly still be hiding somewhere? Or had he been taken to one of those godforsaken prisoner of war camps?*

Families could only wait while Krebs and Cannon ran their obstacle race between hideouts, waiting for the Allies' advance to their corner of the war.[8]

Uncertainty stains all in war. Aircrews, airborne combat forces, sailors, and troops on the ground all shared the uncertainties of death, serious wounds, lifelong disability, running out of ammunition or food, and being left behind when the shooting stopped.

Second Lieutenant Eugene Shauvin had been worried long before he was among the first six aircrews to enter Holland on September 17 with a load of eleven pathfinders. While on leave, the pilot had told his wife, Phyllis, on their last night together in Chicago that he had a premonition that he would not return from his next mission. He and Phyllis had a daughter, Linda. He was twenty-five years old.

He held steady after flak disabled an engine. But not long enough for all the paratroopers to jump. Later, nearby villagers recovered eight bodies and buried them in a common grave.

THE SECRETARY OF WAR DESIRES ME TO EXPRESS
HIS DEEP REGRET THAT YOUR HUSBAND SECOND
LIEUTENANT EUGENE P SHAUVIN HAS BEEN
REPORTED MISSING IN ACTION SINCE SEVENTEEN
SEPTEMBER OVER HOLLAND IF FURTHER DETAILS …

The Shauvin family would be among dozens of others across England and America who received similar telegrams in the weeks following Operation *Market Garden*'s D-Day. In the days ahead, Field Marshall Montgomery's two-day battle plan would stretch across several more sunsets and prove as costly as it had been fanciful.

8

Facing the Enemy

Weather is undefeated in war.

Immune to the hopes and plans of others, it persists and shifts on a whim, unalterably advances at its own pace, and changes course when it chooses. Late on D-Day, General Brereton pushed back D+1's mission by four hours due to persistent English fog and also combined serials onto the southern route due to clouds and rain over the Channel, Holland, and Belgium. Then, when a heavy cloud cover developed on the southern route early on the 18th, Brereton moved the day's airborne missions all to the northern route with a 1400 hours departure.

It became a staggering start to the day's massive glider resupply battle plan spanning 1,336 US troop carrier aircraft, 340 British troop carrier aircraft, 1,205 gliders, and then 252 bombers on resupply sorties.[1]

IX Troop Carrier Command had judged D-Day's airborne missions to the 82nd and 101st to be eighty-five percent effective and one report characterized the 1st Airborne's arrival by RAF aircrews at Arnhem as precise as a "parade ground drop." They had been costly, however. Almost one in four planes sent to the 101st had been shot down or damaged by enemy fire on the more threatening southern route. Of those sent to the 82nd from the north, the aircraft casualty rate was closer to one in ten.

On the ground, Field Marshal Montgomery's plan had frayed from north to south. Lieutenant Colonel Frost's battalion had seized the north end of the Arnhem bridge but was badly outnumbered. The Germans held a vital Nijmegen bridge as the 82nd focused on its priority of protecting its flank to the east. The Germans had destroyed a key bridge in the 101st's sector. Most alarming, the XXX Corps had advanced only four miles on the first day.

Over the next two days, multiple battles unfolded. Against the weather, against unexpected German firepower in Arnhem, and against the German gauntlet, the length of Highway 69 from Belgium to Arnhem. Finally by late afternoon on the 18th, the sky filled with Allied aircrews. The American glider pilots and their infantry confronted brutal turbulence over the English Channel, generated by the C-47s, Dakotas, and bombers. Roiling prop wash shattered the front-facing Plexiglas in several gliders, creating a 100-mile-per-hour gale in the cockpits. One in five communication cables between the gliders and C-47s and Dakotas failed or malfunctioned. Paratroopers in back passed vomit buckets toward the cargo door as the glider pilots gritted through a three-hour flight without trained co-pilots to share the duty.

The Germans now knew the airborne approach routes and had concentrated artillery crews before RAF aircrews arrived with more than 1,900 paratroopers, the remainder of the 1st Airlanding Brigade, and then with sixty-eight tons of supplies in heavily congested airspace.[2]

Flying "low and slow," all aircrews became ideal targets for enemy gunners. For many aircrews, their supply or reinforcement objective transformed into one of survival.

The smoke erupted from 1st Lieutenant William McCormick's left engine near Breda, Belgium, forty miles from his glider's landing zone near Eindhoven. Like others, McCormick faced a critical decision, mostly based on unanswerable questions. *How long before I lose power in the left engine? Any fuel leaks? Are we going to explode? Do I take the chance, keep going, and hope I can release my glider over the LZ? Engine's running rough. Will it hold together?*

At the back end of his tow rope, Flight Officer Herbert Bollum confronted a similar conundrum. He could abandon the mission and release right away or trust McCormick would get him to the LZ.

"Hang on, I see a field straight ahead."

Once Bollum released less than two minutes later, McCormick turned back toward the coast as oily smoke filled his aircraft. *Where's the fire?* Radio operator James Powell spotted it. Under the fuselage's floor, much too close. When his engine quit, "I looked down at the hydraulic pressure gauge ... it was indicating 'zero'." Pilots knew three systems were vital to their engines' health. Hydraulic fluid was likened to an aircraft's blood system and manifold pressure gauged how much fuel and air each engine was receiving. Flight required all three.

The flashing red lights across his controls painted a dire prognosis. Shrapnel had destroyed the radio. Fuel and oil spill valves had opened. The landing gear was engaged, not good if they reached the English Channel and had to ditch. But it became McCormick's only choice.

He climbed on one engine to 4,000 feet, turned into a steep dive reaching 220 miles per hour, cut his fuel mixture to bleed altitude as quickly as possible, and then leveled at 1,000 feet. Tail down, he set down on the water. Smoothly, he thought, until the cockpit dug in. The crash sent his plane's rubber dinghy flying across the cabin. With effort, the aircrew managed to get it into the water and inflated. Once in the dinghy, the crew fought a strong current to clear the aircraft's battered wing, far enough away before the C-47 inevitably sank. *Is that a boat headed this way?* The entire aircrew was rescued. McCormick was awarded a Distinguished Flying Cross for "remarkable display of technical proficiency ... devotion to duty ... leadership."

Other aircrews faced harrowing return flights to England as their blood soaked their uniforms. The Horsa cut off from Flying Officer Ed Henry's Dakota seconds after he had taken a direct hit and had died. Every other member of the crew had been wounded from the shrapnel, including Warrant Officer Bert Smith, the co-pilot. *How do we get back?* Smith's navigator had no ready answer. His equipment had been destroyed by shrapnel. Smith set a westerly course and hoped. *There! Dunkirk!*

With that landmark, Smith set a course for England, even though a good portion of his tail and rudder had been shot away. Somehow, he reached a British airfield and landed, despite the shrapnel wound in his arm. The rest of his crew survived as well. The next day, Smith was interviewed by the BBC, later flew two more *Market Garden* missions, and also received the Distinguished Flying Cross for his devotion to duty.

Few have less room and fewer routes to survival than the pilots strapped into side-by-side seats in a C-47 or Dakota cockpit attached to a cigar tube fuselage. For some, survival rested on squeezing through the two-foot square escape hatch in the cockpit's roof, assuming the aircraft had not turned over on its side or nosed down into a vertical dive. But pilots knew the men back in the fuselage had almost no hope if the pilots climbed out. "If we don't survive, they don't survive." Stay with the aircraft, no matter the cost.

First Lieutenant Frederick Hale, Jr, was flying Tail End Charlie at the rear of his formation, never a good place to avoid enemy fire. When a 40mm shell knocked out his right engine and set it on fire, Hale ordered the eighteen paratroopers aboard and his crew to bail out. But seconds later, as 2nd Lieutenant Thaddeus Harvey and Technical Sergeant Milfred Harrold stood to follow the paratroopers out the door, another direct hit under the cockpit killed both as well as the right engine; burned three paratroopers; blew the leg off a fourth; and set the cabin on fire.[3] Except for the three burned men, the paratroopers – including the one who had lost a leg – jumped clear. A third direct hit severed Hale's aileron controls and destroyed his instruments.

He looked up at the emergency hatch above his seat as the fuselage filled with smoke. He unstrapped, squirmed through, and pushed off the plane's roof with only 150 feet left before the crash. His parachute opened, he swung once before hitting the ground miraculously uninjured.

After rescue by a member of the Dutch Resistance, Hale met other pilots who had confronted a similar fate and rescue.

"Hey, I know you!"

"Yea."

"Who are you?"

"I'm Freddy Hale."

Hale and 2nd Lieutenant George Merz had crossed paths in earlier postings. Merz had shocking news for Hale. After Merz had crashed and also was rescued by the Dutch Resistance, Merz had spotted Hale's crewmen listed in a Dutch cemetery's logbook.

"I told them to bail out!" Hale exploded in a burst of expletives, only then realizing he might be the sole survivor of his crew.

Merz's crew, meanwhile, had experienced a grizly fate. Second Lieutenant Russell Stephens' parachute had not opened as he plunged 200 feet to his death. One of the aircraft's propellers struck Technical Sergeant William Buckley's head as he jumped from a door near the cockpit and killed him. Crew chief Richard Eastman's body was found in a field several hundred yards from the crash site. He had been shot twice in the chest and once under his chin by the SS. Only the co-pilot, 2nd Lieutenant Ernest Haagensen, had survived along with Merz.

With the help of the Dutch, Hale and Merz returned to their commands about a week later. Their crews remained buried in Holland and Belgium.

For the second day, aircrew performance appeared to exceed expectations. The airborne delivered approximately 4,500 troops along with 250 jeeps, trailers, and even two bulldozers. About one in four C-47s returned to Britain damaged while achieving a ninety percent effectiveness rate.

Later analysis presented a different diagnosis. Enemy resistance had stiffened considerably. British paratroopers jumped prematurely as British aircrews arrived over drop zones that had been overrun by Germans. American aircrews had tightened their formation so significantly that the parachute drop was completed through the enemy's artillery and small arms fire in only nine minutes.

Other aircrews delivering the 1st Airlanding Brigade took evasive action by climbing, forcing their glider pilots into precariously steep descents toward pastures riddled with abandoned gliders from D-Day's first lift.

Operation *Market Garden* meanwhile had seriously fallen behind schedule on the ground. Frost's beleaguered men still held one end of the Arnhem bridge, but the XXX Corps advance had stalled when the Germans destroyed a bridge at Son near Eindhoven. *Market Garden* was unraveling by the end of the second day, and its key ally, the weather, threatened to swamp any remaining prospects for victory.

Once again weather dictated battle on September 19. Rain, fog, and clouds plagued the southern route, but could General Brereton afford to send aircrews on the northern route for the third consecutive day? No. He rolled back the day's plan to only a mission for the 101st and it would fly through the weather from the south. If Brereton harbored any doubts, he hedged his bet by delaying the takeoff for the 101st until 1130 hours. The scheduled mission to resupply General Gavin's 82nd was nixed. Gavin would have to defend a twenty-five-mile perimeter without reinforcements. RAF missions to reinforce Major General Urquhart at Arnhem with a Polish parachute brigade also were aborted.

Brereton had settled on a mission concentrated on a known route at midday with no chance of escaping a prepared and primed enemy.

"Hand me a chute and bail out."

For the last eight miles, Captain Charles Stevenson's right engine had been on fire as the resupply mission had approached its objective. Towing his glider on one engine had not been part of the flight plan. First Lieutenant Judson Ball flying nearby had used his radio to alert Stevenson after tracers had riddled Stevenson's fuselage and had found an engine.

"Bail out!"

Stevenson had begun flying while attending Akron University and had been a member of a civilian pilot training group at the Akron airport. Married and with a young son back home in the US, now he intended to fly solo over Holland. Except that his navigator, 1st Lieutenant Kenneth Okeson, disobeyed and entered the cockpit to stick with his skipper.

Stevenson's co-pilot, radio operator, and crew chief followed orders, jumping several miles short of their glider's landing zone. First Lieutenant Robert Moore, Technical Sergeant Clinton Perry, and 2nd Lieutenant Lawrence Borland were captured immediately and sent to a German prisoner intake center.

The C-47's remaining two-man crew pressed ahead and released its glider.

Time to get out.

Stevenson put on his parachute, climbed out his cockpit's escape hatch, and jumped. He had not secured the chute's leg straps. He fell out of his chute and plunged 500 feet to his death. He managed to say his name and troop carrier group number to the paratroopers who ran to him before dying. Okeson died as well, presumably in the plane crash.

Shortly before his mission, Stevenson had written a letter to his wife, Katherine, noting, "If I go, I want to go quickly." His fall took approximately six seconds. He never met his son, Charles.

Stevenson's heroism lingered long after this death. Radio operator Lawrence Borland later wrote to his superior officers, "Captain Stevenson showed outstanding courage above and beyond the call of duty and I consider having served with him a very great honor. May I please have the name and address of his next of kin?"[4] There is no known record on whether his request was granted.

Like Stevenson, many British and American aircrews fought not only the enemy but fire on their missions. A fuselage in flames brought nightmares. A pilot and co-pilot could become trapped as their cockpit heated faster than an oven before dinner. Engine and wing fires threatened explosions of the wings' fuel tanks a few feet behind the cockpit. Or a wing collapsing into molten steel.

No aircrew wanted to make more than one pass through fountains of enemy fire and risk an onboard fire on a second run, yet many did not hesitate.

Flight Lieutenant David "Lummy" Lord had studied for the priesthood before enlisting in the RAF in 1936. At a steady 120 miles per hour, he descended to 500 feet for the last two minutes of his approach to his drop zone. On an approach as predictable as a duck silhouette passing broadside in a carnival shooting gallery.

He stayed on his course despite taking two hits in his starboard wing. His aircrew ignored the fire as supply cannisters were dropped. But not all of them. *Do we make another run?* Although starved for power, Lord banked to make a second pass, ignoring the smoke frothing from his starboard engine and shrapnel slicing into his Dakota's skin. The last of the supplies were cast out the door.

"Bail out! Bail out! ... For God's sake, bail out!"

Lord's orders came too late. The airframe's explosion collapsed the starboard wing. The ground shuddered under the crash, ending a mission whose final eight minutes had been flown while on fire. It had not gone unnoticed.

"... troops on the ground, who were so mesmerized by this single plane that they stood up in their trenches to will it on ... They were all highly moved, in some cases in tears ... by this tremendous display of courage and self-sacrifice on their behalf."[5]

Lord posthumously received the Victoria Cross, the only RAF transport pilot to be so honored in World War II with Britain's highest award for valor. Heartbreakingly, Germans had overrun his drop zone. Not only did his aircrew supply the Germans, but two-thirds of his 164-aircraft armada was damaged or shot down.[6]

A Missouri farm boy now married, 1st Lieutenant Jesse Harrison was still five miles from his glider's 101st LZ when flak set his aircraft on fire. *Had the glider, carrying troops and artillery, taken a direct hit, too?* He could not be sure. While holding firm on his course, Harrison was hit again. Seconds later, fire creeped into the cabin as he steadily lost altitude.

Who goes first?

Harrison ordered his crew chief and radio operator to bail out at once, while he pressed ahead toward the glider's landing zone. The C-47's lurch forward told him the glider pilot had released.

Once Harrison dropped the tow rope, there was only one route to survival. The closest escape hatch. Harrison suffered serious burns as he crawled through the fire and then parachuted at only 300 feet. He heard his C-47 die when it crashed.

Pilots often believed "there's a bullet that has my name on it." Others simply trusted each mission to fate or luck. After two passes over his drop zone in Normandy three months earlier, Harrison's crew had counted sixty-seven bullet holes. On an earlier *Market Garden* mission, he had delivered a planeload of troops to Holland. This time, Harrison suffered second and third degree burns to his waist and face that required skin grafts. His recovery would be long, painful, and include reconstruction of his ears and nose.

Second Lieutenant Alan Boyd could feel the weight of the glider behind his aircraft as he crossed the English Channel toward a dull gray wall of clouds a few miles ahead. The water below was as smooth as the beaver ponds that many pilots recalled from their rural boyhoods. Soon like other aircrews, the Florida native would be faced with a decision that fused fear and courage in a microsecond.

Suddenly, when the clouds and water blurred into a monotone mist, devoid of landmarks and points of reference, his brain spasmed into vertigo. The sense of suddenly flying with one wing pointing down at the sea in a vertical left bank turn was over-whelming. Boyd became convinced a crash was imminent. Staring at the instruments in front of him, Boyd's silent debate between terror and training raged for ten minutes before the vertigo eased and sanity returned. Minutes later, his echelon received orders to return to England due to the foul weather over the Continent.[7]

An Army general once said, "war is fear cloaked in courage."[8] Fear among some *Market Garden* aircrews became as deadly as a curtain of enemy fire.

American 1st Lieutenant Walter Hultgren and his co-pilot, 2nd Lieutenant Harold Horowitz, neared their target destination, LZ-W north of Eindhoven on D+2. Their plane caught fire three minutes from the LZ. The sudden shudder told Hultgren that flak had cut the tow rope of the glider he had been pulling, sending the glider crew and eleven glider airborne to their deaths. Hultgren knew his C-47 would soon follow as he ordered his crew to bail out.

Activating the autopilot servo unit at the base of the center control pedestal gave Hultgren and Horowitz time to unbuckle, head back toward the tail, and join their radio operator and crew chief to help open the cargo door so they could parachute out. But Staff Sergeant Elonzo Fenner and Technical Sergeant James Sarginger sat paralyzed about ten feet from the door.

Hultgren later reported the two were in "a condition of shock, refusing to jump. I tried to get [them] to [their] senses so [they] could help us push the [cargo] door out in order to jump but it was impossible. So the co-pilot and I managed it ourselves."[9]

Hultgren and Horowitz later returned to duty after bailing out. Fenner's wife, Virginia, and Sarginger's mother, Catherine, later received killed in action telegrams.

Knowing whether or when to bail out and admit a mission's failure tormented aircrews. *Do I wait for the pilot to make that call? What if I can see the flames better back here than he can? He's the captain of the ship but …* Crew chief Alvin Harrison stood on a stool behind his C-47's cockpit, peering out the astrodome past his plane's tail when his plane took a direct hit. The technical sergeant called down to his pilot, 1st Lieutenant Raymond Francis, to report the fire.[10] The co-pilot, 2nd Lieutenant Samuel Troncalli, left his cockpit seat and headed back to the cargo door. Once he took off his flak jacket and strapped on his parachute he jumped. A passenger, Staff Sergeant James Godfrey, had tried to stop him, knowing the fire had been extinguished.

Troncalli was the only crewman to jump. Francis successfully landed the plane in Belgium while enemy troops captured Troncalli, who spent the rest of the war in a German prisoner of war camp.

More than 350 gliders delivered 2,300 infantry to the 101st on September 19. But it was a hollow win on a day of losses. The mission suffered the heaviest one-day loss of gliders to date in World

War II. By one account, 172 glider landings also were judged to be ineffective, an attrition rate of close to fifty percent.[11]

The RAF scorecard was even more dire. One hundred sixty-four transports failed to link with planned fighter escorts. Losses mounted as aircrews held their course over five enemy artillery emplacements at 900 feet toward drop zones not fully secured. Ninety-seven aircraft were damaged and thirteen were shot down.[12]

In Arnhem, German counterattacks again inflicted heavy 1st Airborne losses. To the south, the XXX Corps finally advanced ten miles once the bridge at Son had been replaced, but the prospects for establishing a bridgehead on the far side of the Rhine in Arnhem now "were very, very small," according to one postwar analysis.[13]

A cold, windy rain soaked more than 2,200 men gathered in defeat along the Lower Rhine on the night of September 25. Operation *Market Garden* had failed. All that remained was evacuation. More than 6,000 non-ambulatory wounded had been left behind as more than 150 crossings by small boats in Operation *Berlin* carried the survivors to the far side of the river before sunrise the following morning.

Losses from Montgomery's plan were among the worst of the war. The 1st Airborne Division was destroyed, losing more than eighty percent of its 10,600-man force. 38 Group RAF alone had recorded 118 damaged aircraft.

RAF officers earned thirty-four Distinguished Flying Crosses "for an act of valor or devotion to duty whilst flying in the face of the enemy." More than one RAF summary cited flying at 6,000 feet over clouds, dropping to tree level with as little maneuverability as a B-17 bomber for the final approach due to a low cloud base, climbing in the last few minutes to 800 feet through the enemy's artillery onslaught to make a supply drop, and then returning to England at 7,000 feet. The six squadrons of 46 Group RAF flew 512 Dakota sorties, split evenly between glider and resupply missions. About one aircraft every twenty sorties was lost, forty-seven crewmen were killed, and twenty-two were taken prisoner.[14]

War often lingers. Triumph or retreat rarely marked the end of battles, assaults, landings, or invasions. *Market Garden* may have become a lost cause, but its aftermath still rested on a pipeline through the air that required penetrating enemy positions, landing, unloading, taking off, and making the run back to base over enemy territory. The 82nd Division alone would require 200 C-47s delivering 265 tons of supplies daily.[15]

Less than eight hours after the British had completed their bloodied retreat across the Lower Rhine, crew chief Winfield Wood made sure the vehicles in his C-47 remained secure for landing on a crude dirt strip, 100 yards wide and 1,400 yards long, carved into a cow pasture bordered by four canals.

The technical sergeant's plane was among more than 200 flying up from the south on September 26, inside a designated half mile-wide corridor over Highway 69 to the Graves area. Tanks lined the road and P-51s circled overhead for protection. But a resupply mission could become as deadly as any mission in the heat of battle.

Gunfire flashes over one landing zone on the route revealed German and American troops fighting for equipment scattered among gliders as Wood pressed ahead. Larger flashes erupted from a German artillery battery until a P-51 dove toward it and then pulled out at about 100 feet as the emplacement exploded from the pilot's fire.

By the time Wood's C-47 came to a halt in the pasture designated as a forward landing strip, his crew had unlashed the cargo. They unloaded a motorcycle, jeep, and its trailer in thirteen minutes. Seconds counted as ten more C-47s were inbound with minimal air traffic control support. The crew braced for the short-field take-off procedure. *Set the brakes. Throttles forward. Wait to feel the tail lift. Release the brakes. Throttles all the way. Hold steady through the bounces. We're up! Now a sharp 180-degree turn.* The pilot didn't bother to gain altitude this time. Instead, he completed the U-turn and sped back down the same approach corridor toward safety.

By 1740 hours, all 209 planes had reached the landing zone and unloaded 882 troops as well approximately 380 tons of cargo. "At one time, there were more than 100 C-47s on the field, 100 closely parked, defenseless sky freight wagons," he later recalled. Yet none was lost. The next day, the airstrip became a fighter base, in part due to the buildup of Luftwaffe capability in the area.

Even when a battle's outcome has been settled, indescribable horrors would pair with unimaginable instances of luck, fate, or karma. When and how, no one could predict.

Second Lieutenant Cecil Dawkins was an eager pilot. After recovering from an ear infection, he had flown a mission over Normandy and had asked his operations officer to assign him every mission. His second mission for *Market Garden* almost didn't happen. He had delivered British personnel on the 18th, but foul weather on the 21st again grounded flights, although a paratrooper mission to the 101st stayed on the schedule.

The two flak bursts close to Dawkins' cockpit were a devastating one-two punch. Shrapnel slit his head and face, and killed his left engine. Fire crept across the wing while prop wash pushed flames down the side of the fuselage. Dawkins dropped out of formation so his Polish paratroopers could jump. Now at only 150 feet, which was standard procedure to avoid enemy fire or a midair collision but too low to jump. Dawkins had applied all his power to his right engine. As he began to climb he ordered his crew to jump. His co-pilot, 1st Lieutenant Cleon Worley, Jr, was the last to jump, at 300 feet. Dawkins remained at the controls, too wounded to leave, intent on piloting his ship to a survival landing.

An explosion under the cockpit floor rocked the aircraft. The next thing he knew, he was riding on the back of a German tank on the way to an enemy aid station. Either the explosion or subsequent plane crash had thrown him out of the plane and into a nearby river where German soldiers rescued him. His aircrew naturally assumed Dawkins had died in the crash.

Worley, along with the ship's crew chief, navigator, and radio operator, landed without injury. A Dutch farmer took them to friends who shepherded them to nearby British and American troops.

Six days after they had crashed, Worley, 1st Lieutenant James Wilson, Staff Sergeant John Ludwig, and Technical Sergeant William White, Jr, returned to active duty in Britain.

The day became costly for Dawkins' crew and his American 310th Squadron. Damage forced seven of the squadron's aircraft to make emergency landings at British airfields and five others remained missing at nightfall.

Dawkins, meanwhile, had become a prisoner of war and would be awarded a Distinguished Service Cross eight months after he was liberated at war's end.

"A considerable amount of flak was encountered at the DZ and two aircraft failed to return … J.L. Wilson."[16] Cryptic entries in British squadrons' war diaries rarely captured the individual battles, tragedies, and heartbreaks suffered in many cockpits.

Flight Officer Len Wilson had settled into his final run on his RAF resupply mission, like Lord and others, flying at only 500 feet and at about 120 miles per hour. That would enable his crew to send wickerwork panniers out the door without the necessity of a parachute, since parachutes were in short supply. But that placed the aircrew within range of infantry and artillery fire. The direct hits battered his Dakota, thunderous thuds that pummeled those inside. Three crew members bailed out as Wilson decided to "fight back" with his wounded aircraft.

He turned toward the German 20mm artillery emplacement that had hit him, intending to crash into it. But a nearby RAF aircrew saw him slumped over his controls, likely dead, as his aircraft veered to the left, plunged, and cut a tree in half with a wing before crashing into several houses. He and those still aboard were buried in a nearby cemetery. According to ground personnel in his squadron, Wilson was married and the father of a one-year-old daughter.[17]

Empty cots at air bases across England reflected the aircrew losses suffered in Operation *Market Garden*.

Before aircrew replacements arrived, an important mission remained. It began with a toast in the barracks to the lost officers and crewmen before throwing the empty glasses against the door. Then sorting their personal belongings to remove anything that might be embarrassing before shipment to families back home.

On more than one occasion, a pilot or crew member walked in to find his comrades dividing up his useful belongings, believing he had crashed and died. Not every plunge into a cloud bank or a smoking plane slowing and dropping out of formation ended in death. Every sortie, regardless of outcome, burnished the legacy and honed lessons from the aircrews' fourth major invasion in fourteen months.

The first major daylight airborne campaign of the war was successful, despite *Market* Garden's lack of ground to air communication, unreliable glider communication cables, and the continued need for pathfinders. Invasion rehearsals remained critical in advance of invasions. Chronic shortages of powered and glider aircraft, pilots, and ground personnel that forced multi-day missions proved counterproductive and deadly. The one-day missions over Normandy and in southern France had demonstrated that vertical envelopment required concentrated firepower, not a string of drops vulnerable to the weather and Germans.

The US IX Troop Carrier Command and 38-46 Groups RAF dispatched 3,989 power and glider flights between D-Day and September 30. Aircrews delivered 30,358 troops and 2,856 tons of cargo. The cost paralleled that suffered on the ground. Damaged, missing, or destroyed aircraft totaled 932. In the end, the rugged C-47/Dakota likely saved hundreds of lives in the course of crash landings, ditching, and staggering back to England. One hundred and eighty-six aircrewmen were listed as killed or missing.[18]

Despite the failure of Montgomery's plan, "As in Operation *Neptune*, the progress of the army in Operation *Market* depended, to a considerable extent, on the success of the airborne assault ... All the airborne tasks were accomplished, tasks that could only have been accomplished by airborne forces ... The degree of [drop and landing] accuracy in Operation *Market* could hardly be improved upon."[19]

Yet the ground troops' assault route on Highway 69 proved so narrow that flak suppression missions were almost impossible for fear of friendly fire losses. The re-supply missions could become more deadly than the initial lifts of combat forces. An RAF analysis concluded, "re-supply operations for the 1st Airborne Division were executed with incredible bravery and self-sacrifice by the RAF Transport Force."[20]

To what end? After pulling out of Arnhem, the 1st Airborne returned to Britain on September 29. The beleaguered 82nd and 101st remained on the front line until late November.

USAF historian John Warren concluded, "All objectives save Arnhem had been won … In return for so much courage and sacrifice, the Allies had won a 50-mile salient leading nowhere."[21]

Montgomery, however, stubbornly later wrote, "[I]f the operation had been properly backed from its inception, and given the aircraft, ground forces, and administrative resources necessary for the job, it would have succeeded in spite of my mistakes, or the adverse weather, or the presence of the 2nd SS Panzer Corps in the Arnhem area. I remain *Market Garden's* unrepentant advocate."[22]

In *Market Garden's* immediate aftermath, many upbeat conclusions had dominated the troop carrier group and squadron after-action reports. Issues likewise were downplayed. Few were more specific than "widely dispersed," "a fairly successful trip," "a noticeable lack of fighter support," or "some difficulty."[23] Yet the pain of loss when acknowledging dead friends inevitably crept into narratives, revealing that no battle's true outcome could be summarized by lists and statistics. On September 21, an anonymous American squadron report writer for the 310th shared his unit's grief.

> Nothing has been heard of him [2nd Lieutenant Cecil Dawkins] since that time. The loss of all [that day's casualties], if in truth they are lost, is a great blow to the squadron. Their absence leaves a gap both in operational strength and ability and in the personal, non-operational life of the squadron. They will not be forgotten. They were gallant officers and men and if they died, they died as all soldiers should – facing toward the enemy.[24]

The tactical failure of *Market Garden* was exacerbated by the loss of Allied aircrews, paratroopers, glider crews, and glider infantry as casualties and prisoners of war. Yet tremendous advances had been accomplished in two years. An RAF mission involving the 2nd Parachute Battalion in Tunisia in 1942 had resulted in fifty percent casualties. The Allied Sicily mission in 1943 had been lethally chaotic. In Normandy, seventy-five percent of American paratroopers were dropped more than five miles from their DZ. Although the drop concentration by the British was concentrated, at one target zone only seventeen of seventy-one troop carriers hit the mark and two battalions went into action forty percent understrength.[25]

Yet in victory in Normandy and defeat only a few months later in Holland, the British and American airborne legacy of courage and sacrifice was cemented into the annals of World War II.

> ... it is not the monumental size nor the operational intricacies of [Operation] *Market* [*Garden*] which linger longest in the memory. It is the heroism of the men who flew burning, disintegrating planes over their zones as coolly as if on review and gave their lives to get the last trooper out, the last bundle dropped. It is the stubborn courage of the airborne troops who would not surrender though an army came against them.[26]

Meanwhile, far to the south another cadre of aircrews waged a secret war, one that armed resistance guerrilla forces on the ground, inserted secret agents, and rescued downed aircrews.

9

The Secret War

Supplies sent to guerillas by the Allied Air Forces have recently been on a scale which cannot be permanently tolerated … [German] Second Army has ordered that a coordinated drive against the guerrilla air supplies be carried out with every possible means and by every suitable branch of the army. The code name for the whole operation against the guerrilla air supplies is to be CASSANOVA.[1]

Colonel George Kraigher, a Serbian-born veteran pilot, was a natural choice to lead a key element of a secret airborne war. A battle to arm and resupply underground armies in territory occupied by the Germans and Italians. To rescue downed aircrews, insert specially trained agents, and evacuate the wounded, homeless, and parentless. Missions principally into France and the Balkans in which C-47 aircrews played a frequent and often indispensable role.

Convivial and gregarious with movie star good looks, the fifty-three-old grew up in Slovenia and had flown in the Serbian Air Corps in World War I. He began flying for Pan American Airways in 1929 and later trained pilots to fly the Trimotor, DC-2, and the DC-3, the civilian version of the C-47. Commissioned as a colonel in the Army Air Corps Reserve early in the war, he flew the first Allied survey mission across the Soviet Union in a C-47 and mapped resupply routes in North Africa.

He and hundreds of pilots, navigators, radio operators, and crew chiefs would play a vital role in a secret war waged deep in enemy territory.

From the Norwegian fjords to Belgrade in Yugoslavia, thousands fell killed or wounded when German troops stormed across Europe beginning in 1939. Yet those in their path refused capitulation. Underground resistance organizations took root across the Continent. Airborne operations became the only avenue to support those that ranged from a few thousand to more than 200,000 men and women, years before the Allies came ashore at Normandy. Airborne operations that escaped public notice back home and were vulnerable to severe weather, mountainous terrain, night missions without escorts, and dependence on "reception committees" at remote drop and landing zones. Secrecy and "special duty" bombers and C-47s would be vital.

By 1940, Britain had established the Special Operations Executive. Two years later, the US created the Office of Strategic Services (OSS, the precursor to the CIA). Their joint mission at Special Force Headquarters was to establish, supply, and tap into an existing mosaic of guerrilla militias across Europe. The airborne's objectives were direct and daunting: arm and supply the militias for extended combat, in part to occupy German troops; insert trained male and female agents ("Johns" and "Janes") to conduct sabotage and espionage activities; drop millions of printed propaganda leaflets (called "nickels"); insert radio operators, weather observers, and aircrew rescue units; and evacuate Allied personnel, wounded partisans, agents who completed their missions, and others.[2]

In 1944, Operation *Carpetbagger*, based in England, focused on Belgium, Holland, Luxembourg, and particularly France leading up to the Normandy invasion in June. In the months following D-Day and surrounding Operation *Dragoon*, clandestine missions supported the Maquis Resistance in southern France. Four massive supply and personnel drops took place between June and September.

Navigating by French landmarks and moonlit rivers frequently defined B-24 bomber and C-47 missions in Operation *Carpetbagger*. Oftentimes, the airstrips were as primitive as a country lane between farm fields, usually framed by handheld flashlights for the low-level night approaches.

To the south in November 1943, General Arnold had approved the creation of Special Operations, Mediterranean Theater of Operations. A few months later, the joint RAF and AAF mission would focus on supplying the Maquis Resistance in France in the west and the Balkans – principally what was then Yugoslavia – to the east.

French and Yugoslav ingenuity became critical in the two-front secret war. When Colonel Clifford Heflin set down on a partially harvested wheat field, the Maquis transplanted small trees to shield his C-47 until he took off two days later, carrying downed aviators, a British agent, and Frenchmen bound for sabotage training in England.[3]

Aircrews often grumbled over the Maquis being "not the greatest experts at selecting landing areas." On one occasion, a C-47 plowed into a ditch alongside a temporary airstrip, damaging a propeller and losing hydraulic power to its brakes, landing gear, and flaps, usually fatal injuries in enemy territory. This time, command risked flying a maintenance team to the site to make repairs that enabled the C-47 crew to fly to Italy.[4,5]

Dara and Mirko had become orphans when everyone in their village was killed by Nazis and their collaborators. In another village, Janko and three siblings watched the Nazis arrest their mother because their father supported a Yugoslav resistance movement. They joined others hiding from the Nazis in a group of caves. P-51 Mustang pilot Joe Randerson was shot down, suffering serious burns that would take time to heal after being taken in by Serbian farmers. All in a country fractured by wartime rivalries, cruelty, grudges, vengeance, and legions of innocent victims.

For more than a year beginning in February 1944, missions to the Balkans carried none of the notoriety of the Normandy drama.

Success rarely merited headlines, which suited General Arnold, the mission planners, and aircrews. Yet the secret war in the Balkans was critical to Allied victory. And a matter of survival for Dara, Mirko, Janko, and Joe.

Greece anchors the Balkans in the south. Its border meets Albania, Yugoslavia, and Bulgaria, with oil-rich Romania abutting Bulgaria. Resistance forces ranged from 10,000 to 220,000 in those countries. Their will to resist was unquestioned. It was an ideal opportunity for the Allies to prevent German troops in the Balkans from moving to meet the Allied advances in Normandy, southern France, and Italy. A target rich environment, if C-47, B-17, B-24, and B-25 aircrews could keep the Balkan resistance forces armed and supplied.

Yugoslavia was the cornerstone of the campaign. It had been occupied by Germany since April 1941 when nineteen divisions attacked. The country capitulated less than two weeks later. By late 1943, it had become deeply splintered. The Germans ruled along with their fascist Ustase allies, but two resistance movements had developed, in part due to their mutual hatred. Draza Mihailovich, a royalist and former colonel in the defunct Yugoslav army, led one group called the "Chetniks." Tough, wiry, and shabby, his strategy was to wait out the Nazis and the war's outcome rather than overt confrontation. Josip "Tito" Broz, on the other hand, led the Communist Party of Yugoslavia. Well-groomed by war standards and erudite, his "Partisans" ruthlessly attacked the Germans, regardless of the cost of reprisals in dead bodies. The two factions were as likely to fight one another as the Germans.

The Allies first supported Mihailovich and then switched sides to Tito. C-47 aircrews from the 60th and 62nd Troop Carrier Groups and bombers were caught in the middle, flying missions to supply both, authorized first by the Mediterranean Allied Air Forces and later by the Balkan Air Forces commands. Aircrews flew night missions and later added daytime sorties.

Kraigher, 2nd Lieutenant Morris Houser, and others completed missions across 150,000 square miles of Greece, western Bulgaria, Albania, and most of Yugoslavia. Most missions were less than 300 miles from Italian bases at Brindisi and Bari on the heel of the Italian boot, only about 100 miles from Albania. Although generally less than five hours, flights stretched across 450 miles and eight hours. The route frequently was circuitous to avoid German night fighters, artillery, and to confuse German radar. "The unarmed and unarmored C-47s … were protected only by darkness and the pilot's ability to take evasive action."[6]

The secret war in the Balkans intensified throughout 1944. C-47 aircrews from the 62nd TCG fought brutal winter weather beginning in February. Of 229 missions scheduled for one squadron, ninety-seven were scrubbed before takeoff. In another squadron, thirty of fifty-one failed due to weather conditions en route or over the drop zones. The tide turned in the second phase from April into October when 60th TCG's daytime flights escorted by Allied fighters proved viable. Russian advances on the Eastern Front pulled German troops out of the Balkans late in 1944, adding to the confidence level of mission planners and aircrews. The commitment to supporting Tito required a never-ending airborne parade of C-47s and bombers. The last significant phase in the fall, Operation *Halyard*, centered around evacuation and exfiltration on an unprecedented scale.

Fifty C-47s comprised the largest resupply night missions, although the average was closer to thirty-five. Depending upon the cargo, hours of darkness, and the number of C-47s on a mission, a single aircrew could be assigned one or multiple destinations. On average, about fifteen target zones comprised a C-47 supply mission.

A night mission typically began shortly after breakfast when ground crews began loading aircraft with that night's cargo. About noon, 1st Lieutenant Stephen Thomas, Captain Homer Moore, other pilots, and aircrews were notified they would be flying that night. A bus took them to the airfield mid-afternoon for a briefing that included their mission, target indication sheet reviews, drop altitudes, friendly convoy locations and nearby bomber attack plans, takeoff times that could be anywhere between dusk and 0200 hours, destination targets, how many passes might be necessary to drop all the cargo, regional topography, signals, codes, and weather reports. An intelligence officer subsequently reviewed specifics of the mission, including whether Tito or Mikhailovich would be receiving the cargo. Sometimes introductions were necessary as crewmen were shuffled from one aircrew to another, in part due to a shortage of navigators.

Duties remained for exhausted aircrews after five- or six-hour missions. They first debriefed (described what had taken place on the mission) with an intelligence or assistant operations officer. Then a medical officer often dispensed a two-ounce shot of Gibson's Pennsylvania Rye Whiskey or another favored brand. Some men passed on that opportunity at 0300 hours and on an empty stomach. Discerning crew members took a credit on individual shots until they were due a bottle for more convenient and effective consumption. Usually, thirteen combat missions were enough to earn a bottle. Finally, a trip to the mess hall for a robust breakfast of eggs, bacon, pancakes, and unlimited strong coffee. On top of the whiskey shot, more than one mission ended with indigestion.[7]

Their C-47s were ideal for the missions. With fuel consumption of about two miles per gallon, fuel tanks holding more than 800 gallons gave the aircrews a range of more than 1,500 miles. Although aircraft specifications called for a maximum payload of 5,200 pounds, cargo flown to Yugoslavia could exceed 7,000 pounds. The aircraft nose had been enlarged slightly for more cockpit room and some were outfitted with special floors to support heavier cargo loads. They also had been outfitted with Rebecca equipment.

A C-47 crew could expect to deliver 4,000 pounds of supplies on a mission, plus 150 to 450 pounds of "nickels" bound for specific areas. Guns, ammunition, dynamite, food, clothing, medical supplies, fuel, oil, jeeps, and even mules could be part of the cargo when landing operations became more common.[8]

C-47s resembled moving vans on many resupply missions. Crews packed unbreakable supplies such as shoes, clothing, and blankets tightly into four-foot-square wood boxes. The "stanpacks" were pushed out the cargo door over the drop zones. Breakable materiel such as medical supplies, weapons, and communications gear were tightly packed in crates with a parachute that automatically deployed when pushed out the door. Under the wings, ground crews installed four devices that resembled bomb racks which held and released "parapacks." Those could be canvas bags or hinged aluminum cylinders about six feet in length. Equipped with twenty-eight-foot parachutes, rifles, and related equipment wrapped in clothing for insulation filled the cylinders.

As 2nd Lieutenant Robert Cook approached his target area, the crew's priority became spotting the drop zone. The Rebecca receiver told Cook he was close to his drop zone. *There it is!* First, he circled the DZ until his aircrew and the "reception committee" below exchanged identification signals, usually the "letter of the day." If the guerillas had not already lit them, eight to ten bonfires would suddenly flare. Looking like distant campfires from the air, they formed that day's code letter. "V," "T," and "W" struck one navigator, 1st Lieutenant Richard Kraemer, as the preferred code letters, perhaps because their straight lines were easier than "S," "G," or, "B" to replicate in a narrow valley's pasture. Once identified, the pilot flashed a pre-arranged signal to the reception committee below. The guerrillas responded by flashing a light in code. If it was yellow or red, the aircrew knew the area was not secure and to stay away. If the response was simply the wrong code, standing orders were to return to base immediately, not knowing if the resistance fighters had made a mistake or if the Germans controlled the area.[9]

But when the recognition process was successful and the C-47 had slowed to about 110 miles per hour, Cook's cargo crew – the crew chief, radio operator, and often a partisan dispatcher – mobilized. Containers attached to the plane's belly fell away while the crew pushed others out the cargo door. In seconds, parachutes blossomed in the plane's wake. The pilot or co-pilot could release the exterior parapacks. (On paratrooper missions, a control panel at the jumpmaster's station also controlled releases.)[10]

The best approaches and perfectly timed drops sometimes failed. Culprits included German patrols, poor ground weather, and Gestapo informants.

One of the most insidious enemies of the night missions was vertigo, a whirling loss of balance that can develop from prolonged downward vision at great heights. Exactly what was expected by pilots and co-pilots on long flights over the Balkans. One night as a pilot departed a drop zone, he suddenly banked hard and began losing altitude.

"What are you doing?"

"I'm trying to get back on course and fly straight and level."

The co-pilot forcibly took control of the aircraft to regain a safe flight path. Unexplained crashes in the mountains of Yugoslavia led to speculation within squadrons that the pilot had first fallen victim to a sudden case of vertigo.

Missing Air Crew Reports compiled after a mission were the equivalent of a police investigation or forensic report. Statements of fact, diagrams, witness statements, maps, suspected causes, and next-of-kin addresses usually left little doubt about what had transpired. As thorough as most were, unanswered questions often lingered when a squadron lost an aircrew.

Uncharted valleys between mountain ranges posed unique challenges from one mission to the next. Navigator Kraemer helped Captain Bob Snyder fly through a maze of mountains the night of April 3. Their mission the night before had taken them to Tito's headquarters, but this time the target area in a narrow valley was awash in thick cloud cover. Kraemer's margin of error was perilously thin in the country's Dinaric Alps where mountain peaks topped 13,000 feet. Snyder aborted the mission due to the cloud cover and looked to Kraemer for a heading back to Italy. Six weeks later, Snyder piloted a similar mission into another finger-thin valley. His C-47 stalled during a sharp turn when a cliff appeared in his path. Seconds later, he slammed into the ground, killing himself and all five crew members.[11]

Pilot Stephen Thomas was as popular as any pilot flying missions to Yugoslavia. His build was perfect for the C-47. A broad chest

General Henry "Hap" Arnold overcame a fear of flying when learning to fly biplanes in 1911. A middling US Army Air Corps cadet, thirty years later he established and led the Army Air Forces in World War II, which ultimately became the United States Air Force. (USAF)

In World War I, Brigadier General Billy Mitchell advocated "vertical envelopment," the insertion of troops by air into enemy territory. Operational development finally began in 1940 when the Parachute Test Platoon was established and the C-47 aircraft followed two years later. (USAF)

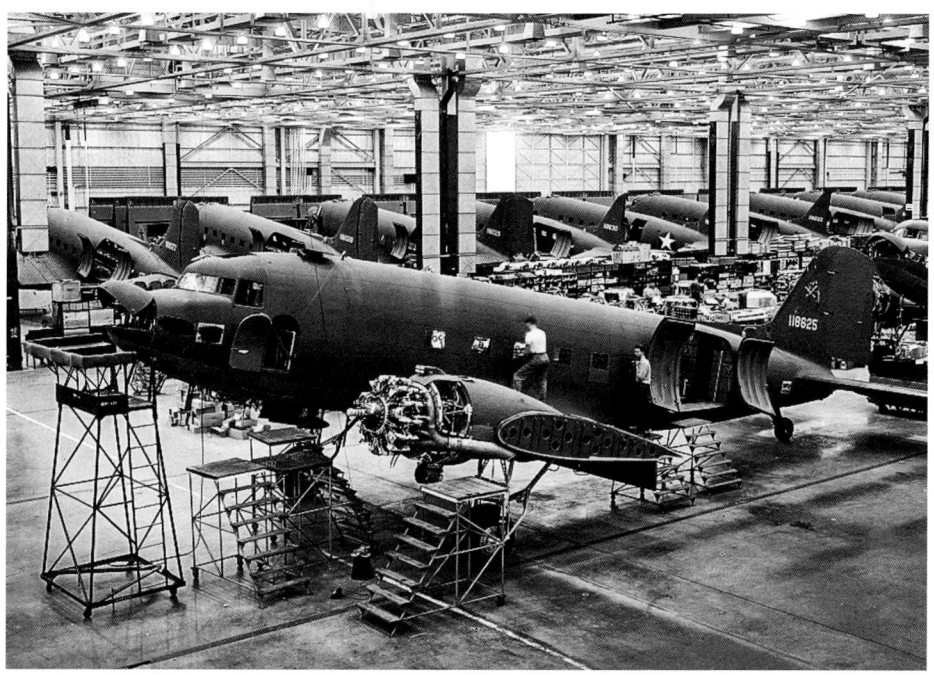

Douglas Aircraft designed the C-47 that made airborne warfare possible by modifying a commercial airliner concept to become a combat plane capable of towing gliders or dropping paratroopers and supplies. Douglas built more than 10,000 C-47s by the end of the war, principally at its plant in Long Beach, California. (Library of Congress)

"Cock O' The Walk" shown here was typical of the US C-47 fleet. The RAF designated its fleet of nearly 2,000 C-47s as "Dakotas." A typical RAF aircrew included a pilot, co-pilot, navigator, radio operator, and often (cargo) despatchers. The C-47 towed a fully loaded glider weighing 7,500 pounds or twenty-eight fully equipped paratroopers. (Silent Wings Museum)

British and American C-47 aircrews faced danger from the moment they were airborne. Here, an RAF C-47 Dakota crashed shortly after takeoff in England where two crewmen were killed and two miraculously survived. (Photo by WATFORD/Mirrorpix/ Mirrorpix via Getty Images)

A C-47's cockpit offered cramped quarters for the pilot and co-pilot. They were practically trapped from the time they buckled in on combat missions. A small escape hatch in the cockpit offered scant hope if a crash was imminent, especially when fire in cabin prevented them from parachuting out the rear cargo door. (Silent Wings Museum)

Aircrews and paratroopers often reported to their aircraft several hours before sunrise. A paratrooper could weigh 260 pounds, including the equipment and supplies he carried. Paratroopers sat on two facing bench seats shoulder to shoulder, sometimes for hours before jumping into battle. (Library of Congress)

C-47 and Dakota aircrews' first objective was to fly in a tight formation, typically 200 feet back and 200 feet to the right or left of each other, often before sunrise. A wingspan of ninety-five feet left little margin of error in bad weather, severe turbulence, enemy fire, or when towing gliders to battle. (Silent Wings Museum)

Aircrews' cargo reflected the nature of the battle the troops were fighting on the ground. In Burmese jungle warfare, a single piece of artillery required seven mules, delivered by aircrews in flying stables. Army artillery pack units could unload and assemble a small howitzer "from mule to firing position" in five minutes. (National Archives)

Highly choreographed US and British aircrew migrations from as many as 24 airfields from England and France delivered 1,600 plane loads of troops and gliders in one hour in Operation Market Garden and two entire divisions in only four hours in Operation Varsity. (National Archives)

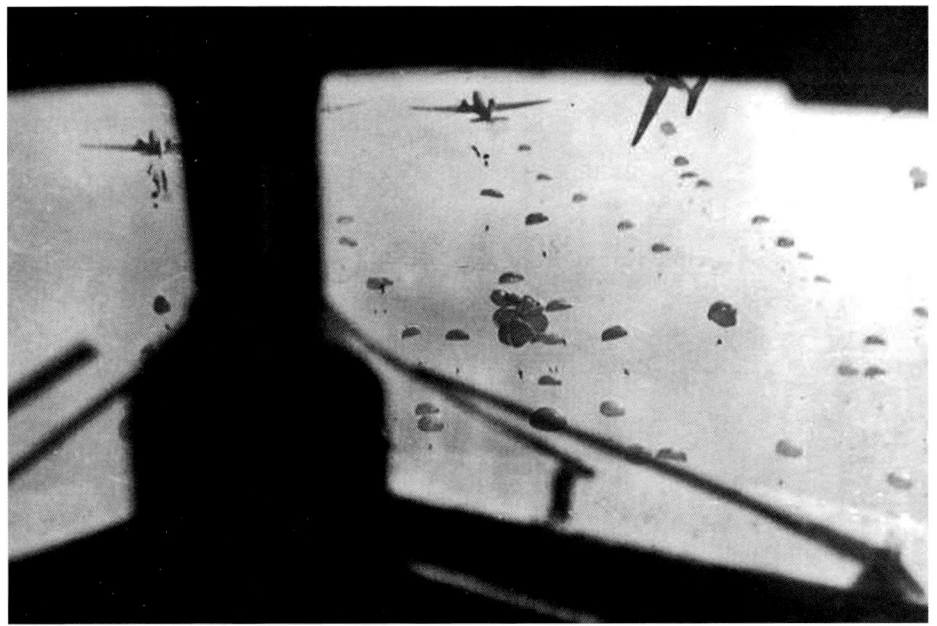

Mission orders prohibited evasive action by aircrews when delivering paratroopers and gliders past the front line. Flying low, straight and level and with no way to "fight back" made them easy targets. Pilots nearby could only watch when enemy fire found a fellow pilot (upper right), perhaps a friend as he lost control of his aircraft. (National Archives)

Aircrews of stricken C-47s and Dakotas sometimes had only seconds to bail out before their plane turned nose down into a terrifying and fatal dive. While some heartbroken families received their loved ones' bodies for burial, others remain buried in Europe cemeteries or were incinerated in crashes. (National Archives)

The Curtiss C-46, far larger than the C-47, was death trap in combat. Design flaws made it susceptible to fires and explosions. Broad fuel tanks in the wings were vulnerable to enemy fire. Pilots called it "Ol' Dumbo" for its dramatic lack of power when it lost an engine. In its only combat mission of the war, Operation Varsity, its 28 percent loss rate proved unacceptable. (USAF)

Aircrews flying supply missions from India over the Himalayas to China endured dastardly flying conditions. Hurricane winds and downdrafts made flights dangerous even on clear days. They flew through thunderstorms, sub-Arctic blizzards and hurricane-force updrafts and downdrafts. Hail pummeled fuselages and windshields. Yet C-47 and C-46 aircrews flew hundreds of missions over the "rockpile" with no emergency landing strips within sight. The crash-strewn route became known as the "Aluminum Alley." (USAF)

As much as 600 gallons of fuel in five-gallon jerry cans filled the fuselages of aircraft bound for the Allies as they crossed Germany in April 1945. Poor visibility sometimes forced aircrews to fly as low as 200 feet, well within range of enemy artillery and small arms fire. A single bullet or shrapnel shard could transform the aircraft into a fireball. (Silent Wings Museum)

Aircrews and paratroopers were defenseless inside spartan C-47 and Dakota fuselages that resembled a large pipe holding two benches. Enemy small arms fire and shrapnel frequently pierced the plane's thin ribbed skin (less than one-quarter inch thick between ribs). The planes' control surfaces were fabric covered. (US Army Signal Corps)

RAF and American aircrews considered the Dakota/C-47 a remarkably sturdy aircraft. On several occasions, pilots returned from missions on one engine or successfully crash landed their crippled aircraft. (Silent Wings Museum)

For many British and American C-47 aircrews in World War II, flying former prisoners of war to England or France became their final mission. Here, their passengers are greeted by volunteers from the Women's Auxiliary Air Force at an RAF airfield in England. (Photo by Haywood Magee/ Picture Post/Hulton Archive/Getty Images)

framed by massive legs and arms set him apart from the rest of the men in his squadron. So did a soft-spoken and tolerant demeanor in a man always smiling and who never smoked, drank, and abstained from begrudging those who did. A true "gentleman," they said.

On the night of April 28, he completed a routine supply mission to Yugoslavia and never returned. Concern morphed into worry, then dread as the hours, then days, passed with no word. On April 30, two reports arrived. He had crashed near Naples and his crew had survived. An hour later, a second report updated the first and rooted everyone's worst fear. He had plowed into a hillside near Naples in severe weather, shattering his aircraft. The entire aircrew had died as the plane's wings and tail had been torn off at the first impact. Why had he overflown Brindisi by 200 miles to Naples on the far side of Italy? No one could know. There were more missions to fly.[12]

The enemies of missions were as stealthy as they were deadly. Navigator Kraemer had guided his pilot's aircraft over three mountain ranges on its way to its "Ballinclay 102" target zone despite murky weather. He had used his dead reckoning skills by spotting a landmark or two along the way, a skill often referred to as "If you don't reckon, you'll be dead."

On the pilot's final approach, he began to lose altitude. He pushed the throttles forward but continued to sink. Now flying below the peaks that bracketed their valley target, Kraemer gave him a new heading, hoping it would keep the approach route parallel to and between the ridges. Despite jettisoning cargo, the plane continued to drop, much too close to the valley floor. Still at full throttle, the plane finally leveled a bit, stabilized, and began a slow climb.

They had exited a severe downdraft, cleared the mountain peaks ahead, and turned toward home.[13]

While America's headlines focused on Normandy in June, Captain Homer Moore scanned the valley below for a crude landing strip in Yugoslavia's mountains. Nothing but a heavy blanket of clouds.

Thick enough to justify aborting his mission. He descended "into the soup," and bounced to a halt between 300-foot ridges. Once Partisans offloaded his cargo, they carried twenty-two wounded Partisans aboard for the return trip to Italy. Moore's courage likely saved several lives, earning him a Distinguished Flying Cross for his bravery.

Five nights later, Captain Howard Colliver looked down on a muddy field. He had grown up in Tulare, California, the heart of the state's cropland. Like a tractor plowing a wet farm field, his C-47 burrowed into soggy soil when he landed. A team of oxen pulled the plane free as the sky awakened in the east. Too late to leave before sunrise, he and his crew camouflaged the plane and hid in the hills until nightfall. After loading thirty-one Partisans, he safely returned to Italy.

Trust among strangers could dictate success or tragedy. As Major Joseph Wimsatt landed near Montenegro, Partisans guided his plane into a bomb crater, damaging a wing tip and bending a propeller. Wimsatt hitched a ride back to Italy and returned the next night with a new propeller. Once his crew had installed it, he completed his mission back to base.[14]

The return to base could threaten lives. When 2nd Lieutenant Robert Cook lost an engine at 10,000 feet, he set a course for Vis, an island 75 miles out in the Adriatic sea. Dangerously low on fuel, he managed to crash land without injuring his passengers.

Crew members sometimes had only seconds to either remain at their posts in a mortally wounded aircraft or jump for survival. Shortly before midnight on July 22, 1st Lieutenant Richard Sams, Jr, had just climbed out of his C-47 after pulling off the airstrip at "Piccadilly Pat," his mission's landing zone in mountainous central Yugoslavia. He watched two aircraft approaching on the midnight mission. Far-off machine gun fire peppered the night sky. Fire erupted from the second plane's left wing. Its pilot, 2nd Lieutenant Morris Houser, held steady on his approach toward Sams.

His co-pilot, 2nd Lieutenant Pinkney Largent, had spotted a yellow light ahead at the LZ, indicating the area was under attack by German night fighters. The aircrew already on alert felt the plane shudder when 20mm shells found its left engine.

"Bail out!"

Largent passed the word from Houser to the rest of crew while the pilot held his rudder and aileron hard against the dead engine's drag. At only half power, he managed a slow climb and banked to circle the LZ. That would give his crew enough time to jump before the fire spread like a rash. Seconds later, the right wing ignited.

"Get the hell out of here!"

Largent headed back toward the cargo door, joining the navigator, radio operator, and crew chief frantically strapping on their parachutes as smoke filled the fuselage. *Would the autopilot hold, giving Houser time to join them?* "I looked back for Houser, the small escape hatch directly behind the pilot was gone, and blazing gasoline was whirling into the cockpit … but [Houser] was still at the controls, being burned alive," he recalled later.

How much longer?

Another direct hit answered, this time in the fuselage a few feet away. "The blazing gasoline was swirling in the open door and breathing was impossible. I closed my eyes and dived for the hole." Largent jumped, not realizing his parachute was upside down. Somehow, it opened.

He did not know that at the same altitude, Houser was headed toward an outbound C-47, piloted by 2nd Lieutenant John Baranich. Baranich "took evasive action by diving to ground level … into the shadows of a high ridge." He continued that course for five minutes before returning to his homebound course. Once there, he learned the heartbreaking outcome of Houser's mission. Baranich had avoided a doomed aircrew, perhaps men with whom he had trained in the States or who had become friends after arriving in Europe. Houser, 2nd Lieutenant Alfred Gunthner (navigator) and Staff Sergeants James Warren (crew chief) and Dick Tschantz (radio operator) had died instantly.[15]

Their Missing Air Crew Report could not answer Largent's lingering torment. "Why I was the only one to escape that flaming inferno I'll never know. Why the navigator, with his chute on, didn't get out, what happened to the radio operator and crew chief, I don't know."[16]

Some crew members flew on the brink of fatherhood. Second Lieutenant Hugh McFarland's wife, Dolores, was expecting their first child. On November 12, the co-pilot sat alongside 1st Lieutenant Oren Leeds on a paradrop mission from their base at Brindisi, Italy, to Corenica in central Yugoslavia. They had just gone "feet dry" twenty minutes from their drop zone when an outbound pilot, 1st Lieutenant Lawrence Carlisle, Jr, checked in over the radio for a weather report along the coast.

The weather had been rough, responded Leeds, but he and McFarland had flown over it at 10,000 feet while avoiding any German artillery storms. Meanwhile, conditions had been "CAVU" (ceiling and visibility unlimited) over the DZ, according to Carlisle. It was the last time Carlisle heard from the aircrew flying the C-47 they had named "Bar Fly." Leeds and McFarland never reached their designated DZ as scheduled.

According to a Yugoslav Partisan named Dozvak who was aboard as an interpreter, Leeds and McFarland could not locate the DZ and as their fuel ran low decided to return to Italy. Although he did not hear the direct hit as they were outbound toward the Adriatic Sea, the C-47 lurched upwards and then settled as the bail-out alarm bell triggered. The right engine was on fire. Only Dozvak bailed out as the plane lost altitude, careened off a hill, and crashed on the southern tip of Rab Island. No one survived the impact.

Guerrilla fighters spotted Germans milling about the wreckage afterward. The entire crew was listed as missing in action and added to the list of "unsuccessful" resupply missions that sometimes plagued the Allies. Weather, enemy fire, and inability to identify drop zones were common explanations. All three contributed to the loss of the crew aboard Bar Fly.

Later, the bodies of all five crewmen were discovered buried in a nearby ditch. Nine months passed before Dolores and her infant son, Dennis, received word that army personnel had listed Hugh as killed in action. Dozvak had parachuted into the sea, had swum to the island, and was hidden by local partisans. They gave him a partially burned document from the wreckage that identified Leeds. More than fifty years later, an aviation archaeologist found the dog tags of the crew's navigator at the crash site.

By August 1944, more than 350 bombers had been shot down in the Balkans, many of them concentrations of enemy artillery, on their way to pound Ploesti, Romania's oil complex and a vital resource for Germany. More than 500 aircrew members had survived, about half in mountainous Chetnik territory near Pranjani. A sea of 400 named mountain peaks harbored Chetnik militias in the region while villagers hid the Americans in barns, cellars, attics, and haylofts.

Colonel George Kraigher received orders in July to command a new Air Crew Rescue Unit (ACRU). He knew the region and had flown numerous C-47 missions into enemy territory. Two OSS-based teams (ARCU #1 and ACRU #2) were established for insertion into Yugoslavia to spearhead airstrip construction, communicate and coordinate with officers in Italy, and prepare for C-47 evacuation flights in the coming weeks.

While the combat supplies delivered to the Balkans might become predictable, Richard Kraemer did not remember whether mission briefers had described the cargo the navigator and his aircrew would deliver on August 5. That night, 2nd Lieutenant Antoine Denis "Frenchy" Lanaux walked around his aircraft, conducting the usual pilot's pre-flight checks. All was in order, the New Orleans native concluded. But when his navigator climbed aboard, four hitched Missouri mules stared at him. They filled the fuselage with bent heads and flattened rabbit ears to avoid the ceiling. Their new horseshoes gleamed, ready to kick through the 3/16-inch sheet aluminum between the fuselage's ribs, triggering alarm bells in Kraemer's mind. *We won't have a muleskinner aboard,* Kraemer wrote later. *What if one of them became really fractious? I'd survived a midair explosion over the Mediterranean. Would I now, over the Adriatic, succumb to mules suffering from a fear of flying?*[17]

Mission planners schemed supply missions to match specific guerrilla forces' requests. When it became clear that landing strips would be necessary to ferry downed aircrews and others back to Italy, mules would be a tremendous asset to the ACRU teams in clearing rocks and trees. Lanaux and the rest of the aircrew would be responsible for flying a livestock trailer into combat. Fortunately, they were quiet passengers, "no more concerned about their flight than corporate CEOs flying first class on Delta," recalled the aircrew's navigator in his memoir more than sixty years later.[18]

Nine days after ACRU #1's arrival near Pranjani, Chetniks had carved a 2,100-foot airstrip into a hilltop, flanked by a forested slope at one end, and a cliff at the other. An airstrip so short that passengers were limited to only twenty-five in each takeoff.[19]

Four of six C-47s reached Pranjani the night of August 9, the start of Operation *Halyard*. The forty passengers on return flights to Italy marked the start of a massive evacuation.

Captain Caleb Moberly had enjoyed playing games of cribbage with his navigator when they were off duty. They flew the lead aircraft the morning of August 10, one of six escorted by P-51 fighters. Six more would follow about an hour later. Compared to previous night missions, this one was easy until the crew spotted "an open area of sandy meadow hanging on the side of a small mountain, with a sheer drop-off at the near end and a high rock wall at the other [and] it pitched sharply from left to right." *That can't be more than 1,400 feet long, maybe a long par four,* speculated one member of the aircrew.

The sandy field braked Moberly's runout before he reached the end of the airstrip. The first phase of Operation *Halyard* that day, Moberly and other aircrews returned 192 downed airmen safely back to Italy. More than a few were barefoot, having tossed their shoes after boarding to the Serbs who had made their rescue possible. Those airmen flew home with their feet wrapped in canvass bags to stay warm. Two more missions in August, another in September, and a final one in December would be successfully completed.

The hole in the cloud cover over Boljanic, Yugoslavia, was a godsend for Colonel George Kraigher on his two-aircraft mission on December 27. Far from a solid runway, the barely frozen 1,700-foot airstrip somehow withstood the C-47s' landing. It marked the last mission of Operation *Halyard*, led by Kraigher to collect the last two members of the ACRU #1 team, its senior officer and radio operator, along with Yugoslav, French, and Italian personnel. The return flight to Italy ended one of World War II's most remarkable rescue missions. In all, 512 airmen were rescued, in what became known as the rescue of the "Forgotten 500."

By Christmas 1944, the Allies' "secret war" had begun to wind down. Airborne operations in support of resistance forces had reached every corner of the ETO. German troop withdrawals had begun when Romania and Bulgaria had surrendered in September as the Russians approached from the east. By the end of the Balkan campaign, roughly 18,000 tons of supplies, and more than 1,000 OSS agents had reached Yugoslavia and Albania. Despite often horrendous flying conditions, mission evaluators considered seventy-five percent of 12,305 missions to more than 350 drop and landing zones successful.

Skilled pilots and resolute aircrews had overcome weather, turbulence, enemy night fighters, mountain ranges, enemy fire, sabotage, and sometimes poorly organized resistance forces. Of the failed missions, half were due to weather conditions and one-third to "ground failures." Yet only one C-47 was lost for every 458 sorties, an extraordinary accomplishment.

Yet it had been a campaign marked by civil war as much as against the Germans. The Chetniks and Partisans viciously vied for control of a postwar Yugoslavia while fighting the Germans. America's aircrews had often been caught in the crossfire.

Among many, OSS Major Linn Farish agonized over the injustice of war. "It is not nice to see arms dropped by one group of our airmen to be turned against men who have rescued and protected their brothers-in-arms. It is not a pleasant sight to see our wounded lying side by side with the men who had rescued and cared for them and to realize that the bullet holes in the rescuers could have resulted from American ammunition, fired from American rifles, dropped from American aircraft flown by American pilots."[20]

On the final day of Operation *Halyard,* fifty aircrews in Chateaudun, France, climbed aboard their aircraft to prepare for a low-level approach at 400 feet toward Bastogne, Belgium. Each towed a glider to resupply the 101st Airborne Division that had been surrounded by Germans since December 22 in the Battle of the Bulge. Their cargo reflected the battered troops' need for ordnance, ammunition, surgeons, and shrouds for their dead.

December 27 would become a shooting gallery and one of the Allied C-47 aircrews' deadliest days of World War II.

Annihilation

December 22nd 1944

The fortune of war is changing. This time the USA forces in and near Bastogne have been encircled by strong German armored units. More German armored units have crossed the river Ourthe … There is only one possibility to save the encircled USA Troops from total annihilation: that is the honorable surrender of the encircled town … If this proposal should be rejected the German Artillery Corps and six heavy AA Battalions are ready to annihilate the USA Troops in and near Bastogne.

General Heinrich von Luttwitz

Men, we are surrounded by the enemy. We have the greatest opportunity ever presented an Army. We can attack in any direction.

Brigadier General Anthony McAuliffe

General Heinrich Freiherr von Luttwitz saw no way out for the 101st Airborne surrounded in Bastogne by his troops on December 20.

Brigadier General Anthony McAuliffe, acting commander of the 101st, had become a *de facto* Sun Tzu philosopher to bolster his troops' spirit.[1] First, with his stalwart "Nuts!" reply to Luttwitz's offer, and then encouraging his men to be optimistic, even bold, in the face of disaster. But from the day McAuliffe's men had become trapped, radio messages to command headquarters seventeen miles away had pleaded for hundreds of tons of fuel, ordnance, combat gear, ammunition, surgeons, and medical supplies.

His troops had moved forward on short notice, drawing only two days' supplies before climbing into trucks for the sprint to Bastogne. McAuliffe's reply on the 22nd to Luttwitz was largely a bluff. The eighteen artillery guns in one of his twelve battalions had 200 rounds left. Others were firing only their charges (artillery propellants) as a ruse for lack of artillery shells. Some units had only ten rounds of long-range ammunition. On one occasion, McAuliffe told an artillery officer, "If you see 400 Germans in a 100-yard area, and they have their heads up, you can fire artillery at them. But not more than two rounds."[2]

Fumes outweighed fuel in many of his armored vehicles' gas tanks, forcing drivers to forego warming their motors in frigid temperatures before engaging the enemy. Conserving the last 445 gallons of fuel on hand had become critical.

Six days earlier, steam had billowed from 1,000 German tanks in Belgium's Ardennes Forest two hours before sunrise on the kind of morning that crusted windshields, thickened oil, and made breathing painful. Across a seventy-five-mile front, Hitler had ordered an invasion his senior officers considered lunacy. In the heart of one of the coldest winters in decades, he envisioned punching through the Ardennes with 250,000 men, crossing the Meuse River, taking Brussels, and capturing the port of Antwerp.[3]

In theory, the Germans would deny the Allies a critical port and potentially cut off twenty divisions.

He envisioned success by Christmas Day partly on the strength of shock and newly created yet undermanned divisions filled with the aged, youngsters, and derelicts from the Eastern Front. They would attack through waist-deep snow and across tortuous terrain pockmarked with rivers in deep ravines, forests, farm fields, rocky bluffs, and peat bogs. So rugged that it would prevent his field commanders from deploying four tanks abreast, much less armored divisions. Somehow, this would take place across 120 miles of

Allied territory at a time when skies did not brighten before 0800 hours and dimmed at 1600 hours.

Bastogne might well be the linchpin to Hitler's battle plan. With few all-weather roads in the region, seven converged on Bastogne, along with three railroad lines. Taking Bastogne could become the springboard for the German march west toward Belgium's coast.

Thanks to the Allies, the unexpected might be his ace in the hole. Intelligence officers had told General Eisenhower that the Germans had lost so many men and equipment since Normandy that an offensive was not likely until spring. Several Allied divisions had left the region (about the size of Connecticut), leaving only four largely inexperienced divisions in place.

Army officers thought the region was safe enough for a USO show starring Marlene Dietrich and a group of touring major league baseball players headlined by New York Giant Mel Ott to visit a town within thirty miles of the front.

Combat mayhem erupted on the 16th when thirteen infantry and seven armored German divisions caught the Allies napping. The Western Front in Belgium shuddered and then fractured into a three-mile gap, creating the invasion's ultimate monicker, the Battle of the Bulge.

Designing a coordinated counter strategy out of chaos became the Allies' top priority. The next day, plans were laid to stop the German advance at the Meuse River in central Belgium and to reinforce troops in Bastogne. That would become the mission of an exhausted 101st Airborne Division that had only recently come off the line after seventy-two days' combat in Holland. Replenishment became deployment on the 18th when the "Screaming Eagles" climbed into nearly 400 trucks headed for Bastogne. They reached the town's outskirts only eight hours ahead of the Germans.[4]

A few days later, the 101st had become a battered and staggering combat force. One night, Germans captured more than 150 medical officers and enlisted personnel when they overran a division hospital. When McAuliffe refused the surrender offer, more than 120 wounded men urgently needed surgery in a converted maintenance garage, 250 more lay on litters, and 400 more were wounded. A quartermaster (supply) unit had been captured, in part forcing many of the 101st's 18,000 soldiers to scrounge and scavenge among Bastogne's residents, farmers, and destroyed buildings. Discovering a town warehouse holding supplies in 2,000 burlap sacks was a godsend. Personnel ferried the emptied sacks out to the soldiers living in frozen foxholes who had not received Arctic-issue shoes.

General George Patton's army had changed course for Bastogne but remained several days away. Advance elements would have to break through positions held by an estimated 45,000 Germans, including three panzer divisions that had bypassed and encircled Bastogne. Meanwhile, foul weather in England had grounded troop carrier groups poised to send hundreds of C-47 aircrews on supply missions to Bastogne and nearby towns where the 82nd Airborne and others also hungered for resupply drops. In France, C-47 aircrews and glider personnel stood by. Not surprisingly, shortly after the 101st had arrived, pleas for medical reinforcements, food, and ammunition became strident and frequent, one with a poignant "We're the hole in the donut" sidenote.

The day after General McAuliffe's bravado, clear skies on December 23 finally enabled supply missions that became tinged with anger, bad luck, and frustration. Two C-47 aircrews in England took off long before sunrise, bound for the Bastogne area with pathfinders. Promised fighter escorts failed to appear over a designated airfield on the route. Regardless, the aircrews pressed ahead on a straight line following a highway toward Bastogne. By noon, the pathfinders' navigational aids were operational, just as men in foxholes heard the far-off groan of approaching C-47s.

Like the pathfinders earlier, twenty-one supply aircraft flew directly over a German panzer division. Though their artillery fire was relatively light, it was accurate.

First Lieutenant Robert Anstey had no training for flying in an inferno. When red-hot tracer fire hit his left wing's fuel tank, fumes swamped the parapacks attached to the fuselage's belly a few yards aft.

Another round of tracers ignited the fumes, turning his plane into a Roman candle.

"The strips on the [cabin] floor, the door load cases, as well as the seats on both sides, the top litters, and the whole left side of the center section [of the cabin] were in flames. The forward half of the aluminum door frame had melted away," Anstey later wrote. After ordering the crew to jump at only 300 feet, Anstey bailed out, his clothing on fire, his nose and ears burned, and so close to the ground he did not remember his descent.

He later found what remained of his burned-out plane near a stream and stand of trees, two miles short of Bastogne. Troops had recovered six cases of ammunition that apparently had cleared the crash on impact. Germans took Anstey's crew prisoner, following the first shootdown of the first supply mission of the day.[5]

Not long after, forty aircraft neared the end their 375-mile flight from Membury, England. Foul weather had forced the aircrews into takeoffs of small groups and the lack of fighter support made them easy marks for the alerted Germans, who had time to reload between serials. It became a skeet shoot as only twenty-eight of the forty reached the drop zone area. Just three of the forty returned to Membury undamaged. Most needed all-night repairs. Those wounded or missing in action amounted to almost ten percent of the airmen on the mission.

That included Staff Sergeant Andre Mongeau.

Improvisation became the battle plan after crashing. On the final and largest supply mission of the day, radio operator Mongeau pulled his parachute's ripcord four times before it opened. It had barely "blossomed" before he settled into a tree, three feet short of the ground. After slipping out of his harness and completing his jump, he hid from nearby Germans until a farmer approached and drew a map in the dirt showing American positions in Marcouray, northwest of Bastogne.

Mongeau might be able to solve one of the biggest challenges to the resupply missions yet to come, a lack of ground-to-air communication with the incoming relief flights. Real-time reports of enemy artillery locations and less-defended approach routes would be invaluable. After joining American troops in the area, he repaired a radio in a damaged tank and sent encoded messages to incoming supply aircraft on two channels. But only the escorting fighter aircraft pilots heard them. The C-47 aircrews continued to fly in silence, oblivious to any new, last-minute threats to their mission and their lives.

As they approached Mongeau, it appeared the fighters tried to "herd" the C-47s toward his position near Marcouray. They failed as the aircraft turned away without making any drops. In the coming days, dozens of aircrews would have benefited from up-to-the-minute ground reports of enemy positions and visibility conditions.[6] They had been complaining for six months that improved ground-to-air communication capability at the DZs and LZs would improve mission success and save lives.

December 23 marked a modest turning point in the 101st's crisis. More than 300 aircrews from six troop carrier groups flying in three waves at various altitudes dropped more than 330 tons of ammunition, rations, and medical supplies. Many were veterans of multiple combat missions while others had flown their first mission as replacement pilots. Lee Whitmire had earned his wings before his twentieth birthday. A dual-rated pilot for C-47s and gliders, his Bastogne cargo drop would be at 380 feet, the lowest TCG on the mission. "Great, we won't have time to jump if we're hit," muttered a pilot next to Whitmire in the pre-flight briefing.[7]

Some of the day's loads would not be useful. "It took only a brief check … to see that the supply problem was far from being solved. The contents of the bundles were not in balance with the real needs of the troops." Ammunition was the wrong size for the 101st's weaponry, penicillin supplies were inadequate, and blankets remained in short supply.[8] Messages from the 101st on the 24th pleaded for more, noting their hope that gliders could also deliver medical personnel.

Christmas Eve brightened the siege's prospects a bit, largely due to flight plan changes based on lessons painfully validated the day before. Four groups of aircraft would each drop at different altitudes.

The first group would drop from 300 feet, the second group at 2,200 feet using parachutes, the third at 800 feet, and the final drop at 350 feet, all within a span of twelve minutes. Their tight formation, minimal time over enemy territory, and a change in their route delivered approximately 160 tons that included ammunition, rations, and 10,000 bottles of Halazone tablets to disinfect water.

Yet many critical supplies required gliders, particularly adequate volumes of fuel and artillery shells that could weigh ninety-five pounds each. Additional medical personnel remained paramount as some battalions limped along with one surgeon and three medics. A message sent at 2230 hours on Christmas Eve again painted a dire situation.

Fog shrouded much of England on Christmas morning, dampening spirits and plans to resupply the 101st. Visibility of less than 100 yards at the British airfields kept close to 300 crews on alert until mid-afternoon when the resupply missions were postponed to the following day. There could be no more delays.

At a meeting at 0200 hours on December 26 at Supreme Headquarters Allied Expeditionary Force at Versailles, senior supply officers reviewed a massive "want list" from the 101st: 300,000 rounds of .30 caliber machine gun and carbine ammunition, 15,000 rations, 12,500 howitzer and mortar shells, 5,000 gallons of gasoline, 2,100 grenades, nearly 200 radios, 80 miles of communications wire, and 50 litters, among other requests. The quantity aside, the real issue was whether enough supplies could reach the 101st in time. A supply officer at the 101st headquarters harbored serious doubts.

> Providing an attack, in strength, from the north, is not
> launched, the Division can fire a few rounds of ammunition for
> about two days. If an attack is launched, then it [101st] would
> be in a position to hold out for only a few hours.[9]

As the sun rose a few hours later on December 26, weather remained the enemy. Heavy fog limited visibility so much in England that

290 aircrews could only kill time and wait while their loaded
C-47s sat on airstrips. In France where frost coated the aircraft,
aircrews waited for the delivery of ammunition they would carry
to Bastogne. Hardly a promising start on a day when resupply was
critical to the 101st.

"Okay, I'll go."

Second Lieutenant Corky Corwin, Jr, shook the cobwebs from a
Christmas Day meal the day before that featured free drinks while
volunteering to fly the lead glider on an eleven-glider mission
to Bastogne a few hours later. Captain Ray Ottomann and 2nd
Lieutenant Allen Kortkamp's C-47 would tow Corwin, his co-pilot,
Flight Officer Benjamin Constantino, and nine medical personnel
to Bastogne. Medical supplies filled the aisle between the glider's
facing benches that somehow lacked seat belts. The surgeons would
literally have to "hang on" if Corwin and Constantino encountered
trouble on the thirty-minute flight. Ten C-47s would follow,
towing gliders that each carried 300 gallons of 80-octane gasoline
in five-gallon cans.

Finally, a day of across-the-board success. Although Corwin
released two miles early, he was able to set down in a field inside
the 101st's perimeter and only 1,000 yards from the frontline.
The panel markers on the field did not designate his landing zone.
Corwin had landed near the markers for the bombers to make
sure they did not pound the 101st's position. All ten supply gliders
landed successfully despite enemy fire, delivering their entire load
of gasoline. "Thank God! We're at the bottom of the barrel," said
one soldier as he carried a jerrican to a waiting jeep.[10]

One C-47 aircrew counted seventy bullet and flak holes upon its
return. It had been a miracle that no incendiary bullets had hit any
of the gasoline cans.

Five troop carrier groups took off from England shortly after
1200 hours, not knowing if the foul weather would clear before
they reached the mission's initial point to begin their approach to
Bastogne. The plan was to stagger their drop altitudes if they made
it to Bastogne. The 434th and 437th would drop at 300 feet, then
the 435th at 350 feet, the 436th at 2,000 feet (using parachutes),

and the 438th at 400 feet. When the weather cleared for their run into Bastogne, the priority became maintaining a tight formation, giving German artillery crews little time to track and fire at one aircrew and then the next when their altitudes varied by more than 1,700 feet.

As was typical on past missions, the first two TCGs encountered minimal enemy fire. But the third, the 435th at only 350 feet altitude, was an easier mark.

After missions in Operations *Overlord*, *Dragoon*, and *Market Garden*, Captain Paul Dahl and his crew chief, Technical Sergeant George Gazarian, knew that their position in the 289-aircraft resupply mission that day would influence their odds of survival. Over Bastogne, they would be in the middle of the group. More than 125 aircraft ahead of them would have alerted enemy artillery crews to their speed and direction, but not necessarily to their altitude.

Blood splattered Dahl's cockpit two minutes from its drop zone, not far from 1st Lieutenant Zeno Rose's navigator seat. A machine gun burst and artillery flak had destroyed co-pilot William Murtaugh's instrument panel and had ripped into his shoulder. The second lieutenant remained at his post. Rose sat wounded as well. Dahl held his course until they reached the DZ. Once Gazarian had jettisoned the parapacks and bundle packs, Dahl pulled out of the formation. Enemy fire followed, setting the cockpit on fire and wounding Dahl. He had to stall his crash to save his crew. He set for full power and rolled the trim back for a steady, climbing course so the crew could bail out of the doomed plane on his orders.

Rose left his navigator's station, headed back to the tail and jumped, followed by the radio operator, Staff Sergeant David Lifschutz, and Gazarian. Only then did Murtaugh and Dahl jump last, just as the C-47 stalled and nosed toward the ground. Dahl had climbed to 800 feet, giving his crew enough time for their parachutes to open. Several landed remarkably close to each other and not far from an aid station. Dahl jumped at about 500 feet.

Dahl had focused on his mission and then his men before personal survival. He had simply pushed his arms through a seat parachute and jumped. The plane's stall speed kept the chute from being ripped from his arms. Medics treated Dahl's broken arm, lacerations, and neck burns. Second Lieutenant Murtaugh suffered a broken shoulder and several facial lacerations.

Dahl earned the Distinguished Flying Cross for his devotion to duty and for saving his crew, except for his crew chief. Observers concluded Gazarian's parachute had failed to open. He was buried in his boyhood town, Waterbury, Connecticut, where he had graduated Crosby High School and worked for Chase Brass & Copper Company, a major munitions manufacturer. He died eight days short of his thirty-eighth birthday.

The broad fields near Bastogne, framed by threads of leafless trees and crisscrossed by dark tank tracks, offered little cover for the 101st. The daytime glare off the snow hid their foxholes as the aircrews had approached, held their altitude, and spotted Bastogne in the distance. One after another, crew chiefs and others pushed the supply bundles out cargo doors and released parapacks. The moment they hit the snow, like ants mobilizing out of nests, men ran to bundles and dragged them into tree stands, bushy brambles, foxholes, and nearby vehicles. By day's end, the 101st had received 169 tons of supplies.

Two miles south of Bastogne, after destroying a German pill-box, the red, yellow, and blue supply parachutes in a nearby field reminded 1st Lieutenant Charles Boggess of confetti. *We've got to be close to the 101st.* Standing in his open turret, he rode at the point of a tank column as he crept straight ahead on a narrow road bracketed by dense forest, tanks behind him firing at enemy targets on both his flanks. When he spotted foxholes, he stopped. "Come here, come on out!" He repeated the order. The helmets that slowly appeared were American. When a soldier walked up to the tank, Boggess leaned over and shook 1st Lieutenant Duane Webster's hand in the dim, late-afternoon light. The lead element of General Patton's Third Army had reached the 101st perimeter. The German siege had cracked. Surely the next day a ground corridor would be established as additional lead elements entered Bastogne past midnight, enabling a safer airborne supply route, reinforcements, and evacuations beginning at dawn.

Where's the brake fluid?

Under sparkling clear skies on December 27, the sixteen-degree temperature before sunrise coated fifty C-47s and fifty gliders with frost that had set like wet concrete. Scrapers on windshields proved useless, as did a coat of brake fluid on the sheet of crystals that had to be "scraped off the seat with a knife if you were the first one in the outhouse," according to one glider pilot.[11]

First Lieutenants Zeno Rose, James Hurley, Billy Green, and others learned that the cold forced a two-hour delay of their 50-glider mission to 1000 hours. Meanwhile, foul weather in England threatened a 238-aircraft supply mission slated for later the same day. Frost and fog were the first two factors that complicated and threatened the pilots' final relief mission to Bastogne.

There would be no glider co-pilots on this mission. The official rationale cited a shortage of pilots due to the short notice for the mission when many glider pilots were on holiday leave. Years later, the commanding officer of the 439th, Colonel Charles Young, wrote "Since the cargo was HE [high explosive] ammo, it was felt any direct hit would instantly destroy the [highly flammable] glider along with its pilot [and co-pilot] … there was little use in losing two [glider] pilots to a direct hit since there was little hope for survival by either."[12]

Inadequate intelligence information had plagued many airborne missions dating back to Sicily. The aircrews' most common complaint focused on how often it was vague and outdated. On December 26, the pilot towing Corky Corwin and medical personnel to Bastogne had been handed a photograph of the general area of his LZ but no information on its exact location. That had been the extent of his "briefing." On December 24, the largest concentration of German troops had moved west of Bastogne, close to the aircrews' approach route. That intel did not reach Troop Carrier Command for more than two days.

Colonel Young had been so concerned that on December 26 he had driven to Orleans late at night to personally interview aircrews returning from that day's mission. The final officers' briefing summarized what Young had learned at 0230 hours on December 27, less than six hours before the pilots' scheduled takeoffs.

The sun finally warmed the aircraft as pilots and crews climbed aboard their C-47s and gliders. The aircrews were about to start their engines when a jeep stopped next to Young. An intelligence officer had just received a message from the 50th Troop Carrier Wing. "You might want to consider changing the route into the LZ," he said, adding navigation route details. "Why would I want to consider a change in route?" "I don't know. They didn't say."

Taking time to change the route at the last minute would risk missing a scheduled rendezvous with fighter protection. The plan was to follow the same route as the previous day's mission, a route of modest enemy resistance. The December 27 mission probably would be lightly contested as well. "We'll go as planned."

Young did not know that the suggested route would have shifted the aircrews to the secured corridor that General Patton's troops had established less than eighteen hours earlier. A route where most of the enemy had been routed from their artillery emplacements.

The 439th TCG's chaplain, Father John Whelan, was hard to miss. He dwarfed most men with his husky stature crowned by a white-haired crewcut. He did not bother with polished shoes or with sharp creases in his oversized pants. He believed the Ten Commandments were not Ten Suggestions and could be found discussing recipes with cooks in the 439th's kitchen or listening in on pilot conversations in an air traffic control tower.

As the fifty C-47s towing gliders took off on the frosty morning of the 27th, he stood 100 yards past the end of the runway, making the sign of a cross "for my boys" as each C-47 and glider crew passed overhead.

The mission quickly unraveled when delays tripped up the take-off schedule. Rather than a tight formation, the fifty tow planes and gliders stretched across eight miles. The fighter cover from the

Ninth Air Force arrived, but only flew "top cover," on the lookout for enemy fighters rather than attacking enemy artillery positions. Flying only two abreast on a relatively straight line, 88mm and other artillery crews would have plenty of time (up to a minute between C-47 aircrew passes) to gauge their altitude, speed, and take aim as they passed. Like hunters drawing a bead on one inbound duck slowing for a pond landing and then the next. "The Germans had our altitude down to the foot … I was so scared that I couldn't have remembered my name. How I admired the courage [of] our tow pilots … I wondered how Glennis would make out being a widow," reflected Flight Officer Paul Hower as his glider approached a "wall of flak."[13]

Courage and widowhood were likely on the minds of many as they approached Bastogne.

The distance between survival and death could be a few feet, dictated by the arc of a red-hot bullet, a shrieking artillery shard, or a breeze's direction. Flying into a certain firestorm near the front of the formation, C-47 pilot James Hurley released his glider seconds before a fire belched from his left engine and reached the fuselage. Discretion and discussion disappeared among Hurley, 2nd Lieutenant Lester Epstein (co-pilot), Staff Sergeant Marion McCarter (crew chief), and Sergeant Harry Kortas (radio operator). They would soon crash, perhaps in less than a minute. First Lieutenant Hurley climbed up and out of the way of thirty-eight aircrews behind him before his plane nosed downward into a dive. Pilots nearby reported it appeared he had lost control of the aircraft.

Four parachutes soon appeared in its wake, three landing remarkably close together, and a fourth, Epstein's, settling on the opposite side of a road. Hurley headed toward his limping co-pilot, intent on gathering his crew together. But a burst of enemy mortar fire forced Hurley into a ditch, helpless, where he and the rest of the crew watched Germans take Epstein prisoner and escort him into nearby woods.

Hurley's crew suffered the gamut of fates faced by C-47 aircrews. Hurley became a prisoner of war. Gunfire killed McCarter. Kortas returned to active duty. After the 101st had been rescued and relieved, Father Whelan prowled farm fields, woods, and creeks searching for crewmen. He discovered Epstein's shallow grave. Hands tied behind his back with wire and his crushed skull told Whelan that German rifle butts had killed him. Epstein was Jewish.

While losses were relatively light as the 91st and 92nd Squadrons approached Bastogne, others flew toward an inferno. The glider pilot behind the lead aircrew, 2nd Lieutenant Richard Fort, had landed cleanly and then looked back on forty-nine inbound planes. "The sky was thick with sky bursts," reminding him of "a black summer cloud."[14] An artillery officer in the 101st was equally aghast. "Nothing [compared] with seeing those fellows march headlong through that intense flak … I picked them up when they were about four miles away and could see the flak like sparklers around the formations. Several tows [C-47s] were hit and went down along with their gliders."[15]

The losses mounted as the 93rd and particularly the 94th squadron reached the LZs. There was no mystery, no surprise as it became a game of brinksmanship as the aircrews maintained their straight-and-steady course despite the shrapnel punches from 88mm and larger 120mm German artillery crews as they passed.

"We're on fire!"

No aircrew wanted to be near the Tail End Charlie position, flying among the last few aircraft after dozens, sometimes hundreds, had passed over enemy artillery positions. Far better, experience proved, to fly at the front with a reasonable hope for confounding the enemy. On most missions, those at the end of the formation found themselves as exposed as a newborn. First Lieutenant Billy Green and his co-pilot, 2nd Lieutenant John Bachman, had taken off in the mission's second-to-last position, and then fell back due to engine trouble. Flight Officer Gerald Knott in their glider's cockpit behind them had no choice but to tag along.

"We've been hit again!"

Green was already flying on one-engine procedures when he heard Technical Sergeant Al Sabon's shout a few miles short of the landing zone for Knott. His right engine had been knocked out by enemy artillery. One-engine procedures had been a major part of his training. *Check airspeed, directional control, adjust power, reduce drag, reduce fire hazard, adjust trim, trouble search.* Green held steady long enough to release his glider, dove to extinguish the engine fire, and then headed for home.

Another direct hit ignited a fire between the crew and the rear cargo door. Seconds later, a third direct hit took out the left engine. Green and Bachman had lost control of the plane. Green ordered everyone to bail out. Sabon decided to run through the fire filling the fuselage to reach the cargo door. Bachman reached up, twisted two handles to release the escape hatch above the pilots' compartment, and jumped. The plane was so low his parachute did not open as he crashed into the trees, breaking a leg and fracturing his skull. Sabon did not remember his chute opening after diving out the cargo door, suffering burns from the fire and then compression fractures in his back when he hit the trees. Their aircraft likely had been flying at close to 100 miles per hour, too close to the ground when they jumped.

With no power, his training had given Green and his radio operator, Sergeant Robert Slaughter, just one chance at converting a crash into an impossibly hard landing as gravity took command of the plane. *If you are landing in densely wooded terrain, stall airplane out directly over the tops of the trees and mush into the trees.* Green plowed his aircraft through the trees, recalling later, "Boy, they make a noise slapping the nose of the plane." When Green regained consciousness, Slaughter pulled him from the fileted wreckage. The wings and most of the tail had been stripped away. Green had suffered head cuts and a broken back.

No one saw Flight Officer Knott again after he had released. He simply disappeared without any witnesses. The glider pilot remained on his unit's missing in action list until late January 1945 and then added to the killed in action list later when most of his tow plane's crew still wore casts and burn bandages. Knott had graduated glider training only six months earlier and had died on his twenty-fifth birthday.

Following Green in the forty-ninth position, Technical Sergeant Robert Londo, a crew chief, had watched his plane's glider release as his pilot, 1st Lieutenant Alan Maeder, began his turn to depart the area. The crew chief and pilot were anxious to leave after watching an aircraft on their approach burst into flames, turn its nose up, and then fall into a spin before crashing and exploding. No one had bailed out.

The enemy's artillery shell felt as though a boxer had connected with the C-47's chin. It exploded between Maeder and his co-pilot, 2nd Lieutenant Lee Bachman, setting the cockpit on fire. Machine gun fire riddled the cockpit less than a minute later. Londo adjusted the propellers' pitch forward to generate 2,400rpm and maximum speed.

"Bail out!"

Londo and the radio operator, Corporal Robert Holste, jumped and landed without getting hit. Like others who found themselves on the battlefield, Londo hunkered down, fished the compass out of his escape kit, and took his bearing. *That way, head southwest. If I can find some American troops, maybe they can tell me if anyone else got out.* After he started walking, Londo spotted a parachute but no crewman. Almost three miles farther, he first smelled and then spotted a smoldering C-47 carcass. He paused, and found a logbook in the ashes, labeled with his aircraft's identification number. *What happened to everyone?*[16]

Flight Officer Pete Houck, who piloted the glider towed by Maeder, had no one to worry about since he was flying solo. He had been at the controls of an airborne gas station, his fuselage filled with gasoline cans and ammunition. He had marveled at the "black curtain" of artillery blasts ahead on his route and had watched tow planes that had "dropped like golden balls of fire" not long before his aircraft took the knockout blow. Despite burns from the explosion, he managed to land the glider, only to be captured by Germans.

Shortly after the last C-47 aircrew and glider crashed near Bastogne in the first wave, 129 C-47s arrived from airfields in England, far short of the 238 originally scheduled. Weather scuttled most, leaving the remainder to deliver 127 tons of ammunition and gasoline. In poignant contrast to the fifty-glider mission earlier, every C-47 on the mission returned and no crewmen were injured.

The contrast with the morning mission could not have been greater or more tragic.

Of the fifty-eight crewmen in the 440th C-47s on the mission, thirty-five were killed, wounded or taken prisoner, a loss of sixty percent. Far greater than the sixteen percent loss suffered in *Operation Husky II*, losses that after-action reports termed "appalling." The glider pilots suffered even more. Overall, seventeen gliders did not reach the 101st's perimeter, a loss of thirty-four percent. Worse, of the last twelve gliders on the mission, eleven glider pilots were killed or taken prisoner. Only one returned to base.

The next morning, ambulances evacuated 260 of the most seriously wounded in Bastogne on the route carved by the Third Army, the same route that would have been far safer for the fifty tow plane and glider aircrews the day before.

Despite the losses, seventy percent of the cargo carried on December 27 reached the 101st. In missions flown December 23–27, C-47 aircrew drops and glider releases delivered 1,050 tons of cargo, two-thirds of which was ammunition. Adding resupply missions on the 28th and 29th, troop carrier aircraft delivered 2,770 tons, almost matching the 2,900 tons delivered over fourteen days during Operation *Market Garden*.[17]

The German attacks at Bastogne ultimately failed and by mid-January the Germans were in retreat. Hitler's gamble had crumbled and would be the last German offensive of the war at a cost of approximately 120,000 men. By the end of the month, the Americans had retaken their lost territory, but at cost of 75,000 casualties.

Dear General P. L. Williams,

I would like to express to you and your command the admiration all of us in the 101st Airborne Division feel for the grand job of air supply you furnished us during the siege of Bastogne. The IX Troop Carrier Command repeated in this operation the

gallant performance which it had taught us to expect. Despite
the intense flak, the much-needed ammunition and medical
supplies were dropped just where we wanted them.

Needless to say, Bastogne could not have been held without
that excellent support.

Sincerely,
A. C. McAuliffe
Brigadier General, USA
Commanding[18]

Official accounts notwithstanding, the memories that gripped the
Bastogne pilots and aircrews were forged with bravery, focusing on
their mission and a devotion to each other. Colonel Charles Young
later wrote that a visit with a C-47 pilot, 2nd Lieutenant Joe Fry,
crystalized Young's respect for the men he commanded.

When [pilot] Joe Fry returned to Chateaudun [France] from
this mission he came to my office to see me and was still wearing the
jacket he had worn … It was saturated with spots of aluminum
which had hit him in molten form and soaked into the fabric
while he was hanging from the horizontal stabilizer before his
airplane blew apart … Joe believed that his chute hitting the
stabilizer had saved him, both from the blow to his chest, and
by spitting his chute open. Later, I personally flew him in my
airplane from Chateaudun to England, on January 24, 1945.[19]

In three months, new memories would take root among more
than 4,000 Allied airmen and the glider pilots they towed when
they crossed the Rhine River into Germany on their final combat
mission of World War II. The largest one-day airborne operation
in the history of warfare.

Undeterred

... a terrific amount of flak. A number of ships and gliders
went down in flames and after delivering their troops, a
surprising number of troop carrier pilots we saw on their way
back were flying aircraft that were afire. The crew I was with
counted twenty-three ships burning in sight at one time.
But the incoming pilots continued on their course, undeterred
by the awesome spectacle ahead.[1]

Less than ten months had passed since the Allies had first arrived in
France. Thousands of paratrooper and glider aircrews had led the
invasions into the hedgerow country, southern France's vineyards,
and into Holland. Aircrews had waged a secret war in the Balkans
and had become the vanguard of resupply missions in the Battle of
the Bulge.

In March 1945, the Allies stood on the western bank of the
Rhine River, more than 400 miles from where they had first come
ashore. Across the Rhine in Germany, farmers had plowed fields
divided by trees not yet leafed out. A checkerboard of seedlings
on a few and bare, barren loamy furrows on others. Rivers tinged
brown with the last of winter's runoff flowed with purpose. A few
miles away, communications centers and railyards had become
cratered moonscapes. The city of Wesel rested on rubble, its tallest
stone buildings now gutted, their stubborn facades as shallow as

reproductions on a movie studio sound lot. Wesel had become a construction site scrap pile.

The Allied juggernaut had reached the edge of the Fatherland along a front that stretched across 450 miles from Holland to the Swiss Alps. After months of planning and debate among the Allied commands, their dagger would strike along the front's northern flank, not far from Wesel, and only about fifty miles from the disaster that had been Operation *Market Garden*. Field Marshal Montgomery's 21st Army Group's three armies totaled approximately 80,000 men in the Canadian First Army (eight divisions), British Second Army (eleven divisions), and American Ninth Army (eleven divisions). The river crossing, Operation *Plunder*, would establish a bridgehead on the eastern bank of the Rhine that would extend six miles inland to the west bank of the Issel River.

To accomplish that, the largest and most complex one-day airborne lift in the history of war, Operation *Varsity*, would be necessary. US troop carrier groups from the 52nd and 53rd Air Wings would be stationed in France for the US 17th Airborne Division and England for the British 6th Airborne Division. In addition, 38 Group RAF flying modified bombers (298 sorties) and 46 Group RAF flying Dakotas (120 sorties) would deliver 3,900 British paratroopers and glider infantry in 440 Horsa and Hamilcar gliders.[2]

Unprecedented choreography, as well as cooperative weather, would be critical at twenty-three French and English airfields to deliver more than 17,000 airborne troops, seven million pounds of equipment, 130 pieces of artillery, and more than 1,200 vehicles and tanks to the far side of the Rhine. Aircrews would converge over Wavre, Belgium, and then fly northeast across the Rhine north of Wesel.

Vertical envelopment would be tested on a one-day scale that had been approached only once before, at Normandy. Two Allied divisions would be delivered behind enemy lines in less than four hours. On a route as straight as a bowling alley lane, across flat farming country peppered with villages, hamlets, country lanes, and woodlots before reaching ten landing and drop zones in a twenty-five-square-mile area, a few within 200 yards of each other. They bordered mostly the south, north, and east sides of the Diersfordter Forst, forested high ground ideal for observation and artillery. Capturing bridge crossings on the Issel River a short distance farther east would trap the German troops between the Rhine and Issel. Berlin was about 300 miles away.

There would be no pathfinders in Operation *Varsity*, as the DZs and LZs were only a few minutes past the Rhine. The Germans had the invasion plan down pat as they concentrated 88mm artillery crews and others at the suspected DZs and LZs. Farmhouses were fortified with German machine gun crews. Paratrooper drops and glider landings would take place at midday when the enemy could spot the incoming aircraft still miles away.

The massive airlift rewrote the playbook used on previous missions. *Varsity* would be the first operation in which paratroopers had not secured the gliders' LZs in advance. Several aircrews would tow two gliders into combat for the first time, to landing zones only minutes after the paratroopers had landed. About 135 dual-rated (power and glider) pilots would be in the gliders' co-pilot seats bound for a single landing zone.[3]

The C-46 Curtiss Commando would fly into combat for the first time, piloted by the 313th Troop Carrier Group in France.[4] At 51,000 pounds' maximum takeoff weight, wider than a B-17 bomber, and taller than a B-24 Liberator, the Commando looked like a C-47 on steroids. Produced by a different manufacturer, the C-46 was the heavyweight of the IX Troop Carrier Command. Its engines produced twice the power of the C-47, generating a top speed of 270 miles per hour at 15,000 feet and could comfortably cruise at 175 miles per hour. Its bulky fuselage's payload of 15,000 pounds in paratroopers, cargo, and evacuation of the wounded more than doubled that of the C-47s flown on previous missions. Several C-47 pilots were trained to fly the C-46 when it became available.

James Claussen, William Frye, Jr, and other pilots would battle test it for the first time over Germany, carrying 2,071 paratroopers and sixty-four tons of gear. Flying faster than a C-47, they would give their paratroopers a verbal warning at fifteen instead of twenty minutes and the red light would brighten at three minutes instead of four. Big, bulky, and fast, it seemed ideal for airborne combat. Its 3,000-mile range and 24,500-foot ceiling had made it ideal for flying supplies over the Himalayas to troops in China and in other combat theaters.[5]

Market Garden pilot Gerald Hamilton knew the rigors of hours-long flights to the battlefield. The first lieutenant and others would be part of an airborne deluge, taking off minutes apart in England and France, uniting into three lanes over Belgium (with a fourth at a higher altitude), and all arriving in Germany between 1000 and 1300 hours, to be followed by B-24 bomber supply missions only thirty minutes later. To the relief of *Husky* veteran pilots like Thomas Cargill, the ban on friendly fire stretched across thirty miles and would be in effect for as long as ten hours.

First Lieutenant Moorehead Phillips' first mission also had been *Market Garden* six months earlier. A talented artist, he had started painting at nine years of age and sold his first painting at thirteen. He had dropped out of high school to assist noted muralist William Tefft Schwartz on his commission for the 1939 New York World's Fair and study at an art school. He enlisted in 1941. There had been no rehearsals prior to his first combat mission six months earlier. This time, a rehearsal, *Token*, would take place one week before the big day. Aircrews also had flown 50,000 training hours in January on paratrooper flights and 9,000 hours in glider training. Training continued into early March, becoming the largest pre-invasion training effort since Normandy.

Allied bombing of potential mission threats had been intense for weeks and would culminate on D-Day when 1,500 B-17s and B-24s would drop 4,000 tons on enemy positions.[6]

The greatest World War II battle plans, spanning hundreds of miles and hundreds of thousands of men, ultimately rested on a mosaic of young men, now combat transport pilots, who a few years before had been high school dropouts, artists, mechanics, pre-med students, men's clothing store clerks, and textile engineering majors. A cross-section of America, England, and Canada that only had known life on farms and in towns and cities like Marion, Wardensville, and Montgomery. Or Maidstone, London, and Tarpoley. Now they would be waging airborne war in German airspace.

Their fates rested on countless individual decisions. Whether a co-pilot promptly spotted the fire in an engine. Whether the radio (or "wireless") operator overcame his horror when his friend's plane a hundred yards away exploded. Or if a cargo despatcher or crew chief cleared the explosive cargo bundles that sometimes jammed at a plane's door. Or if a pilot chose to stay on his course to the DZ as his aircraft burned or instead ordered his crew to bail out. And if his co-pilot chose to remain in the right seat, despite orders to bail out. A cavalcade of individual decisions, sparks of courage, and a devotion to duty that saved lives and cost lives in the name of accomplishing the mission. Hundreds of individual decisions would face helpless, hopeful, and luckless aircrews on the morning of March 24.

The ground trembled as a thunderous groundswell erupted at 0100 hours on D-Day, three hours after British commandos had led off the crossing of the Rhine. More than 2,000 artillery pieces had opened fire in advance of Operations *Plunder* and *Varsity*. More than 1,000 shells every minute for an hour crashed into enemy positions in Germany. Weighing 25 to 325 pounds each, 65,261 rounds pulverized potential threats to Allied aircrews and troops. Farther from the Rhine, 1,500 heavy bombers pounded a dozen German airfields to pin potential airborne threats to the ground.

By 0300 hours, smoke from the bombing began to cloud landing and drop zones. Worse, Field Marshal Montgomery had ordered fifty miles of chemical smoke machines to blanket the river to conceal the imminent crossing. There would be plenty of time for the smoke to drift on a weakening breeze east to the LZs and DZs, mixing with dust from the bombing attacks. The battlefield chessboard had become murky.

Shortly after 0600 hours in England, two massive migrations rose into the sky. One after another, hundreds of C-47s and British aircraft took off with loads of paratroopers bound for Germany. They would be accompanied by more than Allied 1,300 aircrews towing gliders to landing zones in the same patch of ground east of the Rhine. All were calculated to become an immense airborne armada stretching across 200 miles. Two hours forty-two minutes would pass between the first and last aircraft crossing the Rhine.

Glider pilots taking off in England were tested during the hours-long flights to their landing zones. Massive turbulence from a flying armada often forced each glider's pilot and co-pilot to take fifteen-minute shifts at the controls to relieve muscle fatigue from maintaining position and control. In back, knotted stomachs, sweat, trembling hands, restless feet, and vomit ruled, long before the first German artillery thunderclap rocked each glider.

Thomas Cargill had been on the move since boyhood. Known as "Doc," he had attended Clemson University on an athletic scholarship, majored in textile engineering, set a state track record in the 440 as a freshman, played football, and boxed. He dropped out after his junior year to enlist on October 1, 1941. With less than eight hours' instruction, he completed his first solo flight in pilot training. Cargill was one of those young men to whom everything came naturally, including leadership. In only two years after completing stateside training, he had attained the rank of major and was the commanding officer of his squadron in the 61st TCG.

He had flown through the Sicily nightmare in Operation *Husky*, dropped 82nd paratroopers in Italy, and on his twenty-fifth birthday delivered paratroopers to Normandy. In *Varsity*, his 14th Squadron would ferry Canadian paratroopers from England in "Hard Rock" to their drop zone and then would land at a designated French airfield.

He flew in the second serial departing from England, near the front of the inbound armada. Flying only six miles over enemy territory east of the Rhine, the black-and-white puffs of German artillery in front of the incoming aircraft precisely at Cargill's altitude looked as accurate as a dart on a bullseye. Flak soon bit off chunks of wings, rudders, and engine cowlings. Stabilizers and elevators crumbled. Evasive action was impossible, at least not until paratroopers jumped and gliders were released from the serials yet to arrive.

Once his paratroopers jumped, Cargill put his C-47 into a hard dive for a mile to gain speed before pulling out at about 200 feet and turning into a sharp, thirty-degree, banking U-turn for his route to France. The smoke stream was immediate midway through the turn when he took a direct hit either in the left engine or near his cockpit. Captain James Drake and his co-pilot, 2nd Lieutenant Theodore Walker, flying on his right wing pulled up and sharply to the left to avoid a collision. They could only watch.

One parachute emerged from Cargill's plane, now engulfed in flames. With neither time nor altitude for it to open, its crewman crashed into treetops. Gravity prevailed as the weakened aircraft sank. Its left wing hit a house, the impact pulling Cargill into a nose-first crash. As his tail rose, the fuselage separated and crashed into roadside trees. Black, crematory smoke billowed from a hole in the roof over the pilot's seat. No one survived.[7]

Aircrew fatalities in *Varsity*, like any battle, rippled far from the moment of death to far off the battlefield. Personal effects might not reach grieving families for several months and the remains of those killed might take far longer to be reburied back home. In the meantime, wives and parents desperately sought more information than was typically available "through channels." Anything that might make sense of why their son or husband had died in a fireball or below a crumpled parachute. *Varsity* would produce a heartbreaking list of mysteries.

Cargill's father, Romeo, wrote to one of his son's classmates, Major Roy Pearce, three weeks after *Varsity*, asking for any additional information or perhaps about the return of his only child's remains. Two weeks later, Pearce's agonized reply could only be written by a man who had befriended a stranger in training and who had overcome the same doubts and fears in recasting himself into a combat pilot.

> Clayton and I had a few minutes together in Naples, Italy last spring which was a great help to us both, I think. He is one of my closest friends, and we talked of old times and the future together often. I'm only praying we can both share that in the future we so often spoke of. He was in one of the finest outfits we have in our country ... Clayton was an outstanding officer in that group, of that I know for sure. His ability was only exceeded by his courage. He was never short of that.

Thomas Clayton Cargill was buried at the Netherlands American Cemetery in Margraten.

Flying from France, more than 150 aircraft in four serials had reached the drop zones before the 313th's crews flying the C-46 Commandos arrived. The Germans had ample opportunity to gauge both speed and altitude long before the C-46s appeared over the western horizon.

Gerald Hamilton had not intended to become a pilot when, at the age of twenty-two, he enlisted as an Army private in October 1941. But three months later, the former electrician at the North Electric Company in Ohio transferred to the Army Air Corps when its recruitment efforts intensified. The second lieutenant had flown in *Market Garden* a C-47. This time, he dropped twenty-five paratroopers from his C-46 before turning back over the Diersfordter Forst. It became clear Allied bombers and artillery from the other side of the Rhine had not cleared the forested high ground of German artillery.

Flak caught his right engine, turning his aircraft onto its right side and then into a dive. His crew chief, Technical Sergeant Thomas Klimek, and radio operator, Staff Sergeant Albert Lewis, jumped out of one of the two cargo doors at about 800 feet. According to a pilot flying nearby, the C-46 reached 180 miles per hour as it plunged.

The explosion, like that of other C-46s spitting fire that day, was catastrophic, incinerating Hamilton and his co-pilot, 2nd Lieutenant Wayne Wilson, to little more than a handful of charred remains. "Buckles and part of parachutes were found in the pilot and co-pilot's seats, thus indicating the two were in the aircraft at the time of the crash," noted the crash's post-mission Missing Air Crew Report.

Only two slots behind Hamilton on the runway in France, 1st Lieutenant James Claussen had grown up on a family farm and once, while in training nearby, flew off course to drop a note informing his parents that he probably would not make it for dinner that night. He had enlisted with dreams of becoming a paratrooper, but at five feet, six inches and weighing 140 pounds, he did not meet the physical requirements. He changed course to the next best option. Pilot.

His navigator, 1st Lieutenant Walter Ruzzo, had been flying missions since *Neptune*. Ruzzo had studied journalism at Ohio State University before enlisting in 1942 and marrying Rose Margaret Evans one year later while in training. He shipped overseas the following month.

Like the others, neither had flown in a C-46 in combat. But on March 24, both disappeared with hardly any notice as each pilot and aircrew focused on survival, sometimes only glimpsing a friend or squadron mate's losing battle. First Lieutenant Glen Smith, flying on the right wing of Claussen, saw him make a right turn toward the Rhine River after dropping his paratroopers.

Claussen's left engine was ablaze as he maintained control at 100 feet, according to Smith who lost sight of him seconds later. Claussen's options, were limited at that altitude. Diving to extinguish the fire was out of the question. Climbing likewise was not an option, since C-46s could not offset the loss of an engine by shifting more power to the remaining engine. Friendly territory was only a few miles away. Could he make it that far?

The story of the luckless aircrew's fate could only be surmised, perhaps augmented by a sole survivor's shocked memory. Claussen's wreckage was later found near Wesel, short of the Rhine. A parachute was found with his name and evidence that his body had been removed. Claussen apparently had crashed with a trace of control. His crew chief, Technical Sergeant Charles Williams, perhaps partway out a cargo door, was thrown clear, knocked unconscious, and survived. The rest of the crew died, joining a long list of 48th Squadron casualties that morning.

Losses mounted as burning engines' smoke mixed with flak bursts and red tracers. One after another, aircrews struggled to control their fiery meteor trailing flame and smoke in its wake as it plummeted toward oblivion.

Pilot Moorehead Phillips had drawn sketches of fellow airmen, at least one attractive nurse, life in uniform, and self-portraits on AAF letterhead since his arrival in Europe. A short letter home in March indicated he was preoccupied and would write again "tomorrow night." Prior to reaching his DZ, the first lieutenant took several direct hits, nearly crippling his ability to maintain control. He held steady as long as possible, enabling eleven of his thirty-three paratroopers to jump clear. Then time ran out. The C-46 crashed, killing Phillips, his crew, and the remaining hapless paratroopers.

His father, an accomplished industrial artist, and the mothers of his three-man crew received the dreaded letters notifying them of their sons' deaths.[8]

A fireball shower enveloped the 313th's seventy-two aircrews as they reached their DZs. After-action reports revealed only some of the horrors that swamped C-46 cockpits and main cabins. One in three aircrews suffered beyond the imagination of most civilians. "Hit by antiaircraft fire. Belly of ship caught fire. Right wing blew off." "Right wing on fire before crashing." "Crash landed and burned with all crew members." "Gas tanks were afire with flames lapping into starboard jump door." "Hit in nose, flames observed in pilots' compartment after paratroop jumped."[9]

The C-46 became known as the "flaming coffin" among the pilots, for good reason. Flak damage to its wing tanks produced fuel leaks traveling along the wiring network toward the fuselage. Hydraulic and oil lines running outside the belly of the aircraft were exposed to swarms of shrapnel. Both were design flaws that likely accounted for several fires in C-46 fuselages. Two-thirds of the twenty shootdowns resulted from fire originating in the gas tanks. The wing area totaling 1,360 square feet was a tempting and easy target on low-altitude and reduced-speed paratrooper approaches. Operation *Varsity* would be its only combat mission at the postwar insistence of the IX Troop Carrier Command. It was the 313th's curse to suffer the dangers of flying the C-46 Commando into battle.

Every squadron, it seemed, included a pilot who commanded both respect and admiration. Captain William Frye, Jr, filled that role in the 436th's 81st Squadron, assigned to tow two gliders in Operation *Varsity*. He flew in the third of fifteen serials towing gliders on the heels of the paratrooper serials.

Kind, soft-spoken, and handsome, Frye had enlisted in 1942 after growing up in a town of less than 200 neighbors at the end of a West Virginia rail line that tapped the local lumber industry until the Depression. Unmarried, he had completed one year of college and worked at a haberdashery while living at home before enlisting. He had reached the rank of captain in only three years.

Like others, he had trained for towing two gliders simultaneously, one attached to a 350-foot line, the other to a 425-foot line. Takeoffs could be particularly dicey if the C-47 sat at or near the head of the serial on the runway. That could shorten his takeoff run considerably, forcing Frye and other pilots to "bounce" their C-47s a few times to create more lift just before they ran out of runway. Once airborne, fuel status became a priority given the two gliders' cumulative load, while their two pilots fought turbulence and to maintain 100-foot separation between each other.[10]

When Frye and his aircrew lugged two gliders into the air at 0804 hours over France, no one could know they would meet their fate in front of an audience, a fate that remained fresh for decades.

"Whip it! Whip it!"

Radio operator Hal Friedland heard the alarm in someone's voice calling from a nearby aircraft pleading for Frye to sharply dive and then yank back into a climb to extinguish the fire in an engine. Others called Frye's aircraft. Radio silence. Frye held his course and signaled his gliders to release before turning for home.

Flying on Frye's right wing, 2nd Lieutenant Henry Zimmerman watched with growing alarm. Frye appeared to pull hard into a near-vertical climb. The C-47 rolled over onto its back and sank tail first for a moment, until the nose dropped down into a full-on dive. Somehow, the plane began another climb, as steep as a roller coaster. *Is he doing that, trying to put out the fire or has he lost control?* When Frye's plane fell over onto one wing and dropped again, the crash became inevitable.

Horrified aircrews could only speculate on those final moments. "I had to sit there and watch while the fire must have melted off some of the control surfaces ... the plane went into a dive," speculated one. "... must have caught it right in the cockpit. In his death agonies, a pilot probably would pull back on the wheel, and that plane just went straight up, turned over on its wing and then went straight down. It didn't look as though it went into any spin whatever," mused a nearby pilot.[11]

Uncertainty, blended with interpretation and speculation over the deaths of the entire aircrew, would spawn tears among some squadron mates. A crew chief, Technical Sergeant Cloyd Clemons, was sick on March 24. His flight chief and aviation mechanic, Grover Bension, was ready to climb aboard as his replacement when Clemons announced he felt well enough and that he did not want to miss what might be his final combat mission. Clemons was married and died in the crash.

Frye's co-pilot was 2nd Lieutenant Willard Cooke, Jr. His brother, John, was a pilot in the same squadron. When Frye's plane did not return to its assigned France airstrip, John hovered near the squadron's operations office, grilling fellow pilots about why his brother's plane was late and perhaps missing. In time, John and the rest of the 81st would learn that Cooke had died when the "Nookie Wagon" crashed.[12]

Competitive track and field runners train to "finish strong." To be the fastest down the homestretch. As thousands of C-47 aircrews carrying paratroopers and especially those towing gliders approached the Rhine, the opposite was often the case, slowing to avoid collisions as prescribed separations melted on an unexpected tailwind.

The final few miles to the LZs became a battle to simply land. "We were wallowing just above stall speed. We would creep up on the tail of our [slowing] tow ship, and to avoid running into it, I had to pull up and over ... then settle back in behind again ... the rope would tighten, and then we'd begin another surge forward and repeat the process."[13]

The marionet dance between American CG-4As and C-47s as well as British aircraft towing mostly Horsas began minutes after the paratroopers' aircraft had headed toward Germany. More than 1,300 aircrews in England and France began taking off.

His buddies called 1st Lieutenant William Grieb "Willie," a pilot typical of his fellow 94th squadron's pilots approaching the Rhine River in the middle of more than 900 C-47s towing gliders from France into Germany. Married after three years of high school in Philadelphia, Willie worked as a machine operator before he enlisted on February 12, 1941.

The white and black flak puffs on the approach to the other side of the Rhine did not look as bad as the approach in *Market Garden*, thought Staff Sergeant Wilbur Kline, Grieb's radio officer. The direct hit on the left wing was as sudden as it was unexpected. So, too, was the second jolt in the right engine only seconds later. Their landing zone was only a few minutes ahead. *Now what?*

Grieb struggled to control the wounded plane as he continued his approach, the red glow from his right engine becoming more ominous, the left engine dead. Both glider pilots managed to release from the tow plane, knowing it could explode at any second. Grieb could not be sure it would hold together as he turned back toward Wesel and the Rhine.

"Bail out!" The order was quick and final.

The crew chief, Technical Sergeant Charles Holt, jumped. After a moment's hesitation, Kline followed him out the door as Grieb struggled to keep the plane level at about 1,000 feet as other crews in his formation watched and hoped, unable to do more. A little longer and maybe Grieb's co-pilot, 2nd Lieutenant Ralph Becker, could make it to a rear door and jump. Becker had smiled, waved, and was heading toward the rear of the aircraft as Kline had jumped.

Becker almost made it to the rear door when the plane's left wing dipped, as if to start a left turn. The right side of the plane blazed. When the nose dipped into a moderate dive, the race for survival closed fast. Grieb's plane crashed and exploded, killing Grieb and possibly Becker, although one report indicated Becker had jumped at the last second with too little distance for his parachute to deploy fully or survive.

Weeks later by letter, Mrs. William J. Grieb learned her husband had earned the Silver Star for extraordinary bravery in focusing on both his mission and his men. In England, dozens of intrepid pilots in the front seat would earn the Distinguished Flying Cross and the Distinguished Flying Medal. They too, would focus on their mission and their men, whether at the rear or front of their formation, always straight into the teeth of the enemy.

A Bit Tired

The final turn across the Rhine was made at Weeze [*sic*] at which point the previous monotony of this operation … little different from a practice training exercise, was dispelled, as the Dakota formations ahead were repeatedly hit by flak, which appeared to be quite heavy, a number of aircraft were seen to go down in flames, whilst others exploded in mid-air.

Individual dramas and disasters played out within the British formations toward Operation *Varsity*'s drop and landing zones. "A smoke pall hung over the landing zones … that stuff was thicker than the candles on Grandma's birthday cake … the aircraft was seen to break in two … I began to swing the glider from side to side … several shells exploding between our tug and glider."[1]

While flying as Tail End Charlie in the rear carried no element of ambush and was dreaded by most combat pilots, flying in the front position hardly offered any guarantees. Pilots generally considered flying in the lead group an honor, but they also knew that once awakened, enemy artillery crews could focus solely on them before the skies filled with hundreds of inbound aircraft.

March 24, *Varsity*'s D-Day, had started as early as 0200 hours when RAF aircrews awakened for an eggs, bacon, and beans breakfast, the Americans steak and eggs, and then a ride to their airfields at 0400. At 0600, sunrise crept into the cold night as more than 100 Dakotas in 46 Group RAF and almost 300 modified bombers in

38 Group RAF began taking off, only about one minute apart. Flying at 2,500 feet, aircrews remarked on an emerging dawn's promise over the English Channel, likely reassured by the presence of Allied fighter escorts. But as they approached the Rhine River, their fifteen-mile visibility disappeared in a smoke and haze shroud ahead on their route. Rising to 2,500 feet, it replaced confidence with alarm. Visibility was crucial in Operation *Varsity*, given the dense concentration of ten Allied drop zones for the imminent arrival of 17,000 troops, their equipment, and supplies.

At the spearpoint, the 2nd Battalion Oxfordshire and Buckinghamshire Light Infantry ("Ox & Bucks") would be the first unit of the 6th Airlanding Brigade to land in Germany in LZ-O, sandwiched between Hamminkeln and the Issel River. Objectives included seizure of a key road and railroad bridge across the river to prevent enemy counterattacks.

Leading the glider assault from England was a group of three Horsa gliders, the "Number 1 Coup de Main Force." Flying in the third position, RAF Staff Sergeants Desmond Page and Norman Elton carried twenty-six members of the Ox & Bucks and a trailer. The veterans of *Market Garden* had squirmed at their briefing's orders to conduct what seemed like a leisurely descent once they released from their tug aircraft. They had a different plan.

At eleven miles before the Rhine crossing and another seven to their drop zone, Page's tug plane aircrew began counting off each mile's approach. Enemy flak erupted three miles short of their destination, just as the haze was dimming. *Time to alert the troops in back.*

"Prepare for landing!"

The three gliders released in unison and turned into a single file. There, the flight plan disintegrated, just as it would for hundreds of aircrews in the next three hours.

Page watched the lead glider take a direct hit. In a split second, "the flight cabin, men, and bits of fuselage fell away in front of us." The glider crew and the troops they carried all were killed.

Seconds later, the second glider careened into a sharp starboard dive when artillery destroyed half its port wing. One pilot dead and the other seriously wounded, the dead-weight Horsa plummeted, its flight controls mangled and landing flaps starved for compressed air. The crash resulted in "a pile of matchwood in about one second flat" after the Horsa had skimmed over the drop zone, the Issel River, and then slammed into a group of trees. Only seven men in the center of the fuselage survived, along with one pilot who lost an arm, recalled Page.[2]

Page had weaved side to side behind his Dakota in the last few minutes, hoping to muddle the enemy's marksmanship. Then it was time for his contingency plan. Almost immediately after release, with full flaps he put his Horsa into a steep dive to eat 2,000 feet of altitude as fast as possible. So fast that the troops in back thought the pilots were dead and that they were about to join them.

Then, just one turn to line up as he leveled out at 300 feet, crossed a row of trees, then another, and deployed his parachute (speed) arrestor just as his tail broke apart. He finally stopped with a tree embedded in his starboard wing after plowing through wires, hedges, and ditches. Only one trooper died, another wounded.

Mission accomplished. But it was only the opening jab as the rest of the battalion reached LZ-O and descended into pandemonium. "The Battalion lost half its manpower during the ten minutes that it took all the gliders to land ... By the end of the day the Battalion had lost all but a third of its infantry strength, with one hundred and three dead and a further 100 wounded."[3]

While training far from the battlefield weeks before Varsity, injuries and death draped with cruel horror stalked the aircrews that towed gliders and dropped paratroopers from either the C-47s, Dakotas, or the modified bombers, particularly on non-combat training missions. Six weeks earlier, an aircrew hoped they had escaped the worst of war when most had survived a crash at sea while on a routine navigation training mission. Flying Officer Delmer McGillivray, the pilot; Flying Sergeant James Walker, his navigator; Warrant Officer James Bunn, his air gunner; and Flying Officer George Dixon, his wireless operator had flown to a rocky islet 270 miles northwest of Ireland's Donegal Bay.

In wind so wicked that the local fishing fleet had stayed in port that day, the gale pushed the aircrew off course. Low on fuel on their return, they had ditched in the bay as local lookouts spotted two red flares just before the crash. They dispatched rescue craft but two crew members disappeared when waves drove them off a floating wing.

During Operation *Varsity*, the four members of the Royal Canadian Air Force released their Hamilcar glider over its Germany LZ and disappeared in the chaos overhead. With no witnesses. Their squadron's report only stated, "As two free aircraft only were seen to have been shot down, Duty assured to have been carried out." Air gunner Bunn had married nine days earlier and McGillivray was engaged.

Some US and British power pilots had undergone a wholly unexpected type of training prior to *Varsity*. On D-Day, more than 130 buckled in at the far end of a tow rope. About six months earlier, General Arnold had ordered a group of American C-47 pilots to receive modest glider training due to a shortage of glider pilots for upcoming missions. Records indicate that about more than 1,000 power pilots trained to fly gliders. Two weeks' worth at two US training facilities and in England included ground training, nine days of landings, and one night's landing regimen. Most pilots groused at the prospect of riding behind a tow rope like a water skier heading for battle, a far cry from their standing as twin engine-rated pilots, much less the ultimate insult to their boyhood fighter pilot dreams.

In England, approximately 1,500 power pilots underwent similar training due to the brutal losses suffered by the glider pilots in Holland. Proportionally, the Glider Pilot Regiment had lost more pilots (220) than the 1st Airborne Division (1,175) or the US IX Troop Carrier Command (approximately 30). The power pilots received three weeks' training on small arms and ground combat before transition training in Horsa and Hamilcar gliders.[4]

C-47 pilot Lee Whitmire, sitting in the co-pilot's seat of Flight Officer Otis Cook's glider, had taken a circuitous route into combat. The flight officer joined the 78th Squadron of the 435th

TCG only days before the mission. Cook and Whitmire's first flight that morning aborted while circling their takeoff airfield when an officer they were carrying suspected a wing was cracking. They returned to the airfield and took off a second time, two hours later.

Tow plane traffic congestion leading to their LZ had forced their tow pilot to climb to 1,200 feet, twice their prescribed altitude. When Whitmire hit the glider release, like Page, Cook made a terrifying vertical descent, pulled out, and touched down in a furrowed field. He caromed off a glider, plowed through a fence, and finally stopped when his glider's nose dug into the soft soil. Whitmire and Cook clambered out and promptly "hit the dirt." Enemy fire pinned them down for almost an hour before the German resistance subsided.

The 435th included sixty-nine C-47 pilots ordered to fly as glider co-pilots in *Varsity*, including two best friends, Whitmire and Flight Officer Tom Pleger. Like Whitmire, Pleger also had joined the 78th Squadron the day before to become part of a glider pilot combat unit. He often wrote "My best buddy" on the back of photos he had taken of Whitmire. As both had approached their LZs in their gliders, they knew exactly what was taking place in their tow plane's cockpit. Pleger's tow plane took direct hits, but stayed on course until fire from one hit erupted in the cockpit. Pleger's glider released as the tow plane's pilot, Captain Thomas Tomeny, fought for control. Crews in nearby aircraft were horrified by Tomeny's steep climbs, almost vertical, then two inside loops as crewmen bailed out. His co-pilot, the last man to leave the plane, saw Tomeny struggling with his parachute as the co-pilot jumped. Seconds later, the aircraft crashed, killing Tomeny. His crew survived. Pleger's glider landed safely.

From a platoon's skirmish to Allied invasions numbering tens of thousands of men, the final scorecard of victory or defeat charted triumphs, failures, complications made worse by catastrophes, and losses against objectives met. British aircrews towing gliders were forced as high as 3,500 feet. Half their gliders were damaged, yet most loads remained intact while "many glider men were slain in their seats and many loads were burned or destroyed by mortars."[5]

Overall, Operation *Varsity* became the most accurate and successful large-scale troop carrier mission of the war. Success built upon the bloodied lessons inflicted over the previous twenty months since the Sicily disaster and every subsequent mission flying into the enemy positions at point-blank range. Aircrews flew directly at the enemy, fully exposed, and only a few hundred feet off the ground. On straight-ahead routes with no deviation, minimal evasive action, and often close enough to see German faces taking aim.

"Axis Sally" on German propaganda radio had told the 17th Airborne the day before the mission that "you will not need parachutes; you can walk down on the flak." Yet of approximately 550 paratrooper aircraft carrying 17,000 paratroopers, ninety-nine percent jumped, almost all within two miles of their DZs. All told, forty-three serials from nearly two dozen airfields across 300 miles all arrived within ten minutes of schedule. Of more than 900 aircrews towing gliders (two-thirds on double tows) through turbulence and an unexpected tail wind, close to ninety-eight percent reached the Rhine.[6]

In the big picture, aircrew losses were less than expected. American and British aircraft losses amounted to less than four percent, aircrew losses less than two percent. Those loss statistics were misleading. Recent aircraft replacements with the long-awaited self-sealing fuel tanks were largely immune to small arms fire. But flak, even from the light 20mm artillery that survived the Allied bombers, remained deadly. In some cases, the loss rate approached twenty percent in the last five minutes of the aircrews' approach into flak as dense as a holiday fireworks show.

Glider pilot losses, though, were appalling on March 24. Eighty-one died in about twelve hours (one every nine minutes). That amounted to forty percent of all glider pilot KIAs in World War II and exceeded the combined KIAs in Operations *Overlord* and *Market Garden*. Another 240 suffered wounds and thirty-one remained missing in action. Of the ninety-eight C-47 crewmen killed, twenty-two were towing gliders.

On the ground, the Ox & Bucks' 2nd Battalion had achieved its objectives by 1100 hours that morning, but at a gut wrenching cost. In Page's three-aircraft sortie alone, sixty-one men died or were wounded, a sixty-five percent loss rate. Four companies had lost two-thirds of their combat strength (more than 200 killed or wounded). The next day, only 226 men were combat capable. Just fifteen were officers. "We were slightly less than half strength and were getting tired," summarized its war diary.[7]

General Omar Bradley once remarked, "Amateurs talk strategy, professionals talk logistics." By the fifth major World War II airborne mission in the ETO, bitter experience had honed airborne warfare. The choreography, navigation needs, timing, concentration, coordination to prevent friendly fire, rehearsals, logistics, repairs, maintenance, and other factors had become the cornerstones of Operation *Varsity*'s success. The tactical efficiency and efficacy of the C-47s, Dakotas, and other troop carriers had never been better. Overall loss ratios plummeted unless something went wrong, such as the combat baptism of the C-46.

Losses suffered by the 313th TCG flying the seventy-two C-46s were chilling. Time and again, they became streaking fireballs from leaking fuel, amounting to a twenty-eight percent aircraft loss rate on their only mission of the war. Just thirteen of seventy-two aircraft returned to base (only three undamaged). The enemy destroyed twenty aircraft, damaged thirty-three, and killed or wounded fifty-five airmen. The scorecard was bloody and wretched.

Troop carrier groups' war diaries typically focused on the accomplishments and heroism of a mission. In Operation *Varsity*, the tragedy suffered by the C-46 Commando aircrews surfaced in the 313th TCG's report.

At 0907, the last aircraft was in the air, circled the field, and began its course five minutes late. Late, however, because it was an emergency ship replacing the runway ship that crashed ...

During the long wait for the returning C-46s, personnel were almost jubilant; every indication pointed to a completely successful mission; for it had been skillfully planned, and all indications pointed toward what might be called a "milk-run" mission, without losses and with perfect results. At 1106 hours, the first C-46 circled the field, alone, to land, and a little later there were other ships. The beautiful formations of planes with which the 313th Troop Carrier Group traditionally returned from a mission, where were they? The flak holes in the wings – no "milk run" mission this!

During the afternoon, the grim story began to unfold. From a tactical standpoint the mission was the most successful ever flown by this group. But the rest is tragic.

Used for the first time in combat, the C-46 is magnificent for dropping troops and supplies. It is also a splendid target! Flying at a low altitude and at almost stalling speed, the C-46's maze of intricate hydraulic lines, with great flat gas tanks in the wings, were targets impossible to miss. Many of our C-46s were aflame before they ever reached the drop zone. YET THEY FLEW IN AND DROPPED THEIR TROOPS!

The final score: Twenty C-46s of seventy-three were completely destroyed, and of the remaining aircraft there were only fifteen that returned undamaged.[8]

Every squadron's aircrew in *Varsity* forged a legacy unique to its role, specific mission, and luck's whims. Relief over survival, much less pride in an accomplished mission, extended from the DZs and LZs in Germany to airstrips and the barracks in France and England. Relief that could only be absorbed by an aircrew that had weathered the terror of aerial combat.

At 12:30 they began coming in, scattered, ragged remnants of a formation … the pattern became a nightmare. There was gulping tenseness in the faces of the ground men, as their eyes strained to count their planes. They began to land. Red flares were shot. Some planes began to taxi to the control tower.

Ambulances throttled their engines. Men on the ground knew instinctively from the ragged formation in the air that something had gone wrong, that it wasn't a "milk run." In about 20 minutes all 20 of our planes had come back and no one was wounded. Lucky 44th! Some others were not so fortunate![9]

On the morning of March 24, two men had stood on a hill near the Rhine. Overhead, the massive aircraft fleet headed east, their reverberation making conversation difficult.

"My dear General," Churchill kept repeating to General Eisenhower, "the German is whipped. We've got him. He is all through."

Within a week, Operations *Plunder* and *Varsity* became a knock-out blow on Germany's chin. Four Allied armies had crossed the Rhine River and two more stood ready to join them.

The Allies had pierced the last barrier on the road to Berlin. Within days of Operation *Varsity*, aircrews launched the largest and most ambitious airborne marathon supply campaign over enemy territory to date. The twenty Allied divisions storming into Germany required 28 million pounds of supplies *daily*. Thousands of medical, prisoner of war, and refugee evacuations became equally necessary as the Allies rolled across Germany.

Yet war persisted. To finally bring Germany to its knees aircrews also would become flying gas stations if General Patton's plea, "we got to have gas," to General Eisenhower could be answered.

13

Got to Have Gas

A father in the pilot's seat, a crew chief at the cargo door with an expectant wife at home, and a radio operator planning to write his parents another letter before lights out. None could predict when or how his war would end.

> Harvey put the plane down into a pasture, gear up, and got it down so quickly that all aboard, including the co-pilot, were able to get out the door to safety. All that is, except Harvey. As they tried to reach him, which was impossible because the cockpit had turned into an inferno, they could still see him silhouetted through the flames, but there was no movement at all. He was already dead.[1]

Colonel Harvey Berger had seen action in India, Africa, and the ETO. On April 3, 1945, he had volunteered to fly a resupply mission to Germany so that he could see the city where his mother had been born. But an unexpected shrapnel burst found his plane's fuselage fuel tanks between the wings. Fire erupted immediately as Berger pushed his co-pilot back into the main cabin toward survival. As soon as the C-47 stopped in the plowed field, the crew escaped. Berger was the only casualty, leaving two sons, Gerald Irvin, and Thomas Leland, back in Colorado. They were six and four years old. His fifteen-year career in the AAF and fatherhood ended when he was incinerated less than six weeks before Germany surrendered.

Only two days after Operation *Varsity*'s success on March 24, five armored and fifteen infantry divisions had crossed into Germany. As Allied army groups thundered eastward toward Berlin in a race against the Soviets advancing westward, German troops and Allied bombers had destroyed critical road bridges over the Rhine and Moselle Rivers. Without a reliable motorized river of supplies from France, Belgium, and Holland into Germany, the Allied advance would starve for lack of fuel, ordnance, food, tires, lubricants, medical supplies, and fundamental troop materiel.

Those requirements dwarfed previous campaigns. Organized into three army groups, the Allies' ninety divisions included twenty-five armored divisions. Just one of General George Patton's armored divisions required 75,000 gallons of gasoline every 100 miles. "My men can eat their belts, but my tanks got to have gas," Patton had pleaded to General Eisenhower six months earlier.

Beyond fuel, a typical division required 600 to 700 tons of supplies daily.[2] It all must arrive on time, intact, and to the precise locations where it was needed most by the commanding officers of troops eager to end the war. As German resistance crumbled in isolated areas and stiffened in others, communication and coordination with rear echelon personnel would be as fluid as it was vital.

The IX Troop Carrier Command became the linchpin of the ultimate Allied assault across Germany.[3] The unprecedented air supply campaign became known as "The Flying Pipeline," an endless parade of C-47 aircrews from France and England daring stubborn enemy fire across 350 miles of the Fatherland to airstrips and pastures almost alongside advancing Allied armies. On missions so dangerous that for the first time resupply missions to the frontline were classified as combat missions in the first three weeks of April.

Suddenly, two or three missions per week following an invasion became two or three missions daily for all pilots, deeper into Germany with each passing day. Many were unescorted by fighters as aircrews climbed to 6,000 feet, in part to avoid the barrage balloon cables over the Rhine River. Like a marching band, minutes later they morphed from tight formations into a single line as they approached their assigned airstrip.

Second Lieutenant Donald Walch and his co-pilot, 2nd Lieutenant Burton Culp, faced all-day missions that sometimes resembled a postal delivery route, starting with breakfast at 0500 hours, landing in a German pasture to deliver rations a few hours later, then continuing to a dirt strip to load radio equipment, making a third stop to offload that equipment, and returning to base in France at dusk, in time for dinner at 2100 hours. A mission to an airfield in what later became East Germany would be close to a 1,000-mile roundtrip. Shorter missions could result in two roundtrips before dinner. Instrument flying in foul weather over unfamiliar terrain and despite exhaustion joined enemy fire as ever-present threats.

The 441st TCG kept seventy-five of its seventy-seven C-47s in operation, only because crew chiefs and mechanics worked through the night to maintain the fleet. Officers suspended standard 50-hour mechanical inspections along with the usual engine replacements after 650 flight hours. Ground personnel staged the next day's prescribed cargo at each plane and refueled it while its aircrews searched for a few hours of genuine sleep.

The Pipeline became a unique airborne marathon of daily two-way relay races, made possible by nightly "pit crews" keeping aircraft airworthy.

Hundreds of aircrews flew in narrow corridors cleared by Allied armored units low enough so that they could track the battlefield terror that had preceded them, sometimes only the day before. A landscape – from one village to the next, from one home to the next – often pockmarked by war's carnage and sometimes blessed with luck.

Colonel Charles Young and other aircrews traced the trail of war on their missions. They noted the Siegfried Line's "dragon's teeth," the tightly packed concrete pyramidal blocks that slowed Allied tank advances. Zig-zagged trenches in open clearings, fields, and pastures where crouched infantry had returned fire knowing their trenches' design limited casualties from direct hits or from the enemy overrunning their position. Aircraft wreckage on a ridge blackened beyond recognition. Gutted factories missing their roofs. Untouched fairytale German houses, others with white flags hanging from their windows. Decapitated homes, a family's debris scattered in the yard as if a tornado had touched down on the roof. A twisted railyard. Fields churned by hundreds of tank tracks. Farmers plowing untouched fields. Ribbons of Allied truck convoys heading east. Cities afire in the distance. An approaching C-47 flock on its way back from one of hundreds of airstrips, so temporary and fluid that their names were only numerical: R-16, R-48, R-70, etc. Closer to an aircrew's destination, a standing-room-only POW camp. More airborne troop carriers heading east off in the distance.[4]

As the Germans retreated, new airstrips a few miles closer to Berlin commandeered by the Allies supplanted those used the previous day. It became a nightly game of hopscotch for the IX Troop Carrier Command's operations planners. Bomb and mortar craters pockmarked most. Ground personnel raced to fill in as many as possible before the laden C-47s arrived. Heavy April showers muddied unpaved and slickened grass airstrips, making landing a long shot and taking off even more dangerous. More than a few destinations simply were pastures, a few nothing more than plowed farm fields. Landing in line with furrows eased the impact a little, but flattened and cut C-47 tires plagued resupply missions day after day.

The German war zone was as fluid as the tides as unseen pockets of German soldiers leaned into the relentless Allied advance. Every flight was vulnerable, particularly when aircrews descended toward their airstrips. Snipers, artillery crews, mortar units, and rogue German fighter pilots making strafing runs could kill, maim, damage, and destroy as aircrews landed, taxied, helped unload, and prepared to take off as quickly as possible. Regardless, enormous amounts of daily supplies reached the troops on the ground. On a single day in early April, fourteen aircrews in one squadron carried

94,500 pounds of gasoline to a German airfield. The aircrews logged a total of fifty hours' flight time in what became combat conditions.

Shortly after they landed, German mortar crews opened fire on aircrews. In one instance, Technical Sergeant Thomas Woodcock suffered a broken leg and lacerations to his scrotum and left thigh from artillery shrapnel while unloading fuel. His plane took several hits, leaving a large hole in a wing, another in the fuselage near the latrine, and another in the bulkhead near the navigator's station. Bullet holes riddled the right wing faring, rudder, and stabilizer. Other aircraft on the mission suffered damage to a fuselage, vertical stabilizer, rudder, and elevator.

No pilot wanted to see a red flare on his final approach to an airstrip. A red flare told the C-47 aircrews to pull up, circle, and possibly abort their landing altogether, perhaps due to the enemy or because earlier arrivals remained on the airstrip. A sudden mortar attack on crews unloading parked C-47s could threaten another half dozen planes on their final approach.

On April 10, flight leader Captain Merril Meaker was minutes away from landing when he pulled his landing gear up and aborted his approach as a flare arced across his airstrip. Behind him, 2nd Lieutenant George Fillman brought his ship in and parked near C-47s that had already landed. When German artillery erupted and enemy fighters arrived, Fillman and other crewmen sprinted to what might have been and old ditch and dove in. Fillman dared to look around for the enemy fighters. Black smoke rising on the far side of a stand of trees in line with the runway, perhaps two miles away, drew his attention. *Who didn't make it?*

Second Lieutenant Clifford Katz also had landed just before the fighters appeared. He suspected they had shot down Meaker as he made his second approach toward the small, sloping airstrip. His instincts were spot on. Meaker, his crew chief, Corporal Michael Barbero, and his radio operator, Staff Sergeant C. A. Smith, were killed two miles short of the runway. The body of his co-pilot, 2nd Lieutenant Robert Maneman, was missing when ground personnel reached the site several hours later. They learned he had been badly burned, someone had completely bandaged him, and a 436th aircrew had evacuated Maneman a short time later. Unconscious when the aircrew had taken off for France, he died in mid-flight.

He had been a bomber pilot until transfer to C-47s only a week before his resupply mission. Although memorial services at home in central Iowa were held a month later, it wasn't until November 6, 1948 that his remains were buried only a few miles from where he had graduated high school. Survivors included his parents and nine brothers and sisters.

The mysteries surrounding other aircrews that disappeared while flying the Pipeline could take weeks, sometimes months, to solve.

Four days after Meaker's mission, Captain John Cosgrove led a flight on a resupply and evacuation mission on a dull, gray day. Flying in a line ("trail formation"), the overcast thickened as they crossed the Rhine. Cosgrove ordered his pilots to make a turn and climb hard to break out of the overcast. Watching for one another, 1st Lieutenant Myron McEllech lost sight of the leader of one flight element, 1st Lieutenant Frank Yakos, as McEllech climbed. *Where did Yakos and his element go?* After McEllech broke out of the clouds, he noticed the column of black smoke rising from the cloud bank.

Who's that?

Not far away, Yakos had decided to drop "down to the deck" to fly under the cloud cover. First Lieutenant Paul Lee followed. The overcast seemed to follow them as "visibility decreased considerably." A hill emerged, dead ahead. After Lee and the others climbed hard to break out of the cloud bank and then leveled, he noticed a plane was missing. They circled for a time, but the missing aircraft never appeared. The group "made a few more turns and then proceeded [to] our destination."

Combat veterans knew a mysterious column of black smoke when an aircrew was missing rarely ended well. Empty bunks in their barracks often confirmed a mission's destiny.

A month later, Captain Charles Harris stood over Yakos' wreckage in a wooded valley not far from the Rhine River. Its tracks indicated he had gone "straight in," steady on the route of flight. It appeared that Yakos had barely missed a stone silo before slamming ten to twenty feet higher up into an upslope. Perhaps the aircrew had not noticed the rise in terrain as Yakos stayed below the low cloud cover. It seemed the only explanation.

He and his crew had died in an impact explosion that had left seat belts, paper, a left foot, combat boot, "the top of a skull with fleshy matter thought to be a scalp, and other small piles of fleshy material in states of decomposition."[5]

Evacuating the wounded on return flights to France or England bedeviled pilots and their aircrews. Some took time to say hello to the eighteen to twenty casualties on litters as personnel lifted them aboard. Those with serious head injuries or sucking chest wounds were rare but sometimes gingerly carried to a rack. Burn bandages or immobilizing casts covered many.

A flight nurse and medical technician from a Medical Air Evacuation Transport Squadron accompanied them, each patient wearing an emergency medical tag outlining the man's condition and treatment, as well as an envelope filled with his medical records and x-rays. Their litters clamped down onto aluminum racks three high that ran the length of the fuselage. Medical personnel laid those with heavy casts and the wounded requiring more intensive care on lower racks.

Each C-47 became a flying aid station, equipped with plasma, oxygen, morphine, portable heaters, first aid medications, blankets, and splints. If a patient died in flight, medical personnel typically turned his body toward the outside of the fuselage. They then tried to act as normally as possible, while the fuselage often turned hot or cold, and sometimes the smell of burned fresh became nauseating. Smoking might be allowed but only if oxygen was not in use.

The aircrews, meanwhile, pressed ahead without the benefit of a red cross painted on their fuselage since they also carried equipment and supplies, often on the same day. No two flights were the same.

On April 9, an armored unit ran out of gas. German troops had destroyed a twenty-two truck refueling convoy, forcing thirty-four C-47s from the 441st TCG to fly from a base near Paris across the enemy sky with more than 160,000 pounds of gas, 37,000 rounds of ammunition, and 5,400 pounds of K-rations.

Through most of the war, only aircrews that had crashed experienced German mortar fire. Now, after landing, mortar attacks erupted as aircrews helped unload cargo. The German *Granatwerfer* 42 could fire 120mm shells as fast as every six seconds, as far as three miles from the airstrips. Its high rate of fire was as deadly as its accuracy when aircrews and ground personnel gathered around aircraft. Even a short lull in mortar fire could offer hope if the wounded were carried aboard quickly enough. One aircrew waited out a mortar attack and then took on forty-two patients for a hair-raising flight through uncertain skies back to Allied territory.[6]

Among the liberated prisoners of war flown to France were C-47 aircrews whose missions had ended in a crash at Normandy, in Holland, and elsewhere. The chaos they endured under fire became a precursor to how some left Germany after months spent as POWs.

First Lieutenant Robert Webb had been shot down on a supply flight to Bastogne. Artillery fire knocked out his left engine and his elevators. He crash landed, short of his LZ. The engine fire spread to the fuselage, burning Webb on his hands, wrists, face, and neck as he pulled his co-pilot, 2nd Lieutenant Wilson Scott, clear. Scott had suffered a broken leg. Germans captured both immediately.

Following Webb's liberation, he and another C-47 pilot walked eleven miles to an Allied airfield near Giessen.

On April 2, Webb approached Colonel Charles Young who had flown supplies to Giessen. Webb's appearance after three months at the Dulag Luft prisoner camp's evacuation hospital stunned the commanding officer of the 439th TCG. "His faced looked like a skull, he was so thin. He began to talk but could only speak in a very weak voice … [he] started to climb aboard but was too weak to make the first step. He fell, and I caught him … he was only a bunch of bones … [he] had been starved by the Germans. Lieutenant Webb wouldn't have lasted much longer."[7]

"Welcome" parties for the evacuees at French airstrips resembled county fairs, complete with bands, flags, and smart salutes. After the survivors staggered or were carried off C-47s in France, at least one pilot reported his plane was fumigated with DDT powder for lice. Meanwhile, some POWs surrendered to their wounds aboard their liberty aircraft bound for Allied territory.

Some pilots flew POWs in the opposite direction. C-47 pilot Alan Boyd received orders to fly liberated Russian POWs to Russian-held Dresden. Men who "looked like apparitions, walking human scarecrows. They had sunken eyes and hollow cheeks. I didn't know men could be so thin and still be alive … The first man to board the plane fell to his knees and kissed my boots. I'd never felt such a welter of emotion. Shame and pity mixed with riotous other emotions."[8]

Boyd had heard that Russians considered those captured to be cowardly. For the rest of his life, Boyd wondered if the men he had flown to Dresden, so grateful to be alive and perhaps harboring a slim hope that their families, too, had survived, had been executed.

By the end of April, 233,000 POWs had been flown to freedom. On just one day, 19,000 had returned to Allied territory on their journey home.[9]

The stampede across Germany eased with Germany's surrender on May 7. Although supply missions continued, thousands of C-47 pilots, co-pilots, radio operators, navigators, and crew chiefs became aircraft and ship passengers on their way home.

In April, IX Troop Carrier aircrews delivered 60,000 tons of freight that included more than ten million gallons of gasoline. More than four times the freight and fifteen times the volume of fuel delivered in the previous three months combined. Patton and the other Allied generals had received the fuel for which they had pleaded as, more often than not, the aircrews not only delivered the fuel and supplies, but also helped unload it, one five-gallon jerrican at a time, before returning to base.[10]

Approximately 1,500 heavy-duty aircraft had flown 21,000 sorties in just thirty days. Hundreds of those flights were heart-breaking. More than 46,000 wounded troops departed by air, nearly 100 percent of those wounded following Operation *Varsity*. For the first time in World War II, military hospitals remained up to 300 miles behind the frontline, only due to the valor and dedication of the aircrews and flight nurses on the medical evacuation flights, sometimes nonstop to England.

Some, like Flight Officer Lee Whitmire, had flown a circuitous route of service before turning for home. After "The Battle of Burp Gun Corner," he flew C-47 Pipeline missions less than a month later, in part picking up liberated French and British prisoners of war, and in May flew eighteen resupply missions, again returning with freed POWs and slave laborers.

The multi-dimensional role of the C-47 aircrews in the ETO throughout the war and its aftermath would remain unmatched. In Whitmire's case, he finally reached the United States as a second lieutenant in late January 1947, along with Rose-Marie, his wife of one year.

Meanwhile, families of too many aircrew families waited, wondered, and wept as waves of despair swept aside flashes of optimism. The formal letter from Major General J. A. Elio, received by the mothers and fathers of aircrews – such as 2nd Lieutenants Donald Walch and Burton Culp, Staff Sergeant Norman Waxelman, Technical Sergeant George Kelley, and Medical Technician Lloyd Rutan following their disappearance in a cloud bank on April 13 – had offered scant solace.

> "missing in action" ... is not intended to convey the impression that the case is closed ... Experience has shown that many persons reported missing in action are subsequently reported as prisoners of war ... the War Department is helpless to expedite such reports. However, in order to relieve financial worry, Congress has enacted legislation which continues in force the pay, allowances and allotments to dependents of personnel being carried in a missing status. Permit me to extend to you my heartfelt sympathy during this period of uncertainty.[11]

Only eight hours of war in Europe remained at 1600 hours on May 8, 1945. The Germans had surrendered the day before and Hitler had been dead for a week. By the end of April, IX Troop Carrier Command aircrews had used 240 airfields between Cherbourg and

Leipzig. On average, three new airfields joined operational plans every day throughout the marathon.

Not everyone was coasting until they received orders for home, however. At a German airstrip near Czechoslovakia, 179 C-47s had landed, each with a load of gasoline for Allied tanks and trucks. Just across the border, German troops still were fighting.

"Bandit!"

The radio call to a C-47 aircrew that had just landed came as a German Me-109 fighter aircraft circled the airstrip. A quick push of the throttles and a hard turn got the plane off the runway as the German pilot landed.

He had taken off with three other aircraft. One had been shot down, the other two had disappeared. He was alone. Once he disembarked, turned, and faced a group of Americans, he handed over his pistol, knife, and wristwatch.

Captain Richard Overfield, a squadron's commanding officer, stepped forward to give the pilot a cigarette and return his pistol. An officer's gentlemanly gesture between two aviators as the German began to cry. After a moment, he pulled out of his emotional dive, wiped his face with a sleeve, and turned toward the American personnel who had gathered. Perhaps unwittingly, he spoke for all them.

"It's been a long war."[12]

While the Allies' march across Europe dominated much of America's headlines, Allied aircrews flew into the howling sands of the Sahara, deep into South Pacific jungles, and over winter-encrusted Himalayas into China. Supplying. Evacuating. Rescuing. In dust storms, dangerously thin air, blizzards, and terrifying turbulence – as part of an aerial network that stretched across 180,000 square miles.

PART TWO

From the Himalayas to the Sahara

14

Over the Rockpile

We are paying for it in men and airplanes. The kids here are flying over their head [*sic*] – at night and in daytime – and they bust up [the aircraft] for reasons that sometimes seem silly. They are not silly, however, for we are asking boys to do what would be most difficult for men to accomplish; with the experience level here, we are going to pay dearly for the tonnage moved across the Hump … With the men available, there is nothing else to do.[1]

Two weeks after the Japanese had attacked Pearl Harbor, they had invaded Burma, an ideal staging location for attacking India once the Allies had retreated there in May 1942.

Meanwhile, the lion's share of the Imperial Japanese Army had deployed to China, intent on seizing control of its coastline, seagoing ports, and natural resources. Supplying the defending American and Chinese forces in China became critical. When the Japanese cut off the Burma Road supply route to China, the Tenth Air Force's supply campaign over the Hump from India became a primary Allied response to keeping China in the fight and engaging Japanese troops. Retaking Burma to reopen the Burma Road to China also became a priority.

In December 1943, Brigadier General Cyrus Smith, president of American Airlines before the war, was appalled. The US Air Transport Command's attempt at supplying Chinese troops and

American forces by air on the far side of the Himalayan Range from India over the preceding eighteen months had carried a brutal price. In the preceding six months, 135 aircraft had crashed on the Hump route with 168 fatalities. The preceding month, more than one aircraft per day crashed, and now aircrews piloted by mostly first and second lieutenants like Jack Hunter, Peter Dominick, Gibbs Montrose, and others also would be flying night missions for the first time.

To date, their missions had received little notice at home. Many pilots who took off in sweltering monsoons where visibility ended at their wingtips and hours later crossed over the Himalayas in arctic flying conditions considered themselves the "FBI."

The Forgotten Bastards of India.

Supply lines can be any fighting force's Achilles heel. Starving the enemy as a battlefield tactic dates back at least to Sun Tzu's *The Art of War* in the 5th century BC.

By early 1942, Japan had seized China's ports and the southern two-thirds of Burma. General Chiang Kai-shek's nationalist Chinese army and American Brigadier General Claire Chennault's China Air Task Force (the "Flying Tigers") still held much of China's interior. Both had become dependent on a single railway and the Burma Road, a switchback-riddled 717-mile gravel road snaking through jungles and cutting across knife-edge ridges from Lashio in eastern Burma to Kunming in China's eastern Yunnan Province.

When the Japanese cut off the road in March, a new World War II theater metastasized. Four months later, the China–Burma–India Theater (CBI) was established, becoming the western flank of the Allied war against Japan. A viable Chinese fighting force would prevent Japan from moving troops into combat elsewhere and the American air bases in China would be within bombing range of Japan. But only with steady and reliable supplies.

Lieutenant General Joseph Stilwell commanded all US forces in China, Burma, and India. Numbering only about 250,000 personnel, the priority became continuous airborne supply missions to air bases in the Kunming area and in Burma from a cluster of air bases in eastern India's Assam Valley.

No airborne route in World War II approached the dangers and uncertainties of crossing "the rockpile" into China. Once airborne, aircrews looked down on jungles that stretched across the breadth of Burma. They flew over the Patkai Range and cut across the Chindwin River valley framed by the Kumon Mountains rising to 14,000 feet. A series of 15,000-foot serrated ridges loomed ahead, barren rock barriers separated by the West Irrawaddy, East Irrawaddy, and Salween Rivers. Then the Santsung Range, on the far side of the Mekong River, the final obstacle in the steeplechase route flown by often overloaded aircrews.

The missions of 1st Lieutenant Thomas Caldwell and his co-pilot, 2nd Lieutenant Robert Samuel, could not have been more different than their fellow C-47 pilots crossing the English Channel and then France, Holland, or Germany.

Instead, Caldwell and Samuel would push their C-47 beyond its published limits, stretching its 12,000-foot ceiling to 20,000 feet in the Himalayas, despite the lack of engine turbochargers that made higher altitude missions possible. Sturdy, reliable, and "loyal" in many pilots' views, its limited payload became a drawback when Tenth Air Force units – later under Air Traffic Command (ATC) – began operating in the summer of 1942 and soon expanded operations.

In early 1943, the Curtiss C-46 augmented the C-47 force, featuring twice the payload and far more power and a higher ceiling for flying "over the roof of the world." Seventy-six feet long with a 108-foot wingspan, a 15,000-pound payload, 27,000-foot ceiling and maximum 3,000-mile range, it was ideal for the Himalayas. But the C-46 was rushed to India and would require hundreds of modifications as design and persistent operating defects became evident and deadly.

The two aircraft would ultimately account for nearly two-thirds of the planes flying over the Hump. The C-47s and C-46s would carve out a unique legacy, long before they joined forces in Operation *Varsity* two years later. The four-engine Douglas C-54 (twice again as large as the C-46) and two variants of the B-24 Liberator bomber (C-87 for cargo and the C-109 tanker) would augment the airborne fleet flying into China.

The steadily increasing supply demands of General Chiang and those of General Chennault's troops would place extraordinary demands on Stilwell's aircrews and fledgling aircraft fleet. Even a 5,000 ton-per-month goal bordered on unrealistic. Every gallon of fuel, all weapons and the ammunition and even food and all living supplies needed by American troops in China had to be flown in across hundreds of miles over perhaps the most treacherous terrain on earth.

Perhaps "Ol' Dumbo" might meet China's supply needs. Second Lieutenant Jack Hunter, 1st Lieutenant Harry Poppell, Jr, and others would wrestle an aircraft with a massive payload, turbo-charged power, and that featured a ceiling approaching Mount Everest's summit. Ideal on paper, Hunter, Poppell, and others learned its design flaws made it marginally better than an experimental aircraft still in development. "The C-46 had a pretty rough time in the early days of the war. Military necessity put it to work in a faraway theater before all the bugs were worked out it," admitted General Arnold in the introduction to the 1945 C-46 training manual.[2]

The defects that would make it deadly in Operation *Varsity* were equally lethal in clear skies. Engines tended to fail on takeoff, causing crashes with four tons of high-octane fuel aboard. As pilots pushed their throttles forward, even in ideal conditions, training had taught them to always anticipate that something would go wrong. That could eliminate a split second's indecision and disaster.

Fuel leaks in flight were prevalent, leading to midair explosions from a wayward spark. Heaters malfunctioned at 20,000 feet. In the monsoon season, it leaked like a colander through cock-pit windows. "Ol' Dumbo" rivaled "Flying Coffin," "Curtiss Calamity," and "Plumber's Nightmare" as various pilots' preferred nicknames.

"Mayday! Mayday!"

No war zone flight route approached the severity and unpredictability of that faced by 1st Lieutenant Gibbs Monrose and hundreds of other C-46 co-pilots, navigators, radio operators, and flight engineers. From India's sauna jungles over the Himalayas to a mile-high plateau in western China and back, aircrews endured a bevy of enemies unique in World War II.

Seasonal weather over the Himalayas conspired against every supply mission. Pilots learned to scan for cumulus clouds that held lightning and rain that pummeled the fuselage as if a popcorn popper had gone berserk and that forced the aircrew to shout. In the spring, thunderstorms billowed to 38,000 feet, beyond the aircrafts' maximum ceiling. Icing conditions developed at 15,000 feet where crystals "the size of rocks" hid. Turbulence, unimaginable and hidden within the thunderstorms, threatened to pulverize planes as aircrews pitched and rolled in an airborne rodeo. The pounding some aircrews endured resembled a prize fight with an unseen foe.

Winds reaching 100 miles per hour glanced off barren slopes to create updrafts as powerful as a rocket launch and then their mirrored downdrafts on the ridges' far sides into desolate valleys forced descents up to 5,000 feet per minute (eighty-three feet per second). In a split second, the next updraft could yank an aircrew back toward the stratosphere. Wind so severe that it was difficult to focus on the cockpit's instruments as it jammed bodies against seatbacks and yanked against harnesses.

> I was forced to turn back in a C-47 on account of heavy ice
> and violent updrafts associated with turbulence … Ice was
> encountered at 16,000 feet … A free air temperature of plus
> 2 degrees Centigrade … [After changing course to a lower
> altitude] updrafts struck the airplane … very clear ice formed,
> blacking out all radio reception and covering the side windows
> of the windshield so that the wings were no longer discernable.
> I judged this ice came from freezing rain …[3]

Prophetically, pilots in C-46 aircraft had learned in training that "it is possible to meet gusts which impose greater stress on the airplane than that for which the structure was designed."[4]

With mountain ridges at 20,000 feet topped by thunderstorms or lashed by polar-worthy gales, only the captains of ships cresting the North Atlantic's forty-foot waves, icy water, and freezing, horizontal sleet experienced anything similar.

Aside from gut-wrenching storms, 100-mile-per-hour winds directly from the south at every flyable altitude pushed aircrews on east–west routes well to the north and into the Himalayas.

May through October brought steaming monsoon downpours totaling more than 100 inches per year. At times, the landing gear of aircraft acted as keels as they plowed to a stop in ankle-deep muck after a mission.

Tumultuous and often unpredictable flying conditions awaiting aircrews flying overloaded aircraft over the Hump increased the risk of crashing. More than half the time, the cargo consisted of dozens of fifty-five-gallon drums of gasoline for ground operations as well as 100-octane fuel for aircraft in China. If one of the notorious C-46s' leaks developed mid-flight or if turbulence knocked a drum loose, the aircrew could be incinerated by a single spark. More benign loads weighing several tons included ammunition, engines, bombs, ordnance, and even Chinese soldiers. If the supply run from India included more than one landing in China, an aircrew sometimes grabbed a meal and coffee at one stop before making their four- to five-hour flight back to base in India.

On one midwinter day, a massive storm brought down fifteen aircraft with winds so wicked that they pushed helpless aircrews fifty miles off course and into mountains, nowhere near their expected route of flight. One C-46 was shot upward on an ascent rate of 4,000 feet a minute by a vicious updraft. Suddenly, dirt from the floor rained down on the pilot, 1st Lieutenant Thomas Sykes, hanging by his shoulder straps, when his C-46 flipped over onto its back. Bailing out was impossible. He and his co-pilot arm wrestled the Commando back into an upright position. *Now what? Do we press ahead?* "We had been in the air quite long and decided that our destination must be closer than the point of departure. We turned and bucked our way through the storm and made it," Sykes reported later.[5]

Just as the C-46 was coming on line, the stakes of conquering the Hump by air increased when Allied leaders attached a greater priority to opposing the Japanese in the Pacific and southeast Asia. That, in part, placed a premium on increasing monthly supply quotas flown over the Himalayas upwards to 10,000 tons per month.

As the supply missions intensified later that year, many aircrews exceeded 100 flight hours a month, returning to their Assam Valley base in the summer when temperatures exceeded 100 degrees in the monsoon season, so hot that ground crews risked second-degree burns by working on exposed aircraft metal during the day.

General Chiang Kai-shek soon pleaded for 10,000 tons a month to supply his army and later would increase his demands further. In the first six months of "uptempo" operations, 150 aircraft accidents and losses caused 160 crew fatalities. "It was safer to take a bomber deep into Germany than to fly a transport plane over the Rockpile from one friendly nation to another," wrote the general who soon would take command of the supply mission.[6] Maintenance inexperience, parts shortages, and the intolerable aircrew losses fueled plunging morale.

From the beginning, the pilot corps had been a mixed bag. Experienced commercial airline pilots had been recruited or called to active duty. Stateside flight instructors were summoned, and freshly trained pilots – their dreams of flying fighter aircraft aside – received orders for the CBI Theater. Many needed C-46 training once they arrived in India.[7]

The deadly ante rose in October when a spate of daytime Japanese fighter attacks led to the institution of night flights. Around-the-clock flight operations began in November, just as winter loomed. At 15,000 feet, night temperatures of -15 degrees Fahrenheit (-26° Celsius) were not uncommon. Visibility was "near-zero" the entire length of several trips, forcing 1st Lieutenant Ned Thomas piloting his C-47 to "trust my instruments" for hundreds of miles. Pilot error crashes jumped from five to nineteen per month.[8]

Night flights over the Hump were otherworldly. On a clear night, an inkwell black coated the sky above the peaks with a salt-shaker's worth of stars ablaze. At lower elevations over Burma's jungles and then the broader expanses of China, cooking fires, torches, and perhaps lanterns revealed otherwise invisible villages, flickering and fleeting far below. The route's recognizable land-marks – peaks, valleys, ridges, open plains, rivers, changes in foliage – had disappeared after sunset. Night flying was instru-ment flying. Faith flying.

The missions, already blind dates in a sense, were exhausting. The call for a night mission often arrived with only a few hours' notice. Thomas often did not know who his co-pilot or his crew would be. An early-night departure might mean he would not "hit the rack" until the sun curtain had risen the following day. In the monsoon season, the heat would be so unbearable that when he awakened four hours after a mission the suffocating, sweaty humidity already had heated his bamboo barracks to ninety-five degrees Fahrenheit (35° C/Celsius).

Gasoline was an omnipresent co-conspirator with weather on missions, especially at night. The fuel capacity in aircraft – especially the C-47 – heading to China had a slim margin of error beginning with takeoff. A timer in the back of every pilot's mind counted down to when his fuel would be exhausted. The slightest delay, unexpected turbulence, or detour threatened survival. Gasoline was so valuable at the Chinese airfields that using it for runway lights was borderline heresy and draining a bit of "excess" fuel by ground crews before an inattentive aircrew's return flight was common. A pilot's fuel was as precious as gold.

Usually about mid-flight, Thomas knew when to initiate Himalayan fuel rationing procedures. First, reduce power and avoid climbing if at all possible. *Keep it at 140 but watch my stall speed.* Then adjust the tank selector to drain one fuel tank "down to the fumes," then switch to another. With luck, the engines gagged and then fired off again, perhaps with a "thunk" that shook the plane with the return of fuel flow. *Watch my wing weight, keep her balanced. How can I increase the distance with the fuel I've got? Time to start a slow descent ahead of schedule. Gotta put gravity to work to build some speed. Enough? Closer now.*

"Hankow tower. Calling for landing instructions. Low fuel, request direct approach to runway."

"Roger. Come in, 1826. Over."

The authorization every pilot wanted, needed really, to hear. Thomas landed at the Hankow airfield, less than a minute before both engines coughed a quick death.[9]

Some aircrew losses in 1942 and 1943 were as baffling as a mystery novel. First Lieutenant Sidney David flew his C-47 toward Kunming on a moderately clear day when "for some reason [it] was lost enroute [to] this station." Second Lieutenant John Lengel was bound for a Chinese airstrip in a C-46. His Missing Air Crew Report simply stated the reason for his disappearance as "unknown." Speculation became Flight Officer William James' epitaph after his C-47 disappeared due to a "lack of proper direction finding radio equipment facilities."[10]

Some pilots who had successfully crossed the Himalayas and had settled into a textbook approach in China flew their planes straight into the ground, killing everyone aboard. The clues led to a startling discovery. A few "tough guy" pilots had eschewed their oxygen masks, despite flying at a 17,000-foot minimum and often at 25,000 feet. The resulting lack of oxygen – anoxia – had clouded their vision and mind up to the moment of impact. Flight surgeons began preaching the value of oxygen, although at least one commanding officer groused about having "to tell men over the age of twenty-one years old that they needed oxygen" for missions over the Himalayas.[11]

As General Chiang pleaded for more supplies, spit-and-polish General William Tunner took command of the China–Burma–India division of the Air Transport Command on September 4, 1944. "A new sheriff is in town," mused one pilot, after learning there now would be strict discipline throughout the ranks, a production-line maintenance program would be instituted, and that pilots would have to stay in theater a full year and fly more hours than had been required to rotate out.

Four months later, the CBI airborne campaign had increased its monthly delivery to 34,000 tons monthly.

The campaign had become "big business." Larger aircraft, C-54s, were arriving in theater, carrying triple the payload of a C-47. Once General Stilwell had captured an airfield near Myitkyina in Burma early in the year, a southern route skirting the bulk of the Himalayas was feasible and considered easier, although those aircrews would be flying across more than 150 miles of Japanese-held jungle.

Shootdowns on airborne missions in Europe ended in one of two places: Allied territory or German territory. In the China–Burma–India Theater, a third fate loomed. Purgatory in Burma's jungles. Hundreds of square miles so dense that a yell for help traveled less than 150 feet. Where Japanese patrols shared footpaths with the affable Abor, the sullen Mishmi tribes in the north, and the head-hunting Nagas in the south.

Survival prospects for downed airmen were generally dim from the outset, often due to their physical condition. Malaria, diarrhea, and dysentery were pervasive enemies at many Allied air bases. A sanitation report at one base in China referred to "dead bodies floating ... above the original source of the base water supply ... Water used for sterilizing dishes ... is, in fact, a form of soup with a basic foreign element of well-cooked feces and red mud."[12]

Yet aircrews stood a chance of surviving Burma's jungles with luck and the modest survival training they had received. They learned panic was an enemy equal to the Japanese. First and foremost, "Don't rush. Think things out, then act." For some, malaria could be a crewman's worst enemy, his doses of quinine and atabrine his greatest friend if he had his first aid kit. Local tribes could be their most valuable ally. ("Jungle natives will be friendly ... don't try to bully them," emphasized their training manual.) Finally, stay with the crashed plane if at all possible. It will be far easier for a rescue plane to spot from the air.[13]

But each crash brought its own opportunities and threats. A wrecked plane in a deep ravine would be difficult to spot from the air. Shelter and water were godsends to a crewman who had bailed out and landed on a mountainside ledge exposed to downpours.

First Lieutenant Harry Poppell, Jr's preflight midwinter weather report had looked benign by Himalayan standards. "Few thunderheads and plenty of hail." "Icing and hail at 17,500 feet." But as he and his crew approached Burma's extreme northeastern corner, their C-46 suddenly felt as though it had taken an overhead karate chop at 23,000 feet. Poppell and his co-pilot, 2nd Lieutenant John Starling, had been flying on instruments while in the clouds. Now, a dastardly downdraft was flying the plane.

Full power and an open throttle were useless as they dropped 2,000 feet per minute. "Push out the cargo and get your chute," Poppell instructed his flight engineer, Corporal John Wyatt. Then, at 19,000 feet, "Haughton, [radio operator] get your chute and help Wyatt." They continued to sink. At 15,000 feet and below nearby mountaintop peaks, Starling strapped on his chute and took control so Poppell could do the same.

"Get out!"

Starling jumped and Wyatt followed. Houghton hesitated.

The explosion seconds later rocked Starling and Wyatt's open chutes. Starling landed in the jungle, Wyatt on a mountain ledge in a downpour with second- and third-degree leg burns. The supply mission had morphed into two missions of survival.

Both were lucky, landing among the Kachin people of Burma. With Japanese troops only one-half mile away, Nee Chiang guided Starling over a 12,000-foot ridge before snow and the absence of food and blankets forced them to return to Nee Chiang's hut. Wyatt had been led to a cave by another Kachin, Yo Yin, because Japanese troops were in Yin's nearby village. Days passed as the Japanese searched the crash area.

Almost a week passed before a group of Kachin carried Wyatt to a British outpost, and days later several Kachin men and Starling hiked over a snow-covered mountain to another outpost. Blisters covered Starling's feet along with hundreds of bites "from every kind of jungle bug."

Poppell and Houghton's bodies remained in the wreckage.

Daily, it seemed, aircrews faced emergencies, many unique, others expected, and some unfolding as quickly as a one-act play.

If an engine suddenly died at 20,000 feet, the pilots knew to feather its propeller, shut off its fuel, turn off relevant switches, and institute an "idle cutoff" by fully closing its carburetor mixture valve. *But don't get featheritis!*, they had been told in training. Make sure the engine could not be restarted and then go to single-propeller flight procedures. *Advance the prop control and throttle on the good engine. Move mixture control to "Auto Rich." Remember, you may have to use fuel from the tanks on the bad engine ... warn the engineer to be ready to turn on the cross-feed valve at your order.*

Aircrews in four-engine aircraft sometimes faced cascading emergencies. On one flight as the aircrew exited a thunderstorm, its number four cylinder head temperature dropped. Closing the cowl flap didn't help. *Is the instrument just bad?* But then its oil temperature shot upward just before its oil pressure dropped. *We're dropping fast. Shut it down, see if we can get back to base.* With only ten pounds of oil pressure, the pilot, 2nd Lieutenant Peter Dominick, decided to restart the engine, searching for any power to claw back up to 16,000 feet. Then the supercharger regulator on a second engine failed. An oscillating manifold pressure gauge hinted at possible piston damage. The aircrew reached their base before the second sickly engine quit that would have transformed the emergency into a crisis.[14, 15]

Experience became the savior for many aircrews as they navigated through one mid-flight crisis after another. On another mission, Dominick fought an unseen downdraft, almost to a draw. "[The aircraft's] controls tightened up. No ice. Next the plane did its best to turn over four times. Schnitz (co-pilot) and I were both using full controls, throttle wide open, and stick full-forward. Sixty degrees from one side to the other it lurched, and then slowly straightened out ... After it was over, the controls felt like mildewed bananas ... all I needed was one engine to sputter, and we would have all jumped ... decided to land, which we did at 150 miles per hour."[16] The two pilots inspected their C-87 once they landed. They could find nothing amiss, yet Peter Dominick felt "we were as close to crashing as I've ever been."[17]

Post-mission reports by others often carried a contemplative tone, recorded in Dominick's diary: "one engine caught fire on takeoff," "lost one engine over the Hump and seen going down on instruments at night on the Hump," "overshot the runway on three engines at night," "chased off a runway by bombing raids," "flown 700 miles by dead reckoning," "lost at night in thunderstorms," "flown through more thunderstorms than I knew existed," "weighted down with ice with a snow storm in the cockpit," "let down [landed] from between thunderstorms from 20,000 feet ... and yet I've never quite had to bail out."[18]

The Hump gods seemed to conspire against pilots on missions. On one occasion, a pilot returned to base when a gasoline drum leaked. On his second takeoff attempt, an engine tachometer failed. Back to base. On his third try, fire erupted from behind his instrument panel. The crew donned parachutes, but managed to return to base. That was enough. Maybe tomorrow. If a high-octane fuel drum began leaking, the aircrew's eyes burned and watered. A leak could become so serious that a momentary electrical short might detonate the flying gas station. Earlier, a fireball twenty-five miles away by an aircraft carrying fuel drums crashed and mesmerized the aircrew.[19]

By early 1945, aircrews and ground personnel had developed an efficient operation worthy of any assault. Monthly deliveries now steadily reached 30,000 tons per month and continued to increase. The relatively new southern "Easy" route was more direct at a lower altitude, but over enemy-held territory. "Charlie," the northern route, crossed more mountains but was now out of the enemy's aircraft range. Together, the airborne "freeway" between the Assam Valley and eastern China grew to 200 miles in width and extended across more than 1,000 miles as aircrews flew at prescribed altitudes ranging from 18,000 to 25,000 feet in each direction.

Six hundred and fifty aircraft were taking off every twenty-four hours (every two minutes) in the push to increase monthly tonnage, weather be damned. It was common knowledge that if a pilot could see the end of the runway, the weather was good enough for takeoff.[20]

Aircrews' nerves became casualties. Poor weather never abated, it seemed. Despite modifications, the C-46 remained a dreaded aircraft. Death loomed in the jungle below. Emergency landing in friendly territory was a fantasy. It was widely believed that a major portion of the supplies delivered by aircrews were used by nationalist General Chiang Kai-shek in his civil war against communist forces or found their way into the hands of Japanese troops via Chinese warlords. At one point, officers transferred one in five pilots home after in-theater treatment for "battle fatigue" proved ineffective.[21] "Fair weather pilots," veteran aircrews called them.

Unexplained crashes and the disappearance of aircrews continued to mount and unsettle.

Some of those aircrews remained entombed in the Himalayas at war's end, covered in mystery. First Lieutenant John Deaux had taken off from Yunnanyi in China, bound for Misamari in India's Assam Valley. A routine mid-morning flight, according to mission planners' reports, with only low clouds in the valleys en route after departing through modestly low cloud cover at Yunnanyi. Second Lieutenant Edgar Corbiere occupied the co-pilot's seat while Corporal Paul Pakari sat at the radio operator's table in front of a full cargo load.

They were never heard from again. No witnesses to their disappearance, no reports of a crash from villagers along the presumed route of flight. The subsequent seven-page Missing Air Crew Report simply concluded, "Information not available."

The ATC's Intelligence Office Rescue Unit ultimately learned what had happened, but only partially. A search party, with the aid of two Tibetans, found the wreckage in northern Burma, spread across a towering mountainside. The tail rested about 900 feet downhill from the bulk of the mangled C-47. Both sections had burned. The remains of Corbiere and Pakari were identified, and a third corpse must have been Deaux. All three were buried at the crash site. The search party's final report became a cryptic epitaph. "The trip required 55 days of very difficult mountain climbing but resulted in solution of a long standing mystery." The where, but not the why. Paraki's sister in Barnesville, Ohio, Corbiere's wife in Las Vegas, Nevada, and Deaux's father in Portland, Tennessee, would only learn a brother, husband, and son had died on a mountain more than 8,000 miles from home.

In August 1945, CBI missions set a twenty-four-hour record with 1,118 roundtrips delivering 5,327 tons, the equivalent of the one-month goal only three years earlier.[22] The fleet averaged two roundtrips per aircraft. An aircrew crossed the Hump every forty seconds. Four times a minute, a ton of cargo arrived in China. Remarkably, there were no accidents in that one-day period.

By the end of the month, aircrews delivered more than 70,000 tons. For the entire month only twenty accidents marred 136,000 flight hours. The accident rate now was one tenth of that which the aircrews had suffered in the previous two years.[23] While still dangerous, pilots had mastered the nuances of the longest and most dangerous airborne supply route of World War II.

By war's end, eighty-one percent of the supplies received by Allied forces in China (650,000 tons) had arrived by a fleet that had grown to 640 aircraft supported by 84,000 personnel. More than sixty percent were C-46s and C-47s.[24] The Hump became "the proving ground, if not the birthplace of mass strategic airlift … even under the most unfavorable circumstances, if only the men who controlled the aircraft, the terminals and needed materiel were willing to pay the price in money and men … [they] made it possible to conceive [and implement] the Berlin airlift of 1948–49."[25]

The pioneering courage of the aircrews came at an extraordinary cost. C-47 and C-46 carcasses became mile markers on the routes into China, leading to its nickname, "Aluminum Alley," by the end of the war. Even with incomplete records in the early years, one historian compiled losses that approached 3,500 crewmen in less than four years.[26] Official Army Air Forces reports pegged the deaths at more than 1,300 in about 600 aircraft accidents and losses, generally considered to be conservative in retrospect.

Since its establishment on June 22, 1942, Air Traffic Command had been responsible for both the accomplishments and costs of flying the Hump in a region that many aircrews believed became the stepchild theater of World War II.

Only five months after ATC's establishment, thirty-nine C-47 aircrews had completed a 1,500-mile, one-way night mission from England to the edge of the Sahara in North Africa. They, too, had endured suspect aircraft, cruel weather, unreliable radio communications, zero visibility, unreliable navigation aids, and the prospect of enemy attack while "flying blind." In their case, not knowing if they were bound for friendly or enemy territory.

Flying Blind

The cadre of strangers had gathered at two heavily guarded airfields on a remote stretch of southwest England – appropriately named Land's End – some arriving on the day of their mission. Speculation among the nearly 200 C-47 pilots, co-pilots, navigators, radio operators, and crew chiefs had evaporated two days earlier on November 5, 1942, when a parade of briefing officers walked them through their first airborne combat mission. Those men – Operations, Intelligence, Weather, Communications, and others – were as green as the aircrews selected for the mission.

Operation *Torch* would become one of the most inadequately briefed, prepped, and equipped airborne combat missions of World War II, as the precursor to the Sicily, France, Holland, and Germany missions that would follow. Thirty-nine aircrews from the 60th TCG would fly the mission, without the benefit of a full rehearsal or recent training flights.[1] They would fly almost 1,100 miles, so close to their C-47s' maximum range that ground crews secured two fifty-gallon drums of additional fuel in each fuselage. Most would carry up to fourteen paratroopers (averaging 260 pounds each, including their gear) and an equipment container weighing 250 pounds attached to a red parachute, totaling two tons of cargo.

The aircrews would be carrying paratroopers on one of the longest unescorted AAF missions of the war in a new, not-yet-fully tested, and unarmored aircraft. At night, from England to North Africa.

Sergeants Michael Saunders, Shelby Wood, Edward Cohen, and other radio operators had not been given adequate time or opportunity to test and familiarize themselves with newly installed VHF equipment. Navigators, including 2nd Lieutenants Harry Boyle, Vincent Pettigrew, and Harold Kenner, later would discover that mission planners had overlooked key topography features in their destination's region. Second Lieutenants Allen Adair, Ira Long, and Edmund Berry III, co-pilots on the mission, would find the "weather guessers" had failed to predict a wicked wind, strong enough to push their C-47s fifty miles off course. One briefing mistakenly focused on the Gibraltar region instead of Oran, Algeria, the mission's objective roughly 260 miles away on the other side of the Mediterranean.[2]

A year earlier, the AAF had received only 255 C-47s. Its fledgling aircrews had rarely dropped more than a company of paratroopers in training. Some were hardly out of school while others were married. Almost none had substantial flying experience. Second Lieutenant William McLoughry had attended a military boarding school and had become an Eagle Scout before dropping out of college after his sophomore year. Newly married, the co-pilot's wife was pregnant back home. After attending Catholic schools as a boy, 1st Lieutenant Joe Beck had graduated Carnegie Institute of Technology in Pittsburgh with a degree in engineering. He had earned his wings eighteen months earlier, McLoughry only seven months prior. McLoughry and Beck had been born only four days apart and were twenty-three years old.

The Allied landings in North Africa would become their battlefield christening, a battalion-sized combat airborne test flight, and an ambitious execution of the battlefield paratrooper strategy.

That baptism had been brewing for more than two years as British, German, and Italian forces fought for control of Libya, Egypt, and the shipping routes through the Suez Canal. Meanwhile, the French Vichy Regime's Marshall Philippe Pétain commanded 125,000 troops in Morocco, Tunisia, and Algeria. The British had advanced 600 miles westward from El Alamein in early1942 before Field Marshal Erwin Rommell and his German Afrika Corps arrived in Tripoli, Lybia in February.

When the Allies agreed in July 1942 to open a second front along the North Africa coast, a new World War II battleground had been set. A three-prong amphibious landing strategy would stretch across nearly 800 miles of coastline from Morocco to Algeria. Three task forces would comprise Operation *Torch*. The 102-ship Western Task Force would arrive from the US with 25,000 troops coming ashore near Casablanca. Taking Algiers would be the objective of the Eastern Task Force sailing from England with 33,000 British and US troops in fifty-two ships. With airborne support, the 39,000-troop Center Task Force in forty-two ships would come ashore near Oran, about in the middle of the Vichy French troops' position. H-hour was scheduled for 0500, more than two hours ahead of sunrise on November 8.

Two months earlier, Major William Yarborough, the airborne advisor to General Mark Clark, commander of the US Second Corps, had pitched the concept of paratroopers supporting a portion of Operation *Torch*. He argued the tactic of confounding the enemy by a seemingly inconceivable airborne mission would batter the enemy's morale when 500 paratroopers suddenly landed in the enemy's defensive center. He maintained there was enough time left to adequately train for the mission and a night flight would not require fighter escort. He acknowledged the risks included the unproven size of the mission, paratroopers in aircraft at 10,000 feet without oxygen, minimal navigation resources, and aircraft without blackout curtains or flame dampeners, the navigation lights of which would be visible from the ground.[3]

Colonel William Bentley, Jr, Lieutenant Colonel Thomas Schofield, Major Jesse Tobler, and Major Frederick Sherwood were among the most experienced pilots in the 60th TCG.[4] They would lead four flights ("A," "B," "C," and "D") of aircrews (three groups of ten aircraft, one with nine) to an airfield, Tafaraoui, about 15 miles south of Oran in western Algeria. About ten miles away, another airfield, La Senia, would be a second objective. The battle plan was straightforward: deliver 531 paratroopers of the 2nd Battalion, 509th Parachute Infantry to Tafaraoui and take control of its hard-surface airfield and then march on La Senia. Both airfields sat on the edge of a twenty-five-square-mile, mostly dry lake, Sebkra d'Oran (Sebkra). The aircrews would drop their paratroopers before dawn near Tafaraoui if they encountered Vichy French resistance. In the absence of any resistance, the aircrews would land at La Senia after sunrise. Seizing the two Algerian airfields would provide air bases for fighter groups staged at Gibraltar, enable air cover for the amphibious landings as much as forty-five miles away, and establish a destination for subsequent reinforcement and supply flights.

Setting down on the dry lake bed was an option for both plans, if necessary. Regardless, it would be a one-way trip with a very slim margin of error in fuel consumption.

Secrecy was as paramount as training. Takeoffs from England would send the aircrews on a westerly heading before turning south to cross the Bay of Biscay west of France (to avoid enemy radar and potential airborne interceptors) on a straight south-southeasterly course to North Africa. There would be almost no visual landmarks on an overnight route that would cross Spain's coastal mountains and continue south, overfly the Madrid region, and then across the Mediterranean to Algeria. Emergency landing locations would be dicey at best, given Germany's occupation of France and Spain's fascist government and Axis sympathizers.

Major Clarence Galligan, Captain Robert Barrere, and the other pilots could not be sure if the French Vichy government (that collaborated with the Germans) in control of Algeria and Morocco would oppose the Allied landings and airborne assault or stand aside. Weeks of negotiations had not yielded solid assurances, and the final decision might become evident only when the aircrews reached Algeria. *Do we make our eight-hour flight in time to drop our paratroopers at 0500 hours if we think there will be resistance or delay our takeoffs to arrive over Algeria after sunrise if we've been assured the coast will be clear?* Uncertainty made both flight plans a gamble.

Although the 60th TCG had several of the AAF's most-experienced pilots (some with more than 1,000 flight hours), the aircrews were impossibly inexperienced and unproven. Only a few navigators had more than fifty hours' experience. Just a handful had demonstrated celestial navigation proficiency on what would be a tar-black night once a sliver of moon set at 0300 hours, possibly about the time the aircrews would be crossing Spain's Sierra Nevada mountains. (The C-47s' overhead astrodome size also limited sextant use.)

Maps and charts were in such short supply that they had been issued only to the flight leaders' navigators, 1st Lieutenant Frederick Jenks and 2nd Lieutenants William O'Conner, Thomas Dukes, and Arnold Anex. Similarly, only the flight leaders' radio operators – Captain Edward Payeski, Technical Sergeant Garard Push, Master Sergeant Carl Hahn, and Staff Sergeant Carl Bixby, Jr – had been issued Eureka equipment to home in on their ultimate destination.

By 1700 hours on November 7, paratroopers filled thirty-nine C-47s, the aircrews of which had settled into their seats and had warmed their engines. Everyone sat, cramped, and waited. At the last minute, an "Advance Alexis" message arrived (known as the "peace plan"), signifying the Vichy government would not oppose Operation *Torch*. After a four-hour takeoff delay in England, a sunrise landing at the two airfields had become the mission.

"Okay, load 'em up. Next stop, North Africa!"

The flare arcing across the airstrip signified the start of Operation *Torch*. The four flight leaders led their groups aloft in forty minutes, starting at 2105 hours. None had flown a "house of cards" mission built on a marathon night route, secrecy, a destination in flux, expected foul weather, and aircrew inexperience. Once all had taken off and assembled into the prescribed formation, they entered an alien universe.

"Blue, red, green, and white running lights ... intermingled with the stars ... It was as if we were circling in a huge planetarium with the universes all around, as if ... we were circling to find a haven on the land there below," recalled Lieutenant Colonel Edson Raff, the tough, fearless, and aggressive commanding officer of the 509th.[5] Cramped paratroopers faced a long flight after the delay. A handful passed out gum, hoping it would stem possible airsickness. Others ate a chocolate bar or gnawed on a hardtack British Army biscuit or two. The steady, growling drone of the C-47s at flying speed put many to sleep.

Almost immediately, the fleet's formation frayed over the Bay of Biscay. Stragglers fell back shortly after takeoff and more fell behind when pilots made the only turn on the mission to a 177-degree heading. Still more struggled to hold their prescribed 135 miles-per-hour speed. Some fell behind as they dodged rain squalls. One of the flight leaders, Major Sherwood, discovered that activating his running lights in hopes of maintaining visual contact and speed between aircrews did not help. When the four groups reached Spain's coast, they had to clear 8,000-foot coastal mountains. Still more aircrews fell behind as they lost airspeed on their ascent to 10,000 feet. The flock had irreparably scattered.

As they met a predicted storm over Spain, the aircrews had become "completely dispersed. Not more than two planes in any element or three in any flight were able to stay together."[6] Flying only with dimmed formation lights, maintaining visual contact had become a memory. Radio operators in each of the four groups called their flight leaders but heard no reply. Or perhaps they did, but the newly installed VHF equipment malfunctioned. Second Lieutenant navigators Richard Smith, Raymond Glasgow, Julius LaCroix, and the rest of the non-flight leader navigators had no detailed maps and only eleven had American-issued navigation equipment with which they were familiar.

A splintered mission of solo flights prevailed by the time the bulk of the aircraft had reached Spain's Sierra Nevada mountains. Working by flashlight, his head navigator sat hunched over his table as Lieutenant Colonel Schofield, the 60th TCG's commanding officer, had reached his 10,000-foot altitude. Cabin lights had been turned off as paratroopers pulled up blankets and fell asleep. Snoring had battled engine noise in the gloom as eleven paratroopers approached their first battle.

They had little choice but to place their trust in the stranger sitting in the pilot's seat. Schofield led "Flight B" and was one of ten aircraft carrying the 509th's headquarters company, including the 509th's commanding officer, Lieutenant Colonel Edson Raff, Major Yarborough, and paratroopers.

As the aircrews struggled to find their bearings and each other, more than 530 paratroopers now were spread across the Spanish night sky, too many headed for the edge of the Sahara hundreds of miles from their briefed destination and mission.

Across the fractured formation, each pilot confronted a critical decision. *Do I circle over the storm until daybreak to find my bearings? Can I rely on the dead reckoning skills of my inexperienced navigator and press ahead? But if we're more than two degrees off course when we reach the Med, we likely will be out of range of the homing beacons. Gotta decide, fuel's getting low.*[7]

The aircrews were flying without visual cues and would become equally deaf. The Royal Navy's HMS *Alynbank* sailed thirty-five miles off Algeria's coast with orders to send homing signals at 1130 hours. The ship's crew also stood ready to flash a "V" signal when the airborne fleet approached within twenty miles. But, incredibly, the crew dialed the wrong frequency. If the aircrews heard anything on the prescribed frequency, it was unintelligible.

Perhaps the radio operators flying with the group commanders would pick up a Eureka radar signal sent by an OSS agent, Gordon Browne known as "Bantam," near Tafaraoui, assuming they somehow still were on course. But he had destroyed his equipment at 1130 hours (as per orders) when he had not received word that the mission had been delayed by several hours.

"Play ball! Play ball!"

Not only had the intended navigation broadcasts failed, but the rules of engagement had also changed since the aircrews had departed English air space. The coded baseball message broadcast separately by the *Alynbank* alerted the inbound aircrews that Vichy Marshal Philippe Pétain had turned on the Allies when he issued a new order to "resist the invaders with every means at your disposal." But, still on the wrong frequency, the alert never reached the aircrews. French fighter pilots and artillery units prepared to engage the inbound aircrews as they scanned the African horizon for anything familiar before they ran out of fuel.

This doesn't look right. Those hills and the shoreline. I don't think that's Algeria. Operation *Torch's* battle plan had been flipped into confusion as the aircrews approached Africa. An unexpectedly stout crosswind from the east had pushed many aircraft more than fifty miles off course to the west toward Spanish Morocco. A few were as much as 250 miles astray toward French Morocco. The briefers' lack of attention to Moroccan topography removed any chance that Captains Jack Worley and William Raymond or 1st Lieutenant Richard Litsey could somehow turn east and reach Algeria. Low on fuel and uncertain on their precise location, the three aircrews landed 250 miles from Oran in Spanish Morocco where they were "interned" by authorities for three months. Captain Ivan Stracener also landed in Spanish Morocco, but managed to unload his troops, refuel, and fly on to the dry lake bed near his original objective.

Two others refueled in Spanish Morocco and continued on to Casablanca in French Morocco. Their flight ended more than 400 miles from their assigned destination.

Two other aircrews landed in French Morocco. Low on fuel, Captain Charles Light ordered his paratroopers to jump before landing where his aircrew was taken prisoner by the French. First Lieutenant George Vaughn and his co-pilot, McLoughry, suffered a similar fate. The wings on their C-47 had iced as they flew through Spain's tempestuous clouds. When a hole appeared in the haze over Africa, they spotted a French flag on an airfield and landed. Their aircrew was also briefly taken prisoner. Both aircrews were released five days later.[8]

Where are we?

One pilot, Colonel William Bentley, had to ask for directions to Oran. Flying the lead aircraft in Operation *Torch*, nothing below looked familiar after he crossed Africa's shoreline. With less than two hours' fuel left, he landed and learned from some Arabs he was

100 miles west of his drop zone. He took off, rejoined other C-47s that had been circling overhead, and headed for Sebkra.

A ninth aircrew with 1st Lieutenant Kenneth McCormick in the pilot's seat never made it across the Mediterranean. Almost out of fuel, he landed in Gibraltar. Nearly all of the aircrews that did not reach Oran were among the fourteen aircrews that had arrived on the day of the mission and likely had not been as fully briefed as the others.[9]

Like every battle plan in the airborne missions over France and Holland that would follow, improvisation in North Africa took command.

Major Yarborough was standing behind Schofield when they reached an invisible African shoreline. After crossing over Spanish clouds, a thick, gray haze blanketing the African coast again made 1st Lieutenant Frederick Jenks' navigating job impossible. Schofield circled, looking for an opening in the clouds as a tide of unease washed across Private Franklin Wolfe and Technical Sergeants Jack Pogue, Cyrus Paks, and eight others in back. *Why are we circling now?* They snapped alert when a speck in the distance grew into an aircraft approaching at high speed. *The enemy?*

"All right, men, take the plugs out of the windows and put the muzzles of your weapons through. If this is an enemy fighter, wait until he's close enough before you fire. He won't think this flying banana has any armament. Maybe we can fool him," ordered Yarborough. Two lines of would-be snipers, back to back and facing outward on opposite sides of the fuselage, waited. Finally, the spec morphed into the shape of another C-47. "I'll bet that son of a bitch is lost," snickered one paratrooper.[10]

Finally, a gap in the clouds appeared. Schofield put his plane into a steep dive, along with his wingman, and likely others who had been circling nearby. A brown, rock-strewn, desolate African landscape appeared, seemingly uninhabited. *There!* A C-47 had landed on the sepia-tinted lunarscape. Perhaps it was Worley or Raymond. Maybe Litsey. Hills nearby indicated they were over Spanish Morocco, 140 miles west of their objective.

Schofield turned east, as did other aircrews who were off course, trailing like puppies. An hour later, an estimated ten C-47s had merged into his formation as he approached Sebkra. Yarborough spotted a dozen C-47s parked on the lake along with about fifty parachutes among hilly, rocky outcrops where troopers had jumped.

"Take your chutes off, get your weapons ready, and let's be ready to bail out of this crate fighting if we have to." When Schofield brought his aircraft to a stop, his fuel tanks were empty.[11]

A handful of remaining aircrews somehow reached Algeria, low on fuel and exhausted, only to face French fighters' machine gun fire, flak from their artillery units, advancing armored columns, and camouflaged sniper fire that they had been assured would not be a factor on their mission.[12]

"Everybody out! Make the for the shore! Get out of here. They're probably going to strafe the airplane!"[13]

Major Clarence Galligan had been near the forefront of Operation *Torch* as the third pilot in the lead flight leaving England. Among the first to arrive at Sebkra, anti-aircraft fire had greeted his aircrew before a French fighter attacked him over the lake bed. His C-47 wounded, Galligan landed. He hustled his aircrew and fourteen paratroopers to the top of a ridge and dug in before the enemy arrived. When a company of French troops approached, Galligan knew his men were outgunned.

When Colonel Bentley arrived from his detour and landed, he and Galligan had no way of knowing if any other C-47s had landed or dropped paratroopers within twenty miles of their position. Bentley had spotted enemy positions on his final approach. The two pilots decided to surrender rather than fight a hopeless engagement with no real expectation of timely reinforcements.[14]

Meanwhile, every aircrew became lookouts as they crossed the Algerian coast near Oran when it became clear they were entering enemy territory.

"All hell seemed to break loose."

In the second aircraft of "Flight C," Captain John Evans flew at the forefront of those on course for the Sebkra lake area. A French fighter pilot's tracers had sliced through his fuselage, forcing Evans to cut power, half roll into a steep dive, and level out just above the ground at a speed beyond his air speed indicator's range. He managed to land as the enemy pilot turned to make another pass at his C-47. Seconds after his crew had scrambled clear, the French fighter made one more run, this time aiming at a stationary hulk and "finished off [our] ship in pretty good shape." Evans would be among several aircrews that flew through enemy fire after taking off on "the peace plan" the night before.[15]

Captain Robert Barrere's angst had been building since he had entered his cockpit in England. Already in the next-to-last position, a dead battery delayed his takeoff, making him the first straggler on the mission. He had never practiced his orders to fly at night in a two-column formation. He had opted to fly over Spain's storm clouds, costing valuable fuel. Like the others, his radio operator, Sergeant Donald Hardwick, reported no signal from the *Alynbank*.

Yet he had somehow stayed on course and, while low on fuel, searched for other aircrews once he reached the Senia area. *There's one down on the lake bed.* Barrere, along with his wingman, 1st Lieutenant Thomas Telzrow, landed alongside. The aircrews and their paratroopers unloaded and established a defensive position against periodic sniper fire. Not long after, ten C-47s appeared from the north, dropping their paratroopers before landing.

Frustration had grown as pilot 1st Lieutenant Joseph Beck lost visual contact with two nearby aircraft as they plowed through the clouds over Spain. Additional clouds over the Mediterranean had left Beck and his navigator, 2nd Lieutenant Bjorn Ahlin, only one viable option. Drop low enough to spot a lighthouse and fly a hopscotched route to the next lighthouse and then the next based on time and estimated distance. Meanwhile, his radio operator, Sergeant Leon Stripe, was unable to reach Beck's command aircraft. "During the night, we heard other ships calling their flight commanders but heard no answers."[16]

Beck and the others who had taken off as a single formation now were piloting thirty-nine solo missions.

He managed to stay on course. After spotting Oran, reconnecting with the other aircraft became the priority, despite relatively light anti-aircraft fire from the French. A short time later, Beck saw other pilots near Sebkra and fell into formation between Telzrow and Barrere. They circled the lake area, reconnoitering other C-47s that had landed, likely paratrooper drop zones, enemy ground positions, and enemy aircraft.

The air space over the lake bed soon resembled an air traffic control pattern at a small regional airport. A new mission plan evolved among the aircrews. Early arrivals alerted inbound aircrews of snipers on one side of Sebkra. Airborne pilots and the paratroopers' commanding officers discussed the possibility of organizing *ad hoc* paratroop drops somewhere on the lake bed and whether other aircrews that had landed in isolated positions should surrender. After landing at one end of the lake, Beck learned others had landed on the west end. He reloaded his paratroopers and took off to join them.

By mid-morning, "the great flight from England [had] ended."[17] Three groups of fourteen, six, and twelve aircraft had reached the Sebkra area, eighty-two percent of those that had taken off from Land's End twelve hours earlier. Most had landed on the damp lake bed with their paratroopers still aboard. Several hundred had unloaded and had taken cover to guard against French snipers and where the 509th had established its ground headquarters.

As the aircrews and paratroopers consolidated their units on the south and west sides of Sebkra, taking the Tafaraoui Airfield became the mission's foremost objective. By early afternoon, the Allies had taken Tafaraoui. The flights had been more treacherous than the objective. With approximately two dozen aircrews in the Sebkra area, perhaps some of those on firm ground could take off with paratroopers for a short hop to Tafaraoui.

Adrenalin pushed aside exhaustion when Beck took off with Yarborough and a load of his paratroopers packed together, shoulder to shoulder, flying at 100 feet, with no plans or hope to jump once they reached Tafaraoui.

I was standing just in back of Lieutenant Joe Beck ... Suddenly
a movement in the air to the right front caught the corner of
my eye. [Joe] slid into a steep bank and cut the motors. The
co-pilot pumped the flaps down, throwing shudders through
the whole ship. My heart jumped into my throat and stayed
there. I could feel the impact of the Vichy machine gun bullets
hit our ship broadside. The fuselage began to leak light as the
rounds poured into the defenseless mass of men seated on
the floor. The noise was deafening. Each shot cracked so loud
that I had the sensation of feeling it as well as hearing it ... We
smashed into the ground doing 130 miles per hour and slewed
around to a violent halt. Again, and again the murderous fire
jabbed through the fuselage.[18]

After Beck slid to a stop short of Tafaraoui, the pilot became the
troops' commanding officer.

The remaining paratroopers started out for Tafaraoui to attack
it and left us with the wounded and the dead. Three paratroopers
were killed outright on my ship, ten were wounded. My
radioman ... was severely wounded and died. My navigator
[Ahlin] was hit in the foot by shrapnel and my crew chief ...
broke his elbow ... When the paratroopers left us, I took
command of the situation and had the less severely wounded
assist ... the paratrooper doctor ... to treat the badly wounded.
We gathered supplies from the planes, organized a guard
for the night, and did what we could to make the wounded
comfortable.[19]

Beck's aircrew was one of several that took severe enemy fire from
French fighters on their last leg of Operation *Torch*.

The aircrews whose planes remained mud-bound unloaded
their troops to stand guard duty or march toward their original
objective. The lake bed, eight miles wide, threatened to sap the last
of the paratroopers' energy. "Each step was a task in itself. Just under
the dry upper crust of the lake's surface was a type of plastic mud

that would have immobilized a dinosaur. Our feet picked up the stuff until each shoe felt like it weighed fifteen pounds."[20]

On the morning of the 9th, the downed paratroopers reached Tafaraoui and that afternoon the remainder of the battalion that had set out from Sebkra reached the airfield and assumed responsibility for its defense.

It had taken close to thirty hours from the anticipated sunrise landing on the 8th for the last of the aircrews to reach the Sebkra area, the 509th paratroopers to assemble, develop an assault plan by air and on foot, and ultimately take control of the Tafaraoui airfield.

At noon on the 10th, Oran capitulated to the Allies. By that point, only fourteen of the twenty-five C-47s at Tafaraoui remained operational. The amphibious invasion had been successful – with no major contribution from the airborne – and became a race between the Allies and the Germans to Tunisia. In that, the aircrews and paratroopers could play a more meaningful role.

Paratrooper missions continued until the end of December, mostly delivering British paratroopers along with ammunition, supplies, and equipment to the advancing troops. Medical evacuation return flights typically carried eighteen litters and three nurses or medics on each flight.

All told, opening the second front and setting the stage in North Africa for the invasion of Sicily was successful. Like future airborne missions over Normandy, Holland, and Germany, *Torch* revealed both the potential and limitations of large, highly strategized airborne formations dropping paratroopers and releasing gliders at concentrated, pinpoint locations behind enemy lines. Too often, those lessons had to be relearned time and again.

Daytime missions proved viable, given Sicily's disastrous night mission and Normandy's pre-dawn dispersal and losses. Poor weather conditions were present across the English Channel, in the Balkans, and over the Himalayas. Accurate navigation over 400 miles was marginally achievable. Given the complexity and choreography of every major airborne mission, *Torch* revealed how adequate time for cohesive training was critical to future airborne mission planning.

Pre-mission briefings with statements such as "[If you encounter] resistance, just keep flying south over the Sahara Desert and you will be picked up, eventually" never sufficed. As one pilot recalled after Operation *Torch,* "total physical exhaustion and ignorance as to what was going on" defined aircrews' flight plans.[21] Inaccurate and incomplete pre-briefing would plague future missions.

Throughout the following three years, the war's tides tested Allied aircrews' stamina and devotion far beyond dry lake beds in Africa, the countryside in Europe, and over the Himalayas. To airstrips etched in Burma's jungle deep in enemy territory.

16

A Better Place to Go

"Say fellers, we've got a better place to go."

Only hours before takeoff, Lieutenant Colonel Philip Cochran stood on a jeep, shaded by towering bamboo, a bedsheet map of Burma hanging at his side. The announcement to his C-47 and glider pilots at a remote air base in India late on March 5, 1944, scrambled several months' training and unraveled preparation for their first airborne mission. Instead of inserting troops in eighty gliders on two remote airstrips in the Burmese jungle, the aircrews would land on just one. It had become an all-or-nothing mission.[1]

Five months earlier, General Arnold had sought a commanding officer for what would become an experimental 1st Air Commando Group in the CBI Theater. The 1st would be an autonomous, mobile fighting force, complete with air transportation capability (Allied troop insertion, supply, and evacuation) independent of other commands. In North Africa, Cochran had earned his reputation as an aggressive fighter pilot who often took the initiative in combat. He had shot down two German aircraft and had earned a Silver Star as well as a Distinguished Flying Cross with two clusters. The epitome of a fighter pilot with boyish good looks, he was confident, "brash" some said, aggressive, and imaginative.[2]

Several months earlier, British General Orde Wingate had arrived in India. He believed in "long-range penetration," far into enemy territory. Eccentric, vain, stubborn, and headstrong, his troops were known as the "Chindits," a derivation of the Burmese word, *Chinthe*, a dragon-like creature in Burmese mythology. Fundamental to his battlefield strategy was timely and reliable air support with supplies, reinforcements, and medical evacuations.

A year later almost to the day on February 8, 1943, Wingate led 3,000 men of the 77th Indian Infantry Brigade in two groups split into eight columns, along with mules and horses, across the India–Burma border. Among Operation *Longcloth*'s objectives was disrupting a key Japanese-held railway in Burma. Although the Japanese were caught by surprise in the early going, a gang of adversaries soon hobbled Wingate's men on a mission critically dependent on almost daily airborne supplies.

RAF Flight Lieutenant Brian Shelley's supply mission role was typical. British and US aircrews assigned to supply Wingate's men often flew three missions every other day. Starting at 0430 hours, aircrews awoke to a breakfast of porridge, tinned bacon, powdered eggs, bread, jam, and tea or coffee that would have to suffice until 1930 hours. Then on to the airstrips for their first mission of the day.

Each of Wingate's columns included an RAF signaler and wireless operator who guided aircrews to patches of open ground in the jungle that varied almost by the day. Signal fires on the long leg of Shelley's L-shaped drop zones directed his approach. Usually he circled at 7,000 feet in a holding pattern with other aircrews until it was his turn to make the final run. Often a warning bell alerted the "kickers," also called "chucker-outers," in the rear to prepare to push their cargo out each aircraft. Then, a steady bell signified "Now!" over the drop zone.

If triple-bagged fifty-pound sacks of rice and mule feed were his cargo – a frequent load – it could take as many as ten passes to jettison it all out the cargo door, as low as fifty feet off the ground at 120 miles per hour. On each pass, the aircrew held its collective breath, waiting for enemy fire to erupt.

Shelley and the others would have to land if their loads were fuel, ordnance, or ammunition. Quickly unload before Japanese mortar crews zeroed in, carry aboard the wounded, empty fuel cans or used parachutes, and then full power toward takeoff on a short, 1,000-yard dirt airstrip. Pull hard out of the drop zone's valley and return to India for a new load, refueling, and another mission before dark.[3]

On the ground, supplies could not offset Wingate's unsustainable casualties. Rampant malaria and dysentery weakened fighting strength. Reinforcements were impossible. Resupply in scattered, postage-stamp jungle openings was spotty, and medical evacuations proved nearly impossible. Dehydration, infected wounds, and armies of stinging jungle insects sucked still more combat strength as the Japanese nearly surrounded Wingate's men.

In late March, Wingate ordered his groups to retreat back across the border, leaving their wounded behind. They had hacked their way across 1,500 miles of jungle by the time stragglers reached India. Ill-fated groups simply had disappeared, likely in unmarked graves or left to wildlife in the jungle. By the time Wingate's survivors returned to India on March 27, he had lost 910 men (about half killed and half left behind). The air support plan had proven inadequate.

A ground assault into Burma had bordered on suicide. If Wingate's long-range troop penetration strategy had strategic merit, it would have to be by air, without ground troops simultaneously coming ashore or crossing a river a few miles away as they would in Operations *Overlord, Dragoon,* and *Varsity.* Or with the massive paratroops drops that later characterized Operation *Market Garden.* A second Burma campaign that would begin three months before Normandy would require Allied air bases far behind enemy lines from the outset.

In the fall of 1943, Arnold approved another attempt to invade Burma (originally called "Project 9"), this time by air to three airstrips carved out of the jungle. Cochran's team had only five months to invent an airborne fleet capable of inserting two brigades more than 150 miles into Japanese territory. The initial flights of the week-long insertion of Operation *Thursday* would be the riskiest phase of the new Allied offensive.

It was an audacious battle plan. On the first night, just twelve C-47 aircrews would make roundtrip shuttle trips under a hazy moon northeast across the Chindwin and Irrawaddy Rivers and over Himalayan foothills at 8,000 feet to three jungle clearings on the far side of Burma, codenamed Broadway, Piccadilly, and Chowringhee. There, they would release their towed gliders carrying the men and equipment necessary to transform rutted, marshy clearings bracketed by 1,000-foot ridges and the jungle's 100-foot canopy into primitive airstrips. Only then could Wingate's combat troops arrive by air. The airstrips had to be operational within a day from arrival and able to accommodate one brigade almost immediately and a second brigade three days later before the Japanese took notice and counterattacked.

Each C-47 sortie would be one-way. It would be impossible to return to India with a glider, given the distance and C-47s' fuel consumption. "The men knew that, because of the distance and heavy loads, the gliders would have to land at Broadway ... They could not be towed home even if the Japs disrupted our plans. There was no turning back," General Arnold wrote five months later.[4]

Once the aircrews spotted a burning smudge pot one mile from a landing zone, they would release their gliders and return to their air base at Lalaghat in India where they would refuel, connect additional gliders, and take off again for Burma. Meanwhile, the glider pilots would turn and drop toward four more smudge pots in a diamond pattern that marked their LZ. Seven air Allied units would support the mission, the 5318th, 27th, and 315th American Troop Carrier Squadrons and RAF 31st, 62nd, 117th, and 194th Squadrons.

But invention had to precede insertion. Dozens of airstrips and air bases along with bamboo barracks, hangars, and ground personnel operations became necessary in India. American C-47 aircraft, gliders, British Dakotas, fighters, bombers, light aircraft, and the AAF's first generation of Sikorsky R-4 Hoverfly helicopters had to be procured. Necessary personnel would exceed 500, two-thirds of them pilots. And training needed to begin just as soon as the newly recruited American volunteers arrived in theater.

At a stateside AAF training center, an officer recruited volunteers for a "very dangerous job. I would not tell what the mission was, where they were going, only that it would be hazardous. We had to turn good people away."

Cochran and his staff also assembled the 1st Air Commando Group "air wing" that at the outset numbered 348 aircraft, including thirteen C-47s, 150 gliders, forty-two fighters and bombers, and support aircraft.[5] Remarkably, 523 men and the aircraft arrived little more than thirty days after Arnold had remarked to Cochran, "To hell with the paperwork, go out there and fight."[6]

Meanwhile, the RAF presence in India underwent a transformation from when its first squadron had arrived almost thirty years earlier. In 1915, the Royal Flying Corps was established in India with a single squadron. By early 1942, the RAF had grown to five groups and two additional squadrons, and soon it would reorganize for an offensive against the Japanese. Two years after the Pearl Harbor attack, the Allies established Air Command, South East Asia for the India, Burma, and Ceylon region. The merged US and RAF air wings, groups, and squadrons would supply and reinforce the ongoing Burma campaign.

The 1944 and 1945 airborne missions in Europe would rely on hundreds of C-47 and Dakota aircrews. Many were fresh graduates from stateside C-47 transition training, while a handful had two or more C-47 combat missions under their belts. But when Cochran forged the 1st Air Commando Group in 1943 before C-47s and their British counterpart Dakotas were widely available, they recruited a handful of highly regarded veteran bomber and fighter pilots who would lead the first glider wave of aircraft in Operation *Thursday*.

Major William Cherry, Jr, flew B-17 bombers. On one assignment in 1942, he had ferried World War I ace Eddie Rickenbacker on a tour of the Pacific Theater. Faulty navigation equipment led Cherry hundreds of miles off course, forcing him to ditch in the ocean.

Cherry, Rickenbacker, and the rest of the crew drifted for more than three weeks before rescue by a Navy ship.

Captain Richard Cole had already flown a groundbreaking mission. He was Lieutenant Colonel Jimmy Doolittle's co-pilot when they launched from the USS *Hornet* on a 1942 Tokyo bombing raid. Cole and his crew then bailed out over Japanese-held China. They evaded enemy patrols for several weeks before reaching friendly forces. Cole later flew dozens of supply missions from India over the Himalayas into China.

Captain Jacob Sartz also had proven his skills as a Hump pilot. On an earlier mission to Burma, he had evacuated seventy-one passengers in a C-47 designed for one-third that passenger load. By the time he landed in India, he was carrying an additional passenger after a woman had given birth in mid-flight.[7]

In Operation *Thursday*, they would pilot the three leading C-47s, each towing two gliders for the first time into enemy territory.

Training intensified when the C-47s finally arrived in January. Even with so few aircraft, there was a shortage of qualified C-47 pilots, forcing Cochran to assign surprised glider pilots to several C-47s' co-pilot's seats. Too few planes, minimal training, a pilot shortage, and a daring two-glider towing strategy defined Operation *Thursday*. All to support a one-way glider flight plan revised at the last minute.

"Nothing you've ever done, nothing you're ever going to do, counts now. Only the next few hours. Tonight, you are going to find your souls." Colonel Cochran laid bare what was at stake in his final pilot briefing when, only hours before takeoff, new mission orders appeared.[8]

Last-minute photography revealed logs stretched across Piccadilly. *Was that a Japanese ploy to consolidate landings onto two clearings where the enemy could concentrate its forces to ambush the aircrews and glider personnel?* No one could be sure. Although a mission to two landing zones would divide the inbound force into two groups separated by a river, the size of the force dictated two destinations. Now, all eighty gliders on the night's mission would have had to land in a single clearing, Broadway.[9] Three waves would first deliver pathfinders, followed forty minutes later by ground troops to secure Broadway, and then heavy equipment, engineers, and construction personnel. Operation *Thursday* had become a go-for-broke mission for the pilots of "Queen of the Ozone," "Hairless Joe," "Peaches," "Tail Wind," "Li'l Abner," and the other C-47s.

Cherry, Sartz, and Cole would lead takeoffs every ten minutes in the first wave, their gliders severely overloaded with Chindit troops, supplies, Gurkhas, and even mules. Seconds after Cherry eased his throttle forward to maximum speed by a count of five, he could feel trouble. Both gliders were so overloaded with weight too far forward that their noses dropped under pressure and dug into the dirt. His C-47 growled as it dragged two four-ton plows. Almost immediately, ground crews ran to as many C-47-glider tandems as possible and pulled down on the gliders' tails as they ran alongside, giving Cherry and his fellow pilots precious time and distance to gain speed.

Once they were airborne, the mission unraveled. Two aircrews returned to base when their aircraft developed electrical issues. Tow lines snapped as glider pilots struggled to stay in their low, double-tow position with little more than their tow planes' blue exhaust to guide them. Communication wires wrapped around tow ropes failed, likely from dragging on the ground during takeoff, an issue that persisted in future missions in Europe.[10] Seventeen gliders released or crashed on the way to Broadway, nine of them in Japanese territory.

About four hours later upon arrival, a demolition derby among those who had survived the flight developed on Broadway. Pilots flying the lead gliders discovered deep ruts, ten-foot-wide water buffalo wallows, and tree stumps that Broadway's photos had not revealed. The tight landing area for overloaded gliders became catastrophic. Most released at 1,000 feet. Their excessive weight brought them in at higher than usual speeds for an aircraft that had as much maneuverability as a rock skipping across a pond. Some undershot, crashing into massive teak trees. Others landed in the clearing before crawling up onto the fuselages of gliders that had preceded them. More than a few caromed off wrecks before sliding to a stop, their landing gear crushed. Wreckage littered the clearing with no way to clear it. Early arriving troops moved the smudge pots to less congested areas of the LZ, but to little effect.

At 0200 hours on March 6, the senior officer on the ground sent a coded message, "soya link," to Cochran signifying an enemy engagement made the LZ unsafe. The reality was that glider wrecks on Broadway rendered it unusable. Cochran recalled the remaining aircrews and changed the flight plan to single glider tows.

Of the fifty-four gliders that had taken off, thirty-seven had landed. Thirty-four no longer were flyable (a ninety-two percent loss rate), thirty-eight men had died, and thirty others had suffered wounds requiring evacuation.[11]

Dawn on March 6 brought despair. Mangled steel tubing, butchered wings, and shredded canvas resembled a salvage yard. Men armed with shovels filled ruts and wallows. Teak logs dragged across the clearing left it marginally smoothed. A member of the engineering crew jumped onto a small bulldozer that somehow escaped a glider crash unharmed and began long passes across the LZ, clearing and leveling as he passed back and forth, much like a farmer preparing his field for spring planting. Somehow from Broadway's junkyard emerged a lighted 4,700-foot operational airstrip by sunset.

That night, sixty-two C-47s landed on Broadway, as tightly as forty-seven seconds apart. Nearly 540 men and fourteen tons of supplies were delivered in the first day's stampede. By the end of March, aircrews had ferried 225 tons, and their gliders had delivered another 155 tons of supplies to multiple jungle airstrips. Only one C-47 was lost after hitting a water buffalo on Broadway.[12]

Operation *Thursday* had set the stage for the C-47 and glider missions that would ensue across Europe. Weight management was a critical factor in glider operations. Adequate time for pre-mission training and advance aircraft availability were critical. Glider double tows at night were problematic at best. Up-to-the-minute LZ and DZ situation reports prior to takeoff could dictate success or failure. Reliable communication between aircrews and glider pilots was vital.

The aircrews of Operation *Thursday* had validated the concept of vertical envelopment deep in enemy territory, even in tropical jungles against an enemy entrenched for three years. As one Japanese general later wrote, "The penetration of the airborne force ... eventually became one of the reasons for the total abandonment of northern Burma."[13]

Operation *Thursday* became the opening salvo of British and American aircrews supporting the Allied Burma ground campaign into 1945. "Routine" resupply and transport missions could morph into battles for survival without warning when heavy fog draped mountain ridges as sharp as a hatchet and monsoon clouds as thick as porridge settled into valleys.

There were no parachutes aboard when RAF Warrant Officer Colin Lynch flew his first 31 Squadron RAF missions over Burma. Low altitude flying under monsoon cloud cover made them worthless. Preferred "four finger" formation flying (with the lead aircraft in the extended index finger position) often became impossible through narrow valleys. Each navigator and his pilot concentrated on their route's topography on every mission. Knowing which valleys were dead-ends and which extended their approach closer to drop zones became critical. Mutual trust among aircrews fueled success on most drop missions.

A warrant officer in 194 Squadron RAF flying a Burma supply mission, Deryck Groocock never sensed an invisible roller coaster ahead on his route. Suddenly, his airspeed approached stall speed. More power, but even slower. Adding more power yanked Groocock's plane into a spin, now dropping 2,000 feet per minute. "This is the end," thought Groocock. "The next second we came out below the cloud at 4,500 feet under control and in a valley with great peaks vanishing in the clouds up on either side of us."

Apparently, when his crew had repositioned rice bags for jettisoning, his plane's center of gravity had gravely shifted. When a few bags had fallen out the door during the spin, the restored balance enabled Groocock to recover. After the remainder was pushed out, Groocock blindly climbed up through the clouds, broke free, and returned to base in bright sunshine. Of twelve aircraft on the supply mission, the other eleven aircrews returned with full loads rather than battle the monsoon season's malevolence.

"All hell broke loose," on one of Flight Lieutenant Brian Shelley's missions – he was in the same RAF squadron as Groocock – when Shelley and his aircrew flew into another monsoon nightmare.

> Our airspeed shot up from the cruising 160 to 300 mph, so we closed the throttles. Next, at a speed of 90 mph, we had the throttles wide open to avoid a stall. We did not know the altitude of the aircraft as the artificial horizon had fallen off its gimbals and was useless … The wireless operator's hand was glued to his table due to the great force of gravity. The rest of the crew was thrown against their harnesses … After a few minutes, which seemed like hours, we broke through the cloud in a steep dive at about 500 feet and just managed to pull out at about 250 feet. We all breathed again.[14]

A different hell awaited when Himalayan winter gripped Burma's north-to-south mountain ranges crested by at least twenty peaks rising more than 16,000 feet.

On December 5, 1st Lieutenant William Clegg II transported twenty-three Chinese Army troops across the Himalayan foot-hills toward Burma. For unknown reasons, he slammed into a mountain near Kuyung. Two weeks later, local tribesmen led army engineers to the site. Everyone had perished, severely burned and a few dismembered. They were buried on the mountain. Almost two years later, personnel recovered Clegg's body for interment in Missouri. He was twenty-two years old when he died.

Two months earlier, 2nd Lieutenant Werner Kriese had headed for Myitkyina in Burma under clear skies and unlimited visibility ("CAVU" in aviation lingo). Later, another pilot noticed an angry fire on a mountainside, flew closer, and then radioed headquarters that an aircraft had crashed. No one had witnessed the impact.

Kriese and his crew of three died on the mountain, alone and unseen. Perhaps on Mount Hkakabo Razi that exceeded 19,000 feet. The crash cause, "Unknown," in his Missing Air Crew Report offered scant solace for the searing loss gripping his family.

The same month, 1st Lieutenant Edward Winston flew toward the same destination in "Frivolous Sal." Like Kriese, Winston and his crew disappeared in the Burmese jungle. To the rescue crew that found the mangled aircraft a month later, it appeared a head-on crash with another mountain had demolished Winston's aircraft from the nose to the center of the fuselage. The wings had snapped off as fire gutted the cabin. Three of the four crewmen, including Winston, "were burned to a point of near cremation." Like Clegg, Winston had flown into the side of a mountain.[15]

Resupply missions for US and RAF personnel were as dangerous as paratroop penetrations under enemy fire. In Burma, a sudden attack by Japanese Zeros loomed over most missions.

On January 18, 1944, three C-47s had headed for a remote area of Burma on a food-dropping mission. Paradrops of durable supplies in canvass bags bounced off the ground several times during multiple low-level C-47 passes while parachutes carried delicate equipment to the troops below.

On this mission, four Japanese fighter pilots ambushed the C-47s, piloted by Captain Joseph Downey, 2nd Lieutenant George Beckwith, and Captain Ferde Larson. They were doomed. Within minutes and with no eyewitnesses, all three aircraft crashed. After listed as missing or overdue, those on the subsequent search missions held little hope of rescue in a jungle expanse split by razor-sharp mountain ridges, and almost no level, open ground within sight of any plummeting aircraft. Particularly after local tribesmen had reported billowing black smoke weeks earlier.

Smoldering, twisted metal in what had become airborne coffins marked each of the three crash sites once ground personnel reached them, often with the assistance of local tribal guides. Twenty-three men had died at a clinical-sounding location, "26° 17' north 97° 45' east," likely on impact. A mountainous area so remote that an Air Force topographical map labeled an adjacent, blank area as "Unsurveyed." After reaching Captain Downey's wreckage, an agent's report from a US Experimental Station in Burma became an eyes-only epitaph.

> Our man returned from crashed DC-3 … portion of wing and tail remaining and contained six burned bodies which cannot be identified … Plane contained tinned milk, rock salt. One roll of super XXRay 35 mm film, possibly already exposed, another roll of unexposed super XXRay magazine type, 16 mm film for V-kodak and film for speed graphic camera were only materials secured from wreckage … Report received here states that some cargo from planes thrown overboard N of Kajitu contained gasoline in drums with Chinese markings.[16]

Operation *Thursday*'s daring shuttle aircrew mission to Broadway ultimately turned the Allied tide against the Japanese in Burma. Supply missions continued as aircrew demands and losses mounted while ground troops advanced, routed, and liberated. RAF aircrew missions totaled monthly flight time of 125 hours in "sustained" operations and as much as 250 hours in "maximum" operations. Of 782 missions flown to the 23rd Brigade in Burma, 560 were successful. In the first four months of 1945, the British 14th Army received 210,000 tons of supplies, all but 44,000 by air. Four months later, Allied forces drove the Japanese out of Burma.[17]

> When you go home, tell them of us and say, for your tomorrow, we gave our today.

More than 1,400 graves sit silently on a battlefield later converted to a postwar Kohima War Cemetery in northeast India. They commemorate the two-and-a-half-month Battle of Kohima, a triumph now considered a Southeast Asia turning point in World War II. The British and Indian victory in 1944 opened a vital supply route from India into Burma, at a cost of 4,000 men. The "Kohima Epitaph," etched on a fifteen-foot stone monolith, memorializes the 2nd British Division's sacrifices and legacy in the battle.

While it has become intrinsic to many British remembrance ceremonies, it has also come to honor all Allied forces who served and sacrificed in World War II. On the ground, at sea, and in the air. Honoring not only those whose airborne service is widely known, but those who flew into enemy fire across skies of anonymity. Risking their lives for thousands of troops on the ground, eyes skyward, desperate for firepower, reinforcements, food, supplies, and hope for their wounded buddies' evacuation.

Allied "transport" aircrews, armed only with training, team-work, and trust, unquestioningly flew missions of unfathomable risk into combat, never truly shared with families back home. Carrying paratroopers and towing combat gliders through geysers of enemy fire that terrorized and tore. Ignoring pained shrieks while surrounded by kaleidoscopes of red tracers and exploding shrapnel's "black roses." Then counting their squadron's returning aircraft to tally each mission's price in blood. Wondering who had been shot down and whether they had survived.

Later, staring at personal belongings boxed on empty cots in hushed barracks before reporting for the next day's briefing. Haunted by the uncertainty of their own fate, wondering whether it would arrive in a swarm of shrapnel, flames, or a hug and tears at the front door.

A brotherhood as tight as any fraternity. A brotherhood that flew in the firestorm of World War II.

17

Epilogue

Warriors come home knowing two kinds of pain. One that hurts. Another that haunts. They also know they might breathe their last on the battlefield. Some expect it.

Dying when the enemy is nowhere in sight or, worse, on the way home salts tragedy with cruelty, shattering the hearts of those left behind. Aircrews and their families could never truly breathe easily until a son, father, brother, or husband knocked on the front door instead of a US casualty notification officer. In England, a Dakota pilot's wife shuddered when handed a telegram at the front door. Written condolences from the King and Queen and the pilot's squadron commanding officer ensued, along with a commemorative scroll following the war "… in honour as one who served King and Country in the world war of 1939–1945 and gave his life to save mankind from tyranny. May his sacrifice help to bring the peace and freedom for which he died."

By the end of the war, in the US 200,000 pilots, 100,000 bombardiers and navigators, 20,000 ground officers, 10,000 glider pilots, and 4,500 four- or five-man C-47 aircrews had been trained.[1] In the UK, enough aircrews were trained for the nearly 2,000 Dakotas that had been provided by the US and to fly modified RAF bombers on paratrooper and supply missions.

Each had confronted his own mortality. The proof often surfaced in the most tragic, crushing circumstances imaginable. At home, their families had fought their own war, wondering, worrying, and waiting for news from or about the man whose family dinner table chair sat empty.

Letters were welcomed, "REGRET TO INFORM YOU THAT YOUR..." telegrams feared. The families of 1st Lieutenant Donald Pahlow's crew and two passengers received telegrams in the weeks following their crash in Operation *Market Garden*.

Natalie Pahlow in Wisconsin and Elsie Wade in New York learned that they were widows after their husbands' crash in Holland. Pilot Donald Pahlow and intelligence officer William Wade had been buried in a church courtyard. Pahlow had studied journalism in Milwaukee before the war before quitting his job in a factory shipping room to enlist in 1942. At thirty-five, Wade was the "old man" on the ship as a passenger. The intelligence officer had graduated Yale in 1930. He had flown three missions on D-Day.

Their stories, their endings, were not unique.

Annice Baker in Alabama, Annie Domitrovich in Illinois, and Irene Ellis in Michigan learned that their sons (co-pilot William Baker, crew chief Christopher Domitrovich, and radio operator Rollin Ellis) were missing in action. Thomas Hoge's father, Albert in New York, now had a son who had been taken prisoner, whereabouts unknown. Baker, Domitrovich, and Ellis ultimately returned to their units in November, 1944. The Allies reached Hoge's POW camp the following April. They owed their lives to Pahlow who had ordered his crew to bail out as he stopped to help one man with his parachute, costing both men their lives.

In a bizarre twist that could only happen in war, death stretched from Holland to 20 West 34th Street in New York City, even after the Germans had surrendered in Europe. On July 28, 1945, Staff Seargent Domitrovich, Pahlow's crew chief, sat aboard a B-25 flying from Massachusetts to New Jersey. In dense fog, the pilot became so lost he flew into Manhattan at an altitude similar to a paratrooper combat mission. The bomber narrowly missed the Chrysler Building before crashing into the 78th and 79th floors of the Empire State Building. After surviving two weeks with the

Dutch Resistance before returning to duty nine months earlier, his mother, Annie, learned her son – who had flown multiple combat missions – had died on a bomber shuttle flight in the heart of New York City.

Weather is war's omnipresent enemy.

C-47 Captain George Miller approached the Billings, Montana, airport in a heavy December snowstorm. He and his co-pilot, Captain Vernon Pfannkuch, carried twenty-one passengers bound for reassignment or discharge to family reunions. Apparently, Miller lost altitude as he made a final turn in the clouds, slamming into a shrouded mountainside a mile short of the runway and bursting into flames. Screams in the fire's glow greeted the responding police officers. Charred and smoldering bodies remained in sitting positions as they were removed. Only four of the twenty-three souls aboard survived.

It was a routine wartime morning flight at 0800 hours between two Allied bases in Italy for five C-47 pilots, including 1st Lieutenant Howard Wank. He and his co-pilot carried African-American soldiers when mid-summer fog conspired against them. As a mountain suddenly emerged from the thick haze, three took evasive action, one clipped a tree and managed to land, but Wank hit the mountain directly. Wank, his co-pilot, and nine of his eighteen passengers died. They share a common grave at a Missouri military cemetery. More than sixty years later, an aviation archaeology team found only uniform buttons, broken eyeglass lenses, melted glass, and a bracelet at the crash site.

Training, war's horrors, and too often tragedy bonded aircrews in ways unfathomable to families back home. Only to be fractured forever in battle by fates as disparate as their missions and crash landings. Pilot Norman Baldwin, Jr's crew over Nijmegen in Operation *Market Garden* never reunited after crashing. Germans captured the badly burned co-pilot, 2nd Lieutenant Burton Squire, when they overran his aid station. Liberation came seven months later. Baldwin never returned to Indiana's farming country to meet his infant son. The pilot died in the crash. Nearby witnesses buried him in a common grave. Radio operator William Armstrong and crew chief George Harrison had survived their last-second, low-altitude jump, only to become prisoners and were taken to Kranenburg, a battered twelfth-century village, by a German officer, Ludwig Kluttgen. With their hands clasped behind their heads, he shot both in the head. Their bodies were thrown over a hedge into a garden. He was convicted of murder in a 1947 General Military Government Court in Dachau, despite his claims of "military necessity" due to lack of available guards. Kluttgen was hung a year later in Landsberg, Bavaria. A single crew splintered into one prisoner of war, one killed in the cockpit, and two murdered.

Lieutenant Colonels Frank Krebs and Howard Cannon had spent forty-two days hiding from the Germans after parachuting out of their dying aircraft on D-Day in Holland. The Dutch Resistance provided forged documents and hid them in closets, under floorboards, in a department store, shed, and finally in a hidden room under a woodpile on the floor of a silo. Then one morning, Cannon heard a voice that could only be American.

Advancing troops had finally arrived. Days later, they reached their base in England still wearing their Dutch farmer's clothes. The first order of business? "What did you do with my footlocker?" Krebs asked a general.

Krebs and Cannon unwittingly had joined 3,000 other airmen rescued by the Dutch Resistance. Some could not go home at the war's end without first retracing their escape route to thank those who had made their survival possible. Sometimes, even before the Allies had cleared the enemy from a region.

A month after they had returned to their unit, Krebs and Cannon flew a C-47 to Holland filled with clothes, food, soap, cigarettes, and sundries donated by 440th TCG personnel. The two traveled their escape route while evading the Germans, expressing their appreciation to those who had helped them survive, return to their unit, and eventually reunite with their families.

Howard Cannon had served as county attorney in Utah shortly before he enlisted in 1941. He resumed his political career after the war, first as elected county attorney in Las Vegas and later for twenty-four years as a US senator from Nevada, rising to become chairman of the Armed Services Committee. For seventeen years, Krebs served as legislative assistant to Cannon and the committee after retiring from the Air Force in 1965.

War has unsung heroes.

A small, little-recognized navy, operated by the Royal Air Force Air-Sea Rescue Service, rescued more than 4,000 British and 2,000 American airmen aboard the C-47s, gliders, fighters, and bombers that ditched in the English Channel in World War II. That included 1st Lieutenant William McCormick, Jr, who had pulled out of a 220-mile-per-hour dive over the English Channel after releasing Flight Officer Herb Bollom's glider near Eindhoven.

On his way to the landing zone four hours earlier, the pilot had flown over seventeen small rescue boats stationed along the airborne mission's northern and southern routes. Overhead, spotter aircraft crews had watched for any plane that was slowing or dropping out of the inbound formations and later for aircraft trailing smoke or a flight path that became erratic on its way back to England. McCormick and his crew were picked up by a rescue launch from the RAF Air-Sea Rescue Service only about fifteen minutes after they had crashed. They were taken to a shore station at Ipswich. Following a medical examination, each received a new set of clothes and was dispatched to the 442nd's air base.

McCormick had flown nearly forty miles with a crippled engine to enable Bollom to land at his LZ, before turning back to England. For the rest of his life, Bollom called McCormick "my life saver." Eleven days after his rescue, Bollom's hero celebrated his twenty-first birthday.

After the war, McCormick married Betty, worked as a supervisor for Bristol Myers in New Jersey for thirty-seven years before retiring in 1982, and following fifty-two years of marriage passed away at eighty-eight years of age in 2011. Like so many others, a silent hero whose legacy was known by few outside the Bollom family.

Like McCormick, pilot Stan Fishel also had leveled his wings to bellyflop onto the English Channel, but too close to the Holland coastline to avoid capture by the Germans. Exhausted when he reached Stalag Luft I in Barth, Germany, on October 8, 1944, he had slogged through twenty-one days since he had crashed. He had marched in a group of prisoners as far as thirty-four kilometers in daily treks, often subsisting on black bread, potatoes, and turnips. After climbing into a prisoner train's boxcar, a P-51 Mustang disabled the train's steam engine on a strafing run. Delousing and solitary confinement added to the nightmare. He never received any of the daily letters his wife, Shirley, had mailed. Walking the prison perimeter, reading, playing bridge and poker, and thinking of her passion warmed him through the German winter on the Baltic Sea.

Yet for Fishel and some others, their POW nightmare changed the course of their lives. After attending a class on house design led by a prisoner architect, Fishel decided to abandon his accounting career plan. After liberation in April 1945, he and Shirley had a son, William, and a daughter, Susan, as Fishel returned to college and then built a forty-year career as a leading architect in North Carolina.

Late in life while waiting for his car repair, he struck up a conversation with a woman with a German accent. The chat led to him mentioning that he had been a World War II prisoner in Germany.

"Where?"

"Barth, up on the Baltic Sea."

"When I was a child," she replied, "I was sent to a summer camp at Barth, and we were housed in a former prisoner of war barracks."

On May 1, 1985, Fishel died in Cary, North Carolina, at the age of eighty-five.

Waiting and wondering were war wounds that plagued the American and British families of missing C-47 and Dakota aircrews. Healing only came to a few who refused to accept the uncertainty.

In Bagley, Iowa, the wife and father of pilot Jack Stiles had launched a personal search after learning that Stiles was "missing in action" as of July 10, 1943. Two months later, a letter from a buddy in his squadron had shed little light. "We kept our course and proceeded to our dropping point in perfect formation. That was the last anyone saw of [Jack's] plane because after we dropped the men we broke formation and came home individually."

Six months later, a query from the War Department to Jack's father brought chills. "A report has been received that among those buried in [the] area where your son was known to operate, was a man who was wearing a gold ring that was engraved 'Virginia – Johnny 2-23-43'. The purpose of this letter is to inquire if you know whether your son owned such a ring, or, in case you do not know, if you could refer us to someone who might be able to inform us."

It was Jack's wedding ring. He had been buried wearing it in Sicily less than five months after he and Virginia had married. His memorial service in Stiles' high school auditorium followed the town's Sunday church services on July 30, 1944, without his body. His family received his Air Medal for his devotion to duty in the Mediterranean. Later, his remains were reinterred in Bayard's cemetery in central Iowa.

Some families would endure the ache of uncertainty for decades until a new weapon against their torment arrived. DNA technology could identify a tooth or sliver of bone, all that perhaps remained of a man who had gone to war for his country.

Second Lieutenant Eugene Shauvin disappeared as one of nine fatalities when his aircraft had crashed in Holland.

In 1996 his daughter, Linda, convinced the US Army Central Identification Laboratory to search for his remains. Only his cockpit was located in 2002. A second attempt at Linda's insistence in 2021 found human remains and possible life support equipment. The following year after conducting an anthropological analysis, the Defense POW/MIA Accounting Agency announced Shauvin's identification. He was laid to rest in 2022 in Spokane, his hometown.

A C-47 aircrew provided a rare flyover during the ceremony, which also included a poem written by Shauvin's widow.

> You left, those wings still gleaming for a job that must be done. So I smiled and said, 'I'll see you when you get that battle won!'... The little one you left with me was comfort to my heart, and we spoke of many future years we'd never spend apart. Your letters stopped. I waited, then the telegram, the dread, we regret to inform you one-half of us is dead ...

The C-47 remained in service nearly as many years as its commercial cousin, the DC-3. As late as 1961, 1,000 C-47s were airborne, despite the advent of the helicopter, development of far larger and more efficient military cargo aircraft, and the dawn of the jet age. Modified versions became warplanes in the Vietnam War. It remained in RAF service until 1970. Air forces around the world – from Canada to India to the Soviet Union to El Salvador – included C-47s and their variants for decades.[2]

Meanwhile, most intrepid airmen who flew them returned home in 1945 to resume lives and roles on campuses, at work, in the yard, and with their families. The man who forged their legacy, General Hap Arnold, saw almost none of it. Heart attacks plagued the founder of what became the postwar United States Air Force as early as 1943. More heart attacks ended his military service in 1945, and his sixth heart attack killed him in 1950. He had become the sole USAF five-star general the year before. Arnold only wore his USAF dress blue uniform once, in his coffin.[3]

In Britain, RAF aircrews returned home, stowed their medals, and resumed their lives. Despite his wounds, RAF Warrant Officer Bert Smith had flown his crippled aircraft back to England with almost no rudder or tail, saving the lives of his crew after his pilot had died. The Distinguished Flying Cross recipient became a teacher after the war, golfed, and fly fished. When asked decades later how he would like to celebrate his golden wedding anniversary with Helen whom he had married in 1941, "with a minute's silence," he responded with a smile. Smith died in 2012 shortly before his ninety-fifth birthday.

After being shot down in Normandy, being taken prisoner and then capturing his guards, another RAF Distinguished Flying Cross recipient, 1st Lieutenant Gordon Thring, never spent much time in England after the war. Thring worked for a shoe company, in charge of operations in Italy and Sudan before taking charge of a factory in Australia. He passed away in Melbourne in 1961 at the age of fifty-two.

RAF Dakota pilot Jimmy Edwards, also a Distinguished Flying Cross recipient, became a radio and television star, famous for his handlebar moustache.

The intrepid RAF and US aircrews of World War II blended back into America, Britain, Canada, and Australia, some arriving with a limp and others with emotional scars that never healed. Yet they started families, built careers, became neighbors, and some made military service their life's mission. Many came home with a new love. A love for an aircraft that saw them through the nightmare and, to their way of thinking, made their family's reunion possible.

> The C-47 groaned, it protested, it rattled, it leaked oil, it ran
> hot, it ran cold, it ran rough, it staggered along on hot days
> and scared you half to death. Its wings flexed and twisted in
> a horrifying manner, it sank back to earth with a great sigh
> of relief, but it flew, and it flew, and it flew.[4]

Their courage, audacity, and selfless sacrifice in the name of freedom often astounded the families who welcomed them home and inspired the officers who had led them in war. General Matthew Ridgway, commanding officer of the XVIII Airborne Corps and who had jumped into combat alongside his 101st and 82nd troops at Normandy, knew better than anyone.

> [Allied troop carrier pilots were] as skilled as any aviators I
> ever knew, and God knows they were brave men, both in the
> air and on the ground. In the run to the drop zone, they flew

formations tighter and more precisely than any the bombers ever flew, and they did it at night. They couldn't take evasive action either, no matter how hot the fire from the ground might be.[5]

Resolute. Never shirking their duty. A World War II legacy that endures. One of almost no public notice. Yet one that is revered by the American and British men and women who today fly into harm's way where hatred and enemy fire still rule, fueled by guts in the absence of bullets.

Acknowledgments

"Guilty, your honor, with an explanation."

For many authors, Acknowledgments can be the most agonizing passage in a manuscript, for fear of overlooking a worthy contributor to the two-year mission. Recognizing an omission after a book has irretrievably gone to print can be terrorizing. Thus, I begin with an apology for any omission coupled with heartfelt gratitude to the following.

I take off with a crisp salute to General Mike Minihan, USAF (Ret.) who authored this book's Foreword. Who better than the former worldwide commander of the USAF Air Mobility Command, the modern-day successor to the US Air Transport Command in World War II? Thank you, sir, for your service, legacy, and contribution to this book.

Patricia Overman of the National World War II Glider Pilots Association once again truly has made one of my books possible. Her father, a C-47 and glider pilot in the war, sparked Patricia's lifelong mission as a topflight researcher who made decades of work available and very kindly reviewed much of the manuscript, just as she did for *Brotherhood of the Flying Coffin*. Sharon McCullar, the Silent Wings (glider) Museum's curator, again was most forthcoming in supporting research and photography search missions. The archives of both organizations truly was indispensable to this book. Hans den Brok and others have created an enormous combat glider archive, intimately bound to the "tow pilots" that this book memorializes.

I am indebted to previous authors who plowed the ground of related topics that support this book's research. They include published authors Colonel Mark Vlahos, USAF (Ret.), James Fenelon, James Mrazek, H. Rex Shama, Colonel Charles Young, Martin Wolfe, Dr Carl Frey Constein, R. D. Van Wagner, Nedda R. Thomas, Lieutenant General William Yarborough, Elmer Wisherd, Gerard Devlin, and John Hoye, among others.

Beyond the Silent Wings Museum's archives, we are the beneficiaries of the dedication of various organizations devoted to preserving the Greatest Generation's legacy in the US and UK. They include the Veterans' History Project at the Library of Congress, National Archives, The National World War II Museum, Air Mobility Command Museum, Royal Air Force Museum, National Museum of the Pacific War, Trustees of the (UK) Airborne Forces Museum, Imperial War Museums (UK), and various county and state historical societies, and universities.

Two gentlemen in particular brought those archives to life, when pilot Mike Nightingale and co-pilot Ron Ley took off from the Palm Springs Air Museum in "What's Up Doc?," a World War II-era C-47 with me buckled into the paratrooper's seat closest to the cockpit. The roars, vibrations, runway seams, smells, turbulence, blurred propellers, turns, and more were invaluable. Interviews with them following the flight were equally enlightening. I remain enormously grateful to both.

I am also indebted to individuals such as Don Patton who established the World War II History Roundtable more than thirty-five years ago and continues to offer his knowledge and contacts in America's military history community. Similarly, I am greatly beholden to family members who preserved the legacy of these otherwise anonymous US and British aircrews by writing their biographies, publishing their diaries, recording oral histories, and preserving a remarkable treasure of artifacts and written documents for more than eighty years.

Many others, such as Ian Murray (Operation *Ladbroke*), Mark Hickman (Pegasus Archive), and Carl Weidenburner (CBI Theater) dedicated years to building online databases. And Russ Picket who has added more than 72,000 entries of veterans to an online database, in part to "remember our war heroes who have given their all for our country," to name just a few. I remain amazed and deeply grateful that people such as Ian, Mark, Carl, Russ, and countless others have devoted decades of their lives to seeking, compiling, and preserving the legacy of these heroes.

The same holds true for the legions of everyday Americans, such as David Iwata, who devote a signification portion of their lives to supporting active-duty personnel, their families, and the legacy of those who have preceded them.

As Pulitzer Award recipient and historian Barbara Tuchman once said, "You must know when to stop. Otherwise, you will never finish." So I extend my thanks to those who supported this book and its predecessors, as the temptation to keep researching has always proved addictive and the willpower to stop in order to finish the manuscript was a constant battle.

Like any successful military mission, each has played a key role, fulfilled his duty, and ultimately has made this book possible. The team at Osprey Publishing, commissioning editor Kate Moore, project editor Serena Kerrigan-Noble and designer Stewart Larking again proved invaluable with their counsel, editing, design, and detailed polishing that turned the manuscript clay into a gem of a story.

The book's marketing team at Bloomsbury Publishing, Marketing and Publicity Director Rachel Ewen and Publicist Robin Wane, have been vital to building momentum for my previous book and now *Into the Firestorm*.

I'm often asked to share my favorite authors. Each remains an inspiration: Truman Capote's *In Cold Blood* makes a nonfiction reader's heart race; John Grisham knows how to build suspense; Ernest Hemingway revealed the unique storytelling power of brevity; David Halberstam made history compelling and thought provoking; Laura Hillenbrand has unearthed the unknown stories that capture readers' imaginations; and Tom Clancy for transforming the grind of mundane research into gripping thrillers, among others.

Every author needs a supporting cast of at least two people: one as a North Star and another as an unwavering cheerleader. Literary agent Scott Mendel's support and patient guidance over the years has kept me on course and on target throughout a journey that has included a *New York Times* bestseller, another book in film development, and now *Into the Firestorm*. His counsel remains deeply appreciated.

Finally, Marjorie. Her steadfast support for more than four decades has been the bedrock of my existence, even when I hatched a crazy notion to stretch from writing 800-word newspaper articles to nonfiction books. I had no idea of the implications, but she did and never flinched at the notion and all that has followed. And so, over the course of 1,000,000-plus words in multiple drafts of twelve books approaching 125,000 copies sold, I still struggle to craft the words that capture all that she means to me.

Glossary

AAF: Army Air Forces

aft: Toward or in the rear

Albemarle: Twin-engine British aircraft utilized on paratrooper and glider missions

Allied/Allies: Principally the United States, Great Britain, and the USSR aligned against Germany and its Axis partners

astrodome: A transparent, bubble window in the top of the fuselage behind the cockpit that enables crewmen to send and receive light signals to other planes and navigators to take celestial readings

C-47: Military variant of the civilian Douglas DC-3, designed for paratrooper, glider, supply, and evacuation missions

CAVU: Ceiling and visibility unlimited

CG-4A: Also called a Waco glider, American combat glider. See "Waco"

control yoke: Cockpit device used to direct an aircraft's direction up and down as well as left or right

cowling: Removable cover of an engine

Dakota: Royal Air Force name for the C-47

dead reckoning: Navigation principally by landmarks and astronomical observations

ditching: A controlled crash and aircraft evacuation at sea

D-Day: First day of several amphibious landings in World War II

D+1: The day following an invasion which is designated D-Day. Format also used as D+2, D+3, etc., as well as D-1, D-2, D-3

DZ/drop zone: Designated area on the battlefield where paratroopers, pathfinders, and supplies were dropped by troop carrier aircraft

elevator: Adjustable surfaces on either side of the tail's rudder to control rise and descent

ETO: European Theater of Operations

Eureka: Ground-based transponder to guide inbound aircraft with onboard receivers called "Rebecca"

fairing: A structure on aircraft wings that reduces drag

feather: Adjust the angle of an idle engine's blades so they do not rotate in the slipstream and create additional drag

feet dry: When an aircraft crosses the coast and proceeds inland

flak: Anti-aircraft shells exploding high in the air

flaps: Hinged panels on wings to control lift and descent

glider infantry: Combat troops that ride to the battlefield in gliders, as opposed to paratroopers who use parachutes

Hamilcar: Large British glider

hedgerow: Concentrated stand or row of trees alongside or enclosing a field

Horsa: Larger British glider made of plywood, otherwise similar to the CG-4A

Initial Point: A designated landmark or location on airborne missions that marked the start of the final run to the target

Intel: Commonly used shorthand for intelligence report

Jumpmaster: Leader of a paratrooper contingent aboard an aircraft

landing zone: A designated landing area for gliders on the battlefield. Also referred to as LZ

Luftwaffe: The air offensive component of the German air force

LZ: See "landing zone"

marshalling: Schemed alignment of tow planes and gliders at one end of a runway in a configuration that emphasized serial takeoff speed and efficiency

milk run: Routine flight

Operation *Bluebird*: Morning glider mission in support of Operation *Dragoon*

Operation *Chicago*: Normandy D-Day early-morning glider mission in support of Operation *Neptune*

Operation *Detroit*: Normandy D-Day early-morning glider mission in support of Operation *Neptune*

Operation *Dove*: Early-evening glider mission in support of Operation *Dragoon*

Operation *Elmira*: Normandy D-Day late-afternoon glider mission in support of Operation *Neptune*

Operation *Galveston*: First second-day Normandy glider mission in support of Operation *Neptune*

Operation *Hackensack*: Subsequent second-day Normandy glider mission in support of Operation *Neptune*

Operation *Husky*: Allied invasion of Sicily

Operation *Keokuk*: Normandy D-Day late-afternoon glider mission in support of Operation *Neptune*

Operation *Ladbroke*: Gliders' mission as part of Operation *Husky*

Operation *Market Garden*: Assault into Holland: *Market* signifying the airborne phase and *Garden* signifying the ground phase

Operation *Neptune*: Gliders' and airborne's mission as part of Operation *Overlord*

Operation *Overlord*: Allied amphibious landing in France at Normandy

Operation *Repulse*: Airborne relief missions in the Battle of Bulge

Operation *Varsity*: The airborne assault across the Rhine River into Germany

panzer division: German armored division

paradrop: Delivery of personnel or supplies by parachute

parapacks: Heavy-duty canvas bags or cannisters filled with various supplies dropped by aircraft to ground troops

paratrooper: Infantryman trained to land behind enemy lines by parachute

pathfinder: Advance paratroopers who were the first to land behind enemy lines and establish navigation aids for incoming paratrooper and glider pilots

prop wash: Turbulence to the rear of aircraft generated by propeller engines

RAF: Royal Air Force (Britain)

Rebecca: Aircraft radio receiver that registered navigation signals from "Eureka" transponders at drop and landing zones

recon: Shorthand for reconnaissance, often in the context of reconnaissance photos used to brief glider pilots in advance of their mission

Rommel's asparagus: Wooden poles (about six inches wide and fifteen feet tall) buried upright as deadly obstacles in potential glider landing zones. Some were wired together and mined to inflict more severe damage and casualties

rudder: Adjustable panel on tail to control turns

salient: A bulge along a battle line extending into enemy territory

seat parachute: Standard issue for pilots, it hung from shoulder and chest straps below a man's bottom

serial: Several aircraft flights in a group at a specific time interval

ship: A commonly used synonym for aircraft or plane

Skytrain: Alternative name of the C-47 aircraft

slip: When a glider is steered into the equivalent of a partial sideways slide, either in the air or on the ground when landing, to slow its speed

small arms: Commonly used reference for rifle and pistol fire

sortie: The use of a single military unit, commonly used in the aircraft context

spoilers: Panels on the back side of aircraft wings that, when engaged, reduce lift and speed

stabilizer: forward edge of tail wings

stanine score: Cumulative assessment of prospective aviation cadets to determine acceptance and course of training

stick: The group of paratroopers carried in a single troop transport, typically between 16 and 20

TCG: US Troop Carrier Group, a unit of C-47s assigned to deliver gliders, paratroopers, pathfinders, or supplies to drop zones and landing zones

tracers: Self-illuminating bullets, typically every fifth round in a machine-gun belt, enabling the operator to adjust his aim as he is firing

trim tab: A small flap located on major control surfaces such as the elevators, used to adjust the pitch of the aircraft

tugs: Glider pilots' nickname for the C-47

Waco: Shorthand for Weaver Aircraft Company which designed the combat glider most widely used in World War II. See "CG-4A"

Wehrmacht: The German term for its army, navy, and air force

Selected Bibliography

SELECTED BOOKS

Astor, Gerald. *June 6, 1944: The Voices of D-Day*. New York: St Martin's Press, 1994.

Bilstein, Roger E. *Airlift and Airborne Operations in World War II*. Stockton, CA: University Press of the Pacific, 2005.

Breuer, William B. *Drop Zone Sicily*. Novato, CA: Presidio Press, 1997.

Brucker, Lt Col, Marshall. *A History of Airborne Command and Airborne Center*. Galveston, TX: undated.

Callan, Robert E. *On Wings of Troop Carriers in World War II*. San Antonio, TX: Burke Publishing Company, 1997.

Constein, Carl. *Flying the Hump*. AuthorHouse, 2003.

Craven, Wesley. *The Army Air Forces in World War II, Volume Seven*. Washington, DC: Office of Air Force History, 1983.

Dank, Milton. *The Glider Gang*. New York: J.B. Lippincott Company, 1977.

Dettore, G.J. *Screaming Eagle Gliders*. New York: Stackpole Books, 2016.

Devlin, Gerald M. *Silent Wings*. London: W.H. Allen, 1985.

———. *Paratrooper!* New York: St Martin's Press, 1979.

Dominick, Peter H. *Flying the Hump, The War Diary of Peter H. Dominick*. Green Bay, WI: M&B Global Solutions, 2022.

Eisenhower, Dwight David. *Crusade in Europe*. Baltimore, MD: Vintage Books, 1997.

Ellis, L.F., and Warhurst, A.E. *Victory in the West: The Defeat of Germany*. London: Naval & Military Press, 1968.

Fenelon, James M. *Four Hours of Fury*. New York: Scribner, 2019.

Ferrin, James. *For Us "Der Var Ist Over."* Tempe, AZ: Desert Hills Publishing, 1987.

Flanagan, Edward. *The Angels: A History of the 11th Airborne Division.* Washington, DC: Infantry Journal Press, 1948.

Galvin, John R. *Air Assault: The Development of Airmobile Warfare.* New York: Hawthorn Books, 1969.

Gregory, Garry. *British Airborne Troops 1940–1945.* London: Macdonald and Jane's, 1974.

Huston, James A. *Out of the Blue, US Army Airborne Operations in World War II.* West Lafayette, IN: Purdue University Studies, 1972.

Ingrisano, Jr, Michael. *Valor Without Arms.* Bennington, VT: Merriam Press, 2012.

Johnson, Jr, John R. *Unarmed, Unarmored and Unescorted: A World War 2 C-47 Troop Carrier Pilot Remembers.* Hoosick, NY: Merriam Press Aviation History No. 4, 2016.

Kaplan, Philip. *Skytrain.* New York: Skyhorse Publishing, 2018.

Knickerbocker, W.D. *Those Damned Glider Pilots.* College Park, GA: Static Line Books, 1989.

Lowden, John L. *Silent Wings at War.* Washington, DC: Smithsonian Books, 1992.

Kraemer, Richard N. *The Secret War in the Balkans.* Bloomington, IN: AuthorHouse, 2010.

Lynch, Tim. *Silent Skies, Gliders at War.* South Yorkshire, UK: Pen & Sword Books, 2008.

McGaugh, Scott. *Brotherhood of the Flying Coffin.* Oxford, UK: Osprey Publishing, 2023.

Mrazek, James E. *Airborne Combat.* Mechanicsburg, PA: Stackpole Books, 2011.

Okerstrom, Dennis. *Project 9, The Birth of the Air Commandos in World War II.* Columbia, MO: University of Missouri Press, 2014.

Shama, H. Rex. *Pulse and Repulse.* Austin, TX: Eakin Press, 1995.

Thomas, Ned. *Flying the Hump.* Palisades, NY: History Publishing Company, 2014.

Tunner, William H. *Over the Hump.* New York: Duell, Sloan, and Pearce, 1964.

Van Valkenburgh, Christopher R. *History of the 306th Troop Carrier Squadron, 442nd Troop Carrier Group 1943–1945.* No publisher listed: 2018.

Vlahos, Mark C. *Leading the Way to Victory, A History of the 60th Troop Carrier Group.* Brentwood, TN: Permuted Press, 2023.

Wolfe, Martin. *Green Light! A Troop Carrier Squadron's War from Normandy to the Rhine.* Washington, DC: Center for Air Force History, 1993.

————. *World War II Glider Pilots.* Paducah, KY: Turner Publishing Company, 1991.

Wurst, Spencer. *Descending from the Clouds.* Philadelphia: Casemate, 2005.

Wisherd, Elmer. *Clear the Prop!* Brule, WI: Cable Publishing, 2018.

Yarborough, William. *Bail Out Over North Africa.* Williamstown, NJ: Phillips Publications, 1979.

Young, Charles. *Into the Valley.* Dallas: PrintComm, Inc., 1995.

SELECTED ARTICLES, ESSAYS, VIDEOS, AND HISTORICAL DOCUMENTS

Anonymous:
IX Troop Carrier Command, Activities, Final Phase-European War. June 1945.

82nd Airborne Division in Sicily and Italy, July 9, 1943, September 13, 1943, January 22, 1944. Army Air Forces, undated.

Airborne Assault on Holland, An Interim Report. Washington, DC: Headquarters, Army Air Forces, 1992.

Airborne Missions in the Mediterranean 1942–1945. Washington, DC: USAF Historical Division, 1955.

Air Invasion of Holland, IX Troop Carrier Command Report on Operation Market. 1945.

Air Phase of the North Africa Invasion. Office of Air Staff, Intelligence, November 1944

Analysis of the Circumstances Surrounding the Rescue and Evacuation of the Allied Crewmen from Yugoslavia. Maxwell AFB: Air War College, 1977.

Bastogne, The First Eight Days. Washington, DC: Center of Military History, 1946.

Bastogne: Supplied on a Wing and a Prayer. Film produced by the National World War II Glider Pilots, December 18, 2017.

By Air to Battle, The Official Account of the British First and Sixth Airborne Divisions. London: His Majesty's Stationery Office, 1945.

D-46 Commando Training Manual. Winston-Salem, NC: Headquarters AAF, Office of Flying Safety, 1945.

Combat reports of the 82nd and 101st Airborne Divisions, 1943–1945.

Combat reports of the 313th, 314th, 315th, 316th, 317th, 318th, 319th, 375th, 433rd, 434th, 437th, 438th, 439th, 440th, 441st, 442nd Troop Carrier Groups, 1943–1945.

RAF combat reports of the Nos 38, 46, and 21 Groups RAF and their squadrons.

RAF combat reports of the 1st and 6th Airborne Divisions, 1941–1945.

Douglas Aircraft Company Long Beach Plant. Historic American Engineering Office, National Park Service, undated.

DZ Europe: The Story of the 440th Troop Carrier Group. United States Air Forces, 1946.

Ever First! 53rd Troop Carrier Wing. Paris: Stars & Stripes, 1944–1945.

Historical Data Headquarters, 435th Troop Carrier Group. March–April 1945.

History of the 38th Troop Carrier Squadron 14 February 1942 to 14 April 1944. Air Force Historical Research Agency, undated.

Initial Selection of Candidates for Pilot, Bombardier and Navigator Training. AAF Historical Studies No. 2, Intelligence Historical Division, November 1943.

Interrogation Check Sheets by glider pilots following each mission.

Missing Air Crew Reports, National Archives.

Multiple After-Action Aircrew Reports. National Archives, various sources.

Narrative of Operation Market. HQ. First Allied Airborne Army, October 9, 1944.

Operation Varsity, 17th Airborne Division Historical Report, undated.

Pilot Training Manual for the C-47 Skytrain, "Restricted." HQ, Army Air Forces, undated.

Silent Wings. The American Glider Pilots of World War II, video released 2007.

Special Operations: AAF Aid to European Resistance Movements, 1943–1945. HQ, Army Air Forces Air Historical Office, 1947.

The RAF and the Far East War 1941–1945. Bracknell Paper No. 6, Royal Air Force Historical Society, 1995.

Troop Carrier Operations, 1944. Headquarters, Twelfth Air Force.

US Army Air Forces Form 5: Individual Flight Record(s). National Archives.

Ashcroft, Bruce. *We Wanted Wings, A History of the Aviation Cadet Program.* Air Force Education and Training Command, USAF, 2005.

Boyne, Walter J. "Hap." Air Force Magazine, September 1997.

Davis, Richard G. *Henry H. Arnold, Military Aviator.* Washington, DC: Air Force History and Museums Program, 1997.

Ellis, Jr, John T. *The Airborne Command and Center Study No. 25.* Army Ground Forces, 1946.

Fetters, Rolland. *Overseas Assignment for the Investigation of Army Air Forces Glider Program in the European Theater of Operation.* Army Air Forces, 1943.

Fish, Robert. *Carpetbaggers' Memories.* 801st/492 Bombardment Group Association, 1990.

Harvey, Thomas Spencer. *Blood, Sand and Silk: The Implementation of Airborne Forces in North Africa by the United States Army, 1942.* Harrisonburg, VA: James Madison University, 2014.

Haulman, Daniel. "Before D-Day Dawn." *Air Power History*, Summer 2014.

Hull, Michael. "The Workhorse Gooney Bird." *World War II Quarterly*, February 2017.

Huston, John W. *American Air Power Comes of Age: General Henry H. "Hap" Arnold's World War II Diaries.* Maxwell Air Force Base, AL: Air University Press, 2002.

Jenkins, Timothy. *The Evolution of Airborne Warfare: A Technological Perspective.* Birmingham, UK: University of Birmingham, 2013.

Johnston, Lewis. *Troop Carrier D-Day Flights.* Air Mobility Command Museum, June 6, 2001.

MacDonald, Charles B. *US Army in World War II European Theater of Operations.* Washington, DC: Department of the Army, 1973.

Martin, Jr, Lawrence Michael. "Fighters or Freighters: US Troop Carrier Aviation, 1941–1945." Master's thesis, University of Nebraska, 1993.

Mason, Jr, Herbert. *Operation Thursday, Birth of the Air Commandos.* Washington, DC: Air Force Pentagon, 1994.

Miller, Charles E. *Airborne Doctrine.* Maxwell Air Force Base: Air University Press, 1988.

Noetzel, Jonathan C. "To War on Tubing & Canvas." Air University, Maxwell Air Force Base, 1992.

Sheehan, Thomas J. "World War II Vertical Envelopment: The German Influence on US Army Airborne Operations." Master's thesis, US Army Command & General Staff College, 2003.

Smith, C.R. "The Pioneering Feats of American Airlines." *Simple Flying*, Sept. 30, 2020.

Spiller, Roger J. *Combined Arms in Battle since 1939.* US Army Command & General Staff College, 1992.

Stetson, Conn. *Mobilization in World War II in 1938–1942.* Office of the Chief of Military History, 1959.

Taylor, Joe G. *Air Supply in the Burma Campaigns.* USAF Historical Division, Research Studies Institute, 1957.

Warren, John C. *Airborne Operations in World War II, European Theater.* USAF Historical Division, Research Studies Institute, 1956.

———. *Airborne Operations in the Mediterranean, 1942–1945.* USAF Historical Division, Research Studies Institute, 1955.

Welter, Frank. *The Wartime Tale of a Tug Pilot.* Self-published, undated.

PARTIAL LIST OF PERSONAL ACCOUNTS

Roger Airgood, John Alison, Robert Antey, Leonard Baer, John Baranich, Robert Barrere, Joseph Beck, William Bentley, Jr, Winfield Bing, Vernon Blowers, Don Bolce, Alan Boyd, Robert E. Callahan, Howard Cannon, Charles Cartwright, Norman Chase, Philip Cochran, Jean Crawford, Cobby Engleberg, Leslie Cruise, Jr, Robert Cristina, John Devitt, Peter Dominick, Robert Dopita, Arthur Een, Stan Fishel, Clarence Galligan, Mike Galligan, Goldie Goldman, Billy Green, Deryck Groocock, Frederick Hale, Jr, John Hanscom, Frank Hansley, Alvin Harrison, Arthur Hopper, John Hoye, Walter Hultgren, John Johnson, Lew Johnson, Carlisle Jordan, Leslie Judd, Pinkney Largent, Charles Lusher, Colin Lynch, Don Manke, Jack Merrill, George Merz, David Mondt, Robert Nelsen, Raymond Ottoman, Desmond Page, Harry Poppell, Jr, Thomas Porcella, Edson Raff, Julian Rice, Zeno Rose, Al Sabon, Richard Sams, Jr, Brian Shelley, Frederick Sherwood, Charles Skidmore, Peter Skyora, Benjamin Smith, Luther Smith, Ward Smith, Allan Sophrin, John Starling, Ned Thomas, Gordon Thring, Richard Welter, Lee Whitmire, Gordon Wilson, Elmer Wisherd, Martin Wolfe, Winfield Wood, Spencer Wurst, Arnold Wursten, John Wyatt, William Yarborough, Godfrey Yardley, Charles H. Young.

OTHER INDIVIDUAL WITNESS ACCOUNTS

150+ American Missing Air Crew Reports and British MI9 evasion reports, multiple after-action troop carrier records, National Archives.

Endnotes

PREFACE

1 Letter written by 1st Lieutenant Billy Green, two weeks after he was shot down on December 27, 1944, when he suffered burns to his head and a broken back.
2 The USS *Midway* Museum has become one of the ten most popular museums of any type (35,000 museums) in America. I served for seventeen years as its founding marketing director and have returned to its board of directors.

CHAPTER 1: A FEASIBLE PROPOSITION

1 Alan Boyd, *A Great Honor* (Portland, Maine: Artisan Pess, 2016), 7.
2 Boyd, *A Great Honor*, 40.
3 AAF estimated only one in ten applicants would become a pilot. Two applicants would be necessary for every technical personnel position.
4 Churchill's comment was part of his speech, "The Few," delivered in the House of Commons on August 20, 1940.
5 *7 Pilots Who Flew in the Battle of Britain*, Imperial War Museum, https://www.iwm.org.uk/history/7-pilots-who-flew-in-the-battle-of-britain.
6 Edward Henry Cecil Stewart, "Letters from the First World War, part one," US National Archives, https://www.nationalarchives.gov.uk/education/resources/letters-first-world-war-1915/trenches-swept-continually-shells/.
7 Gerard Devlin, *Silent Wings* (London: W.H. Allen, 1985), 22–23.

8 Scott McGaugh, *Brotherhood of the Flying Coffin* (Oxford, UK: Osprey Publishing, 2023), 23.

9 Major General John Huston, *America Air Power Comes of Age* (Maxwell AFB, Alabama: Air University Press, 2002), 6.

10 Paratrooper parachutes were attached to a static line that ran the length of the fuselage's interior, forcing the parachutes to open when men jumped, vastly reducing the dangers of human error.

11 Richard Davis, *Henry H. Arnold, Military Aviator* (Washington, DC: Air Force History and Museums Program, 1997), 20.

12 McGaugh, *Brotherhood of the Flying Coffin*, 31.

13 Mark Hickman, *Origins of the British Airborne Forces*, Pegasus Archive., https://pegasusarchive.org.

CHAPTER 2: COMBAT BECKONED

1 "Fighter Pilot," Ministry of Information film, narrated by Air Marshall Sir Philip Joubert, undated.

2 "Glory of the R.A.F.," Gaumont British News, 1940.

3 *Initial Selection of Candidates for Pilot, Bombardier and Navigator Training* (Army Air Forces Historical Studies: No. 2. Intelligence Historical Division, 1943).

4 John Johnson, Jr, *Unarmed, Unarmored and Unescorted: A World War 2 C-47 Troop Carrier Pilot Remembers* (Hoosick, NY: Merriam Press Aviation History No. 4, 2016), 35.

5 *Civilian & Military Applicants for the Army Air Corps Cadet Training* (63rd AAF Flight Training Detachment, undated).

6 Ferrin later transferred into the glider pilot program and flew several missions in Europe.

7 Johnson, *Unarmed, Unarmored and Unescorted*, 48.

8 Martin Wolfe, *Green Light! A Troop Carrier Squadron's War from Normandy to the Rhine* (Washington, DC: Center for Air Force History, 1993), 125.

9 Charles Young, *Into the Valley* (Dallas: PrintComm, Inc., 1995), 66.

10 "R.A.F. Lichfield 27 Operational Training Unit Training Accidents, 1941–1945," Fradley Heritage Group, undated.

11 McGaugh, *Brotherhood of the Flying Coffin*, 39.

12 Ibid., 42.

13 Douglas later constructed plants in Oklahoma City and Tulsa.

14 By the end of the war, Ford produced twice as many gliders as any other manufacturer, at a cost of approximately $15,400 each. Only Ford bettered the AAF's goal of producing gliders for $20,000 apiece. *Development and Procurement of Gliders*, 125.

15 RAF No. 46 Group flew the Dakotas while RAF No. 38 Group flew the modified bombers on paratroop and glider missions.

16 By the end of 1943, of the 400,000 applicants who were processed, 260,000 were sent to pilot training, 40,000 to navigator training, and 40,000 to bombardier training. That left 60,000 who did not make the initial cut for training.

17 "WW2 Glider Crash in Warnford Park," Warnford Village, undated.

18 Wolfe, *Green Light!*, 17–18.

CHAPTER 3: TOO GOOD TO BE WASTED

1 James Huston, *Out of the Blue, US Army Airborne Operations in World War II* (West Lafayette, IN: Purdue University Studies, 1972), 306.

2 General Student had overseen the dramatic capture of Fort Eben-Emael during the France blitzkrieg in 1940 and the use of airborne when capturing Crete a year later. The former was a stunning victory while the latter sustained substantial airborne losses.

3 *Bigot, Appreciation by Air General Student, Commanding 11 Air Force.* http://www.operation-ladbroke.com/german-predictions-for-operation-ladbroke-in-husky-kurt-student/.

4 McGaugh, *Brotherhood of the Flying Coffin*, 61.

5 *Douglas Aircraft Company Long Beach Plant* (Historic American Engineering Office, National Park Service. Undated), 227.

6 McGaugh, *Brotherhood of the Flying Coffin*, 62.

7 "Carrier Command's C-47s Go to War," *Stars and Stripes*, July 17, 1943, 5.

8 Ibid., 5.

9 Warren, *Airborne Operations in World War II, European Theater*, 34.

10 "High-Spirited Stupidity," *WWII* History, October 2018, https://warfarehistorynetwork.com/article/high-spirited-stupidity/.

11 "Carrier Command's C-47s Go to War," 5.

12 Ibid., 5.

13 John Warren, *Airborne Operations in World War II, European Theater* (USAF Historical Division, Research Studies Institute, 1956), 40.

14 Mark Vlahos, *Leading the Way to Victory, A History of the 60th Troop Carrier Group* (Brentwood, TN: Permuted Press, 2023), 233–35.

15 Ibid., 227–29.

16 Maxwell Air Force Base Reel A6000.

17 Warren, *Airborne Operations in World War II, European Theater*, 51.

18 Hickman, Pegasus Archive.

19 *1st Battalion The Border Regiment, 1st Airlanding Brigade July 9/10, 1943.*

20 Hickman, Pegasus Archive.

21 Huston, *Out of the Blue*, 162–66.

22 Paul Gale, *Operation Ladbroke*, Second World War Experience Centre, https://war-experience.org/events/operation-ladbroke/.

23 If a CG-4A carried a piece of artillery, its transport Jeep had to be delivered by another glider. While a Horsa could deliver an entire rifle platoon, the CG-4A's passenger occupancy was far less.

24 Elie Wiesel, World War II Holocaust survivor, 1986 Nobel Peace Prize recipient, author.

CHAPTER 4: GET 'EM OUT!

1 Young, *Into the Valley*, 115.

2 Fighter and bomber groups would depart from more than an additional thirty airfields.

3 On D+1, two additional morning glider resupply missions were scheduled, Operations *Galveston* and *Hackensack*.

4 *87th Squadron/438th Troop Carrier Group History*, June 1944.

5 Elmer Wisherd, *Clear the Prop!* (Brule, WI: Cable Publishing, 2018), 78.

6 Wisherd, *Clear the Prop!*, 71.

7 Hitztaler's younger brother, Tony, died the same day in Normandy when the paratrooper dropped far from his DZ, was captured by Germans, and executed.

8 "First-hand accounts of the D-Day Invasion," *WWII Quarterly*, Winter 2015, https://warfarehistorynetwork.com/article/ww2-paratrooper-first-hand-accounts-of-the-d-day-invasion/.

CHAPTER 5: A NIGHTMARE

1 Sass somehow survived by being catapulted into a hedge, remembered almost nothing of the crash, and following hospitalization in England was shipped stateside.

2 Lewis Johnston, *Troop Carrier D-Day Flights* (Air Mobility Command Museum).

3 Wolfe, *Green Light!*, 96.

4 *570th Squadron/No. 38 Group RAF War Diary*, June 1944.

5 *575th Squadron/No. 46 Group RAF War Diary*, June 1944.

6 Gerard Devlin, *Paratrooper!* (NYC: St Martin's Press, 1979), 412+.

7 Ibid., 414.

8 Philip Kaplan, *Skytrain* (NYC: Skyhorse Publishing, 2018), 145.

9 The C-47 pilots flew in such tight formations that evasive action largely was impossible. On at least one occasion, enemy tracer bullets entered a C-47 cockpit and passed between the pilot and co-pilot.

10 Boyd, *A Great Honor*, 71.

CHAPTER 6: A SILVER RIBBON OF ROAD

1 *440th TCG Terrain Analysis, Operation Dragoon*.

2 Airborne casualties exceeded 2,500 on D-Day, according to "Cross-Channel Attack," published by the US Army in 1951.

3 Warren, *Airborne Operations in the Mediterranean, 1942–1945*, 92.

4 According to C-47 radio operator Martin Wolfe, scarves printed with a map were issued to the troops.

5 The following day, 130 aircrews would fly a resupply drop mission in Operation *Eagle*.

6 At one point, it was planned to coincide with Operation *Overlord*, but a lack of adequate resources for both forced its postponement by nearly six weeks.

7 Hickman, Pegasus Archives.

8 One British paratrooper noted that he had to be awakened from his airborne nap in time to enjoy a flask of tea before reaching his drop zone.

9 Arthur Max, *Men of the Red Beret* (NYC: Time Warner Paperbacks, 1992), page number not shown.

10 Warren, *Airborne Operations in the Mediterranean, 1942–1945*, 99.

11 Devlin, *Paratrooper!*, 455.

12 "Glider Pilots: No Engines, No Parachutes, No Second Chances," *WWII Quarterly*, Spring 2023, 47.

13 Wolfe, *Green Light!*, 264.

14 Young, *Into the Valley*, 225.
15 Glider pilot Ben Ward personal account, National World War II Glider Pilots Association Collection.
16 One smaller airborne mission, Operation *Canary*, took place the same day at 1550 hours, when forty-one aircraft had delivered 736 paratroopers and ten tons of supplies to secured drop zones. In addition, the morning's aborted Horsa serial successfully completed its mission later in the afternoon.
17 One post-mission report indicated only two gliders from the last two squadrons were salvageable.
18 Warren, *Airborne Operations in the Mediterranean, 1942–1945*, 111.
19 Ibid., 112.

CHAPTER 7: BAPTISM OF FEAR

1 "News of the World," by Ward Smith, BBC, September 1944.
2 Private Thomas Porcella, 508th Parachute Infantry Regiment, 82nd Airborne Division.
3 Don Bolce, http://marketgarden.secondworldwar.nl/.
4 Edmund Townshend obituary, *Daily Telegraph*, November 28, 2008.
5 Richard Kraemer, *The Secret War in the Balkans* (Bloomington, IN: AuthorHouse, 2010), 161.
6 Stan Fishel, *World War II – Prisoners of War – Stalag Luft 1*, http://www.merkki.com/fishelstan.htm.
7 The war correspondent, Thomas Hoge, also survived, but was taken prisoner after he landed. He was sent to Stalag III-C, a German prisoner-of-war camp on the Polish border.
8 Young, *Into the Valley*, 291+.

CHAPTER 8: FACING THE ENEMY

1 Warren, *Airborne Operations in World War II, European Theater*, 118.
2 RAF squadron diaries noted that only twelve tons fell in Allied territory, the rest benefitting the Germans.
3 Mission analysts decided later that a fourth direct hit destroyed the toilet near the tail and killed Staff Sergeant Clarence Parson.
4 *Missing Air Crew Report 9921*, National Archives.

5   "Flight Lieutenant David Lord," by Geoff Brookes, *Welsh Country Magazine for Wales,* July 1, 2020. https://www.welshcountry.co.uk/stories-in-stone-95/.

6   *271st Squadron/No. 46 Group RAF War Diary,* September 1944.

7   Boyd, *A Great Honor,* 77.

8   General William Westmoreland, commander, Military Assistance Command, Vietnam, 1964–68.

9   *Missing Air Crew Report 9914,* National Archives.

10 Sightlines from the cockpit were limited. Radio operators, navigators, crew chiefs, and paratroopers watched for engine, wing, and fuselage fires and leaks.

11 McGaugh, *Brotherhood of the Flying Coffin,* 184.

12 *No. 38 Group RAF, No. 46 Group RAF War Diaries,* 1944.

13 Warren, *Airborne Operations in World War II, European Theater,* 133.

14 Royal Air Force No. 46 Group Statistics, https://marketgarden.com/2010/UK/statistics/statis4.html, accessed December 4, 2025.

15 Warren, *Airborne Operations in World War II, European Theater,* 149–54.

16 *271st Squadron/No. 46 Group War Diary,* September 1944.

17 Ibid.

18 Warren, *Airborne Operations in World War II, European Theater,* 226–27.

19 *Air Invasion of Holland, IX Troop Carrier Command Report on Operation Market,* 88–89.

20 "Operation Market Garden: Did Air Power Fail?" (Royal Air Force Centre for Air & Space Power Studies, 2023), 44.

21 Warren, *Airborne Operations in World War II, European Theater,* 146.

22 Bernard Montgomery, *The Memoirs of Field-Marshal the Viscount Montgomery of Alamein* (K.G., London: Collins, 1958), 243, 298.

23 One historian noted the 1st Airborne received less than fifteen percent of supply drops, the 101st less than fifty percent, and the 82nd less than seventy percent. (Warren, *Airborne Operations in World War II, European Theater,* 149–154.)

24 *310th Squadron/315th Troop Carrier Group Report,* September 1944.

25 "Did Air Power Fail?", 30.

26 Warren, *Airborne Operations in World War II, European Theater,* 155.

CHAPTER 9: THE SECRET WAR

1   Richard Kelly, *German HQ 21 Mountain Division, 4633/Ops/44.*
    Subject: Action Against Air Supplies to the Guerillas (Blue Book,
    1946–47).

2   Wesley Craven, *The Army Air Forces of World War II, Volume Six*
    (Washington DC: Office of Air Force History), 493–524. (Nearly
    six billion leaflets were dropped across Europe from June 1944
    to the end of the war.)

3   The B-24s in the 801st Squadron/492nd Bombardment Group,
    painted black to evade searchlights, dropped supplies through
    bomb bay doors and through a modified cargo hatch in ball
    turrets. OSS agents also parachuted out of the ball turrets.

4   Robert Fish, *Carpetbaggers' Memories* (801st Squadron/492nd
    Bombardment Group Association, 1990), 176.

5   More than 1,850 sorties were flown over France, Norway,
    Denmark, and Germany.

6   *Special Operations: AAF Aid to European Resistance Movements,*
    1943–1945, 5.

7   Kraemer, *The Secret War in the Balkans,* 152.

8   *Special Operations: AAF Aid to European Resistance Movements,*
    1943–1945, 46.

9   Kraemer, *The Secret War in the Balkans,* 148.

10 Ibid., 150, 147.

11 Ibid., 139.

12 Ibid., 164.

13 Ibid., 167.

14 *Special Operations: AAF Aid to European Resistance Movements,*
    1943–1945, 123.

15 They were buried in a common grave in the Baltimore National
    Cemetery.

16 Thomas Harvey, *Blood, Sand and Silk: The Implementation of*
    Airborne Forces in North Africa by the United States Army, 1942
    (Harrisonburg, VA: James Madison University, 2014), 319–20.

17 Kraemer, *The Secret War in the Balkans,* 193.

18 Ibid., 194.

19 ACRU #2 would collaborate with the Partisans in evacuating
    aircrews and others.

20 William Leary, "Fueling the Fires of Resistance" (Air Force History and Museums Program, 1995), 44.

CHAPTER 10: ANNIHILATION

1 Sun Tzu, author of *The Art of War*, wrote "Appear weak when you are strong, and strong when you are weak."
2 *Bastogne, The First Eight Days* (Washington, DC: Center of Military History, 1946), 134.
3 Wicked winter winds, heavy snowfall, and temperatures approaching zero degrees had already settled on the Ardennes.
4 Some units and stragglers joined the 101st, but heavy fighting in the region forced the 82nd Airborne and others to be assigned elsewhere. In the coming days, that would create added burdens for the resupply missions.
5 Pilot Robert Anstey personal account, National World War II Glider Pilots Association Collection.
6 Radio operator Andre Mongeau personal account, National World War II Glider Pilots Association Collection.
7 Pilot Lee Whitmire personal account, National World War II Glider Pilots Association Collection.
8 According to *Bastogne, The First Eight Days*, the supplies requested by another unit days earlier had been included in the drop.
9 H. Rex Shama, *Pulse and Repulse* (Austin, TX, Eakin Press, 1995), 185.
10 Milton Dank, *The Glider Gang* (New York: J.B. Lippincott Company, 1977), 212.
11 Glider pilot Richard Fort personal account, National World War II Glider Pilots Association Collection.
12 "Resupply Troops at Bastogne," *Silent Wings Museum Newsletter*, March 1991, 9.
13 Dank, *The Glider Gang*, 217.
14 Fort, National World War II Glider Pilots Association Collection.
15 Shama, *Pulse and Repulse*, 237.
16 The radio operator also managed to bail out and parachute into friendly territory despite serious injuries and burns. Maeder and his co-pilot, 2nd Lieutenant Lee Dahman, died in the crash.
17 Young, *Into the Valley*, 376.

18 General McAuliffe first claimed in *Stars and Stripes* that the 101st had not been in dire straits. Colonel Young of the 439th TCG took offense, writing a letter of rebuttal. General Paul Williams, commanding officer of the IX Troop Carrier Command, forwarded the matter to General Eisenhower. McAuliffe ultimately wrote this post-publication letter.

19 *World War II US Glider Pilot's Briefing*, Winter 2021/22, 32.

CHAPTER 11: UNDETERRED

1 "Airborne Warfare," *Infantry Journal Press*, 1947, 229.

2 The 6th Airborne would be comprised of the 3rd Parachute Brigade, 5th Parachute Brigade, and the 6th Airlanding Brigade (including the Glider Pilot Regiment).

3 More than 925 glider pilots were held in reserve for a potential mission, *Choker II*.

4 The C-46 debuted a year earlier, flying supply missions over the Himalayas in the China-Burma-India Theater.

5 A number of C-46 variants each featured different capacities and capabilities.

6 Warren, *Airborne Operations in World War II, European Theater*, 169–71.

7 2nd Lieutenant Theodore Walker personal account, The Clemson Corps Archives.

8 His artwork was later exhibited in the Drury University Pool Arts Center in Springfield, Missouri.

9 Shama, *Pulse and Repulse*, 357+.

10 When two gliders were towed in tandem, both tended to drift toward the tow plane's centerline, directly behind its tail.

11 Wolfe, *Green Light!*, 395.

12 Ibid., 403.

13 McGaugh, *Brotherhood of the Flying Coffin*, 223.

CHAPTER 12: A BIT TIRED

1 *512th Squadron/No. 46 Group RAF War Diary*, March 24, 1945.

2 Desmond Page, *A Formidable Assignment: Operation Varsity, A Glider Pilot's Perspective,* https://www.paradata.org.uk/article/formidable-assignment-operation-varsity-glider-pilots-perspective-des-page.

3 *2nd Battalion, The Oxfordshire and Buckinghamshire Light Infantry Unit History.*

4 "Stories of Battle of Arnhem Casualties," Commonwealth War Graves Commission, August 5, 2024. It should be noted, however, that The Army Historical Foundation lists IX Troop Carrier Command losses as forty-one killed, 153 wounded, and 163 missing.

5 Warren, *Airborne Operations in World War II, European Theater,* 187.

6 Ibid., 193.

7 *Regimental War Chronicles of the Oxfordshire & Buckinghamshire Light Infantry, Vol. 4,* pages 299–314.

8 Major Gerard Hallock, *313th Troop Carrier Group War Diary,* March 1945, 618–19.

9 Michael Ingrisano, Jr, *Valor Without Arms* (Bennington, VT: Merriam Press, 2012), 269.

CHAPTER 13: GOT TO HAVE GAS

1 Young, *Into the Valley,* 439–94.

2 *FM 101-10: Staff Officer's Field Manual,* October 12, 1944.

3 By 1945, the IX Troop Carrier Command had expanded to four airwings of at least 17 troop carrier groups.

4 Temporary landing locations were called "Advance Landing Grounds."

5 *Missing Air Crew Report 13756,* National Archives.

6 *IX Troop Carrier Command Narrative,* April 1945, 97.

7 Young, *Into the Valley,* 482–83.

8 Boyd, *A Great Honor,* 90.

9 *IX TCC Narrative,* 90.

10 Ibid., 94+.

11 Nine months later almost to the day, Major General Edward Witsell still was seeking eye-witness reports of the incident.

12 Young, *Into the Valley,* 502.

CHAPTER 14: OVER THE ROCKPILE

1 Wesley Craven, *The Army Air Forces in World War II, Volume Seven* (Washington, DC: Office of Air Force History, 1983), 132.

2 *D-46 Command Training Manual, 1945.*

3 *Missing Air Crew Report 704,* National Archives.

4   *C-46 Training Manual, 1945*, 48.

5   "Hump Express," *Air Transport Command, USAF*, January 25, 1945.

6   "Flying the Hump," *Air & Space Magazine*, March 1991.

7   Elements of the China National Aviation Corporation (CNAC) also were folded into the ATC mission. CNAC had established air routes through the Himalayas before the war. In three years, CNAC pilots delivered approximately 114,000 tons of supplies and personnel to Allied forces in China, Burma, and India.

8   Caroline Alexander, *Skies of Thunder* (NY: Viking Press, 2024), 233.

9   Ned Thomas, *Flying the Hump* (Palisades, NY: History Publishing Company, 2014), xxii.

10 Missing Air Crew Reports were compiled on almost every aircrew loss, many of them offering no explanation and listing little more than the aircrews' next of kin for notification purposes.

11 William H. Tunner, *Over the Hump* (NYC: Duell, Sloan, and Pearce, 1964), 106.

12 Peter Dominick, *Flying the Hump, The War Diary of Peter H. Dominick* (Green Bay, WI: M&B Global Solutions, 2022), 85.

13 *Survival Handbook, USAF Office of Flying Safety, CBI Theater*, 1944.

14 Peter Dominick returned to civilian life in 1945 as a captain. It is unclear as to his rank(s) during his CBI service.

15 Dominick, *Flying the Hump*, 60.

16 The prescribed landing speed was about 100 miles per hour.

17 Dominick, *Flying the Hump*, 65.

18 Ibid., 66.

19 Ibid., 67.

20 Tunner, *Over the Hump*, 129.

21 Alexander, *Skies of Thunder*, 224.

22 When operational, the Burma Road had delivered only 6,000 tons monthly.

23 Tunner, *Over the Hump*, 133–34.

24 Approximately 14,000 C-46s and C-47s were built in World War II. It would have required seventy liberty ships or 6,500 American freight cars to deliver a similar amount of supplies.

25 Craven, *The Army Air Forces in World War II, Volume Seven*, 151.

26 Thomas, *Flying the Hump*, 95.

CHAPTER 15: FLYING BLIND

1 Fourteen pilots had received their aircraft only the day before.
2 Warren, *Airborne Operations in the Mediterranean, 1942–1945*, 9.
3 Harvey, *Blood, Sand and Silk*, 22.
4 Bentley also was the commanding officer of the Paratroop Task Force.
5 Lieutenant Colonel Edson Raff personal account, https:// www.509thgeronimo.org/combatjumps/jump1.html.
6 Warren, *Airborne Operations in the Mediterranean, 1942–1945*, 10.
7 Ibid., 11.
8 Less than three weeks later, Vaughn, McLoughry, and their aircrew were killed when their aircraft hit a tree, shearing ten feet off a wing. Speculation on the cause abounded. Were they flying that low to avoid enemy detection? Did the sun's afternoon glare lead to a misjudgment of the tree's height? Bird strike? McLoughry's son was born two months later and the American Legion back home in Delaware established an Eagle Scout award in his name.
9 Warren, *Airborne Operations in the Mediterranean, 1942–1945*, 9.
10 William Yarborough, *Bail Out Over North Africa* (Williamstown, NJ: Phillips Publications, 1979), 44.
11 Ibid., 39–46.
12 60th TCG historian Mark Vlahos and others note that five captains and majors flew in place of radio, navigation, and aerial engineer (crew chief) specialists. Some speculated on whether those senior officers exercised their seniority to take the place of trained specialists on a mission that had been considered to be low risk in return for an air medal.
13 Mark Vlahos, *Leading the Way to Victory, A History of the 60th Troop Carrier Group* (Brentwood, TN: Permuted Press, 2023), 97.
14 Ibid., 97+. The two aircrews and paratroopers were released on November 11 when a cease fire was signed.
15 Young, *Into the Valley*, 11.
16 Ibid., 12+. Vlahos, *Leading the Way to Victory*, 100+.
17 Ibid., 12.
18 Major William Yarborough personal account, https:// www.509thgeronimo.org/combatjumps/jump1.html.
19 Joe Beck personal account, https://www.509thgeronimo.org/ combatjumps/jump1.html.

20 Yarborough, *Bail Out Over North Africa*, 53.
21 Ibid., 9+.

CHAPTER 16: A BETTER PLACE TO GO

1 Dennis Okerstrom, *Project 9, The Birth of the Air Commandos in World War II* (Columbia, MO: University of Missouri Press, 2014), 196.
2 Cochran was the model for a lead character, Flip Corkin, in the popular "Terry and the Pirates" comic strip in World War II.
3 Not only was rice "free dropped," but so, too, was the fodder for Wingate's mules and horses.
4 "The Aerial Invasion of Burma," *The National Geographic Magazine*, August 1944.
5 Herbert Mason, Jr, *Operation Thursday, Birth of the Air Commandos* (Washington, DC: Air Force Pentagon, 1994), 15.
6 Ibid., 10.
7 Other notables became pilots in the CBI Theater. Buddy Lewis was an All-Star third basemen and outfielder for the Washington Senators before enlisting to become a C-47 pilot. He buzzed the Senators' home field, Griffith Park, on his way to war and ultimately flew more than 300 missions. Child actor Jackie Coogan – later Uncle Fester in *The Addams Family* television show – was a glider pilot over Burma.
8 Mason, *Operation Thursday, Birth of the Air Commandos,* 28.
9 Several missions flown later in Europe would be plagued with outdated or inadequate landing and drop zone photography. At the last minute in Burma, a B-25 had flown a photo reconnaissance flight, revealing the dangers at Piccadilly. A lesson apparently lost on future mission planners.
10 Cochran broke radio silence, authorizing the glider pilots to fly in a higher position and that aircrews activate their formation lights as a visual aid.
11 Okerstrom, *Project 9, The Birth of the Air Commandos in World War II*, 32.
12 Mason, *Operation Thursday, Birth of the Air Commandos,* 33+.
13 Ibid., 46.
14 Brian Shelley personal account, https://burmastarmemorial.org/archive/stories/1405920-in-the-air-over-burma-brian-shelley?q=shelley%20brian.

15 *Missing Air Crew Report 9177*, National Archives.
16 *Missing Air Crew Report 2001*, National Archives.
17 *RAF and the Far East War 1941–1945* (Bracknell Paper No. 6, Royal Air Force Historical Society, 1995), 53.

CHAPTER 17: EPILOGUE

1 Bruce Ashcroft, *We Wanted Wings, A History of the Aviation Cadet Program* (Air Force Education and Training Command: USAF, 2005), 33.
2 American and British versions of the C-47 appeared in several films, including *Battleground*, *The Longest Day*, and *A Bridge Too Far* as well as the HBO miniseries, *Band of Brothers*.
3 Davis, *Henry H. Arnold, Military Aviator*, 32.
4 Kaplan, *Skytrain*, 85.
5 Ibid., 77.

Index